T0021841

HANGED!

ALSO BY SARAH MILLER

Violet and Daisy

The Miracle & Tragedy of the Dionne Quintuplets

The Borden Murders

HANGED!

MARY SURRATT
& THE PLOT TO ASSASSINATE ABRAHAM LINCOLN

SARAH MILLER

RANDOM HOUSE STUDIO
NEW YORK

Historical Notes
H Street in Washington, DC, has been renumbered since Mary Surratt's time.
Her boardinghouse, which in 1865 was number 541, is now number 604.

The original spelling, capitalization, and punctuation of quoted material have been preserved,
except for a few instances that threatened to interfere with clarity. In those cases, silent corrections
were made. When a discrepancy in the spelling of a witness's name arose,
I deferred to the spelling used in the trial transcripts for ease of reference.

—

Text copyright © 2022 by Sarah Miller
Jacket art copyright © 1882 by John A. Marshall

All rights reserved. Published in the United States by Random House Studio, an imprint of Random
House Children's Books, a division of Penguin Random House LLC, New York.

Random House Studio with colophon is a registered trademark of Penguin Random House LLC.

Visit us on the Web! GetUnderlined.com

Educators and librarians, for a variety of teaching tools, visit us at RHTeachersLibrarians.com

Library of Congress Cataloging-in-Publication Data is available upon request.
ISBN 978-0-593-18156-0 (trade)—ISBN 978-0-593-18157-7 (lib. bdg.)—ISBN 978-0-593-18158-4 (ebook)

The text of this book is set in 12-point Dante MT.
Interior design by Ken Crossland

Printed in the United States of America
10 9 8 7 6 5 4 3 2 1
First Edition

TO ANNIE

Let the rest of your friends say what they will,
I still remain the same and always to the end.
—MARY SURRATT

The living can write and talk, but the dead must
depend on the supreme right of legal justice
either to justify or condemn their fate.
—JOHN T. FORD,
PROPRIETOR OF FORD'S THEATRE

WHO'S WHO

THE SURRATTS

Mary Surratt: widowed mother of three; owner of a boardinghouse at 541 H Street in Washington, DC, and a tavern in Prince George's County, Maryland

John Harrison Surratt Jr.: Mary's younger son

Elizabeth Susanna "Anna" Surratt: Mary's daughter

Olivia Jenkins: niece of Mary Surratt

John Zadock Jenkins: brother of Mary Surratt

MARY SURRATT'S TENANTS

Apollonia Dean: ten-year-old student at St. Patrick's Institute; shared Mary Surratt's bedroom (not present on the night of the assassination)

Honora Fitzpatrick: seventeen-year-old boarder; shared Mary Surratt's bedroom

John and Eliza Holohan: married couple renting two upstairs rooms from Mary Surratt

John Lloyd: leased Mary Surratt's tavern in Prince George's County, Maryland

Louis Weichmann: twenty-two-year-old War Department clerk and college schoolmate of John Surratt Jr.; shared John Jr.'s bedroom at the Surratt boardinghouse

THE ACCUSED

Samuel Arnold: schoolmate of John Wilkes Booth

George A. Atzerodt: carriage painter

David Herold: former pharmacy student and druggist's assistant

Dr. Samuel Mudd: tobacco farmer and physician

Michael O'Laughlen: childhood friend of John Wilkes Booth

Lewis Thornton Powell (aka Reverend Paine and Mr. Wood): Confederate deserter

Edman "Ned" Spangler: sceneshifter at Ford's Theatre

THE AUTHORITIES

WAR DEPARTMENT OFFICIALS

Edwin M. Stanton: United States secretary of war

Lieutenant Colonel John A. Foster, Colonel Henry S. Olcott, and Colonel Henry H. Wells: officers chosen by

Secretary Stanton to organize the influx of evidence in the investigation of the assassination

ARRESTING OFFICERS

John Clarvoe: Metropolitan Police detective; searched 541 H Street in the early-morning hours of April 15, 1865

George Cottingham: detective under the command of Provost Marshal O'Beirne; arrested tavern keeper John Lloyd

Ely Devoe: assisted Major Smith in the arrest of the occupants of 541 H Street on April 17, 1865

John Lee: detective under Provost Marshal O'Beirne; searched George Atzerodt's hotel room

James McDevitt: Metropolitan Police detective; searched 541 H Street in the early morning hours of April 15, 1865

R. C. Morgan: assisted Major Smith in the arrest of the occupants of 541 H Street on April 17, 1865

James O'Beirne: provost marshal of Washington, DC

Charles Rosch: assisted Major Smith in the arrest of the occupants of 541 H Street on April 17, 1865

Thomas Sampson: assisted Major Smith in the arrest of the occupants of 541 H Street on April 17, 1865

Henry W. Smith: detective under Colonel Wells; ordered to arrest occupants of 541 H Street on April 17, 1865

William Wermerskirch: assisted Major Smith in the arrest of the occupants of 541 H Street on April 17, 1865

General John Frederick Hartranft: special provost marshal of Washington, DC; in charge of the Old Arsenal Penitentiary

Major General Winfield Scott Hancock: commander of the military district of Washington, DC, and General Hartranft's direct superior

George Porter: army surgeon responsible for the health of the prisoners at the Old Arsenal Penitentiary

Captain Christian Rath: hangman appointed by General Hartranft

IN THE COURTROOM

Frederick Aiken: twenty-eight-year-old Baltimore attorney and former Union soldier

John W. Clampitt: twenty-six-year-old Washington, DC, attorney

Reverdy Johnson: Maryland senator and former US attorney general

PROSECUTION

John Bingham: Ohio congressman; appointed special judge advocate in the conspiracy trial

Colonel Henry L. Burnett: appointed assistant judge advocate in the conspiracy trial

Brigadier General Joseph Holt: judge advocate general of the United States Army; presided over the conspiracy trial

HANGED!

CHAPTER ONE

WASHINGTON CITY, APRIL 15, 1865

It was two or three o'clock in the morning when the bell of Mary Surratt's boardinghouse at 541 H Street rang "very violently." On the third floor, twenty-two-year-old Louis Weichmann, a former college chum of Mary's younger son, roused himself from bed. After pulling on a pair of pants under his nightshirt, he ran barefooted down the stairs. Weichmann did not open the door immediately. Wary of middle-of-the-night visitors, he tapped on the inside of the front door to let whoever had clanged the bell know that they should stop.

"Who is there?" Weichmann asked.

"Government officers, come to search the house for John Wilkes Booth and John Surratt," came the prompt reply.

Louis Weichmann had seen John Wilkes Booth—one of the most famous actors in America—that very afternoon. Booth had stopped by to speak with Mrs. Surratt just before Weichmann had driven her into the countryside on an errand. However, Weichmann and Booth's mutual friend, Mary's son John Surratt Jr., had left for Canada over a week before. Through the closed door, Weichmann informed the officers that neither of the men they sought was inside.

"Let us in anyhow," the voices outside demanded, "we want to search the house."

But it was not his house. Weichmann was only a boarder, renting his bed and eating his meals in Mrs. Surratt's dining room. He could not let a group of unknown men into a lady's home in the middle of the night without her permission, and Weichmann told them so.

The officers waited on the porch while Weichmann hurried down the hall and past the parlor to Mary Surratt's bedroom door.

Another boarder, seventeen-year-old Honora Fitzpatrick, who shared a bed with Mrs. Surratt, had also been awakened by the clanging doorbell. Now she heard Weichmann's gentler knock and his voice calling softly through the door. "Mrs. Surratt, there are detectives who have come to search the house, and would like to search your room."

Honora Fitzpatrick and Louis Weichmann would remember vastly different reactions from their landlady—so contradictory in tone and manner, in fact, that it seemed they might have been in the presence of two different women.

One of Mary Surratt's young boarders reported her reply thus: "Mr. Weichmann, ask them to wait a few minutes, and I will open the door for them."

The other would insist for decades afterward that she had said, "For God's sake, let them come in; I expected the house to be searched."

At that moment, this detail mattered little. Whatever Mary Surratt's response, the officers were admitted—six or eight of them, as Louis Weichmann remembered it. There were men stationed in front of the house, and men in the alley behind it. Two detectives went directly to the attic, where Mary Surratt's daughter and teenage niece shared a room. Before Weichmann had time to dress, two more men went into his room and peered under the bed and into the closet and then began examining everything else in sight.

"For God's sake, gentlemen, what means this search of the house so early in the morning?" Weichmann implored.

The young man's confusion startled the officers. "Do you pretend to tell me, sir, that you do not know what has happened last night?" one of them asked. Louis Weichmann insisted that he was completely bewildered.

"I will tell you," said one of them, Metropolitan Police detective John Clarvoe, and he drew a crimson-stained piece of a cravat from his pocket. "Do you see that blood?" Clarvoe asked, brandishing the torn necktie. "That is Abraham Lincoln's blood; John Wilkes Booth has murdered Abraham Lincoln, and John Surratt has assassinated the Secretary of State."

Stunned into momentary silence, Louis Weichmann followed the two detectives back downstairs and arrived just as Mary Surratt was emerging from her room. "What do you think, Mrs. Surratt?" Weichmann said. "President Lincoln has been murdered by John Wilkes Booth, and the Secretary of State has been assassinated!"

Mary Surratt threw up her hands in astonishment. "Oh, my God, Mr. Weichmann, you don't tell me so!" she exclaimed.

CHAPTER TWO

Four hours earlier, Abraham Lincoln had been seated in the president's box in Ford's Theatre, chuckling at a line of the comedy *Our American Cousin*, when a .44-caliber lead ball fired from a single-shot derringer pistol smashed into the left side of his skull and bored its way through the center of his brain.

The revolver's abrupt report startled the actors, who knew there were no gunshots in this production. The audience, however, did not immediately react. The play had already been interrupted once, by President Lincoln's own arrival at the theater twenty minutes after the curtain had lifted. One of the actors on the stage had improvised a line to alert the theater to the president's entrance: "This reminds me of a story, as Mr. Lincoln says . . ." Understanding this impromptu cue, the orchestra launched into a rendition of "Hail to the Chief" as Abraham Lincoln; his wife, Mary; and their guests, Major Henry Rathbone and Miss Clara Harris, made their way to the box that had been specially furnished and decorated in the president's honor.

The spectators treated Lincoln to a hero's welcome. After four years of war at a cost of over 650,000 American lives, Confederate general Robert E. Lee had finally surrendered the Army of Northern Virginia to General Ulysses S. Grant on April 9. Abraham Lincoln had preserved the Union, just as he had promised to do.

President Lincoln acknowledged the standing ovation and "vociferous cheering" with a bow, then settled into a rocking chair in the corner of his flag-draped box to indulge in a long-overdue evening of diversion. "Mrs. Lincoln rested her hand on his knee much of the time," one theatergoer noticed, "and often called his attention to some humorous situation on the stage. She seemed to take great pleasure in witnessing his enjoyment."

Now, seeing a flash and hearing a crack like fireworks, the audience waited to discover what additional surprises might be in store. Indeed, a special song had been composed in the president's honor and was scheduled to be performed by the entire company after the main production, as a kind of patriotic encore.

Major Rathbone, seated at the far end of the box, was the first to realize what had happened. "I heard the discharge of a pistol behind me, and, looking round, saw, through the smoke, a man between the door and the President. At the same time, I heard him shout some word, which I thought was 'Freedom!' I instantly sprang towards him, and seized him."

Wresting himself free, the shooter lunged at Rathbone's chest with a knife of considerable length. The major parried the blow, and the blade slid into the crook of Rathbone's left arm like a sword into a sheath, slicing through several inches of muscle between the elbow and shoulder. Rathbone managed only to snatch at the man's clothes as the shooter rushed toward the front of the box and vaulted over the rail.

Below, the astonished—perhaps even delighted—spectators watched a pale, dark-haired man make a catlike twelve-foot leap from the president's box to the stage. A portion of an American flag, caught by his spur as he jumped, trailed like a banner behind him.

Some witnesses heard the assassin shout *"Sic semper tyrannis!"* (Latin for "Thus always to tyrants") as he paused in the footlights with his knife held aloft before making his exit. Others reported the exclamation as "Revenge for the South!"

It was not the first time that pale, dark-haired man had been seen center stage. Several actors and spectators alike recognized him immediately as John Wilkes Booth, a member of one of America's most prominent families of actors. His presence now, in what seemed to be the most startling of cameo appearances, made no sense.

Booth had timed his attack exquisitely. He knew the play—knew that the audience would be laughing the moment he pulled the trigger, and that there would be but a single actor on the stage who might attempt to intercept him as he fled. His plan worked nearly to perfection. In that brief moment of triumph, Booth had no better accomplices than astonishment and confusion.

"Stop that man!" Major Rathbone cried from above. Only one member of the audience had the presence of mind to bound over the orchestra pit and pursue Booth as he dashed across the stage and out a rear door to the alley, where his horse stood waiting.

Up in the box, Rathbone peered through the gunpowder haze toward the president and understood at once that he was mortally wounded. Mary Lincoln's hand was on her husband's arm. Abraham Lincoln's eyes were closed; his chin drooped down to his chest.

Mrs. Lincoln's scream finally pierced the confusion.

☞

At almost the same moment that John Wilkes Booth fired his pistol, a unexpected knock sounded at the door of the Lafayette Square home of Secretary of State William H. Seward. A nineteen-year-old Black servant, William Bell, opened the door to find an imposing white man holding a small package in his left hand. His right hand was in his over-coat pocket. The fellow said he'd been sent by the secretary's physician, Dr. Verdi, with a delivery of medication. That was no cause for alarm, since Secretary Seward was in considerable pain from the broken jaw and arm he'd sustained in a carriage accident. But the courier's de-meanor quickly put Bell on guard. The man insisted again and again that he could place the delivery into the hands of no one but Secretary Seward himself.

William Bell was no fool. He knew better than to fall for any such thing. The secretary had been agitated and uncomfortable all day, and now that he was at last settled in bed, the entire household was keeping as quiet as possible so that he might sleep. Rest was vital to Secretary Seward, and no one would have known that better than Dr. Verdi. "I told him I would not let him up," Bell said later, "but, if he had any package of medicine for Mr. Seward, I would take it up, and tell him how to take it. But that would not do: he must see him."

Young though he was, Bell did not allow himself to be cowed by the suspicious white man who towered over him. Adamantly, Bell refused to permit the courier to disturb the secretary, even blocking his path bodily as the larger man began to bulldoze his way up the steps toward the family's bedrooms. "I had spoken pretty rough to him," Bell admit-ted afterward—no small risk for a Black man.

Physically, though, William Bell was no match for the stranger. The best he could do was try to stall the fellow's ascent until another mem-ber of the household with more muscle or authority could come help. "When he went up, he walked pretty heavy," Bell remembered—so heavily that Bell had to ask the man to tread more lightly.

The thudding footsteps drew the assistant secretary of state, Freder-ick Seward, from his bedroom. Frederick met the man at the top of the steps, just outside his father's door, where a similar confrontation en-sued over the medicine: the stranger doggedly insisted upon delivering it directly to the secretary of state, and Frederick refused. Thinking to placate the messenger, Frederick opened his father's door just enough to peek inside. "He's asleep," Frederick said.

Just then the door opened again and Frederick's teenage sister, Fanny, leaned out to say, "Fred, Father is awake now." Nevertheless, Frederick would not budge. For three or four more minutes, the two men repeated themselves. "He made the impression on me of being rather a man dull of comprehension," Frederick recalled, for the courier offered no reason or excuse for his peculiar instructions. Finally Frederick lost his patience entirely.

"It is not worth while to talk any longer about it," he said, "you cannot see Mr. Seward; I will take the responsibility of refusing to let you see him. Go back and tell the doctor that I refused to let you see him, if you think you cannot trust me with the message."

"Well, if I cannot see him . . . ," the man mumbled, and started down the stairs.

"Don't walk so heavy," William Bell said, turning back to admonish him yet again.

In that same instant, the man reached into his overcoat and drew out a navy-issue revolver. "There was no time for thought or reflection," Frederick Seward would later say. "I remember only thinking, at the moment, 'There is an additional reason why he should not go in.'"

The man pressed the gun to the assistant secretary's temple and squeezed the trigger. Time slowed to an otherworldly crawl for Frederick Seward. "I remember noticing the shape of the pistol. The next instant I heard the click of the lock and then remember to have thought, 'Well, the pistol has missed fire.'"

Undaunted, the assailant raised the malfunctioning weapon and smashed it into Frederick Seward's skull with such force that as Frederick fell, he did not know whether he was reaching for the wall, the floor, or the stairs to brace himself. At the same time, his left hand rose instinctively to assess his wound. His fingertips found only a hole.

William Bell dashed down the stairs and out into the street, "hallooing 'Murder!'" while the assailant crossed the hall toward his intended target.

Inside Secretary Seward's bedroom, Private George Robinson, an army nurse assigned to care for the secretary, heard the commotion and opened the door. A knife flashed twice before his eyes, and Robinson found himself knocked halfway over, bleeding from the face and forehead. The man slashed at Seward's face and neck with vicious determination, striking at least twice before Robinson could recover himself. "As soon as I could get on my feet, I endeavored to haul him off the bed; and then he turned upon me."

Fanny Seward screamed, awakening another brother, Major Augustus Seward, who came running from his own bedroom. Finding two men grappling at the foot of his father's bed in the dim light of a single gas lamp, Augustus assumed his father was delirious and that the nurse was trying to subdue the restless secretary. Augustus leapt into the fray, grabbing the man he thought was his father. "But," he said, "immediately on taking hold of him, I knew from his size and strength that it was not." If his father was not delirious, it must have been the nurse who was delirious, Augustus surmised, and he proceeded to wrestle the unhinged man from the room. The intruder struck Augustus half a dozen times about the head and arms, all the time repeating, intensely if not loudly, "I'm mad, I'm mad!" In the doorway, the brighter gaslight of the hallway allowed Augustus a glimpse of an entirely unfamiliar opponent: a large, beardless man with straight dark hair.

"On reaching the hall," Augustus remembered later, "he gave a sudden turn, and sprang away from me." The intruder shot down the stairs and out the front door, dropping his knife in a gutter as he fled on horseback.

A scene of horror lay in his wake. Private Robinson was bleeding from the forehead and back. Major Augustus Seward's arms had been slashed three times; two of the wounds were bone-deep. Assistant Secretary Frederick Seward lay insensible in the hallway, his skull fractured in at least five places and his brain exposed. He would not be able to speak more than a single syllable at a time for three weeks.

But in the secretary's bedroom, a traumatized Fanny Seward discovered something akin to a miracle. Her father lay in a heap of bloodied sheets on the floor between the bed and the wall—alive. When Private Robinson had lunged at the attacker, the secretary of state had rolled himself, broken bones and all, from his bed to the floor. His quick thinking had saved his life, but not before the assailant had managed to flay Seward's right cheek wide open and sink his knife into the right side of Seward's neck twice. "I am not dead," he whispered to Fanny after he had been lifted back onto the bed; "send for the police and surgeon, and close the house."

Pandemonium erupted inside Ford's Theatre as the realization of what had occurred ricocheted through the building. Two men pounded on the outer door leading to the presidential box, while a voice from within begged them to stop. The assassin had barricaded the door behind him as he'd entered—every attempt to break it open from the corridor only wedged the brace more firmly into its notch, making it impossible for Major Rathbone, who was himself bleeding profusely, to dislodge the brace.

Rathbone soon pried the wooden brace free, and Charles Leale, a twenty-three-year-old army surgeon who'd been seated in the dress circle, burst in. At the same time, another doctor had climbed to the stage floor, where he was being boosted up over the balustrade into the presidential box. Rathbone approached Leale with his left arm cradled in his right, the surgeon would later recall, "beseeching me to attend to his wound." No one knew it yet, but Rathbone was in far more urgent need of a doctor than the president. Booth's knife had slashed through an artery; blood streamed from the major's arm at a life-draining rate. Rather than examine the wound itself, Leale tipped Rathbone's chin upward and glanced into the major's eyes. Seeing no evidence of "immediate danger," Leale shifted his attention to the president.

"I grasped Mrs. Lincoln's outstretched hand in mine," Leale recalled afterward, "while she cried piteously, 'Oh Doctor! Is he dead? Can he recover? Will you take charge of him? Do you what you can for him. Oh, my dear husband!'" Leale spoke soothingly to the distraught First Lady, assuring her that he would do everything in his power. He called for water and brandy, then set to work. What he saw was not encouraging. "As I looked at Lincoln he appeared dead," Dr. Leale later wrote. "His eyes were closed and his head had fallen forward. He was being held upright in his chair by Mrs. Lincoln who was weeping bitterly." There was no pulse. With the help of three other men who had entered the box, Leale laid Lincoln on the floor to examine him more fully.

At first, no wound was evident. If not for the clot of blood Leale had spotted on the president's left shoulder, Leale might have concluded that he had simply nodded off. The flash of the dagger in Booth's hand as he'd fled, and the blood dripping from Major Rathbone's arm, led the surgeon to believe Lincoln had been stabbed. Dr. Leale ordered the president's collar and shirt to be cut open from neck to elbow and found . . . nothing. Not a scratch, nor a drop of blood. Leale lifted Lincoln's eyelids. Immediately the surgeon understood his error. The president's pupils showed indisputable signs of brain injury. "I quickly passed the separated fingers of both hands through his blood matted hair to examine his head, and I discovered the mortal wound." As Leale's fingers probed the hole, a clot dislodged and the president began to bleed.

Then and there, Leale knew there was no hope for his commander in chief. "The history of surgery fails to record a recovery from such a fearful wound and I have never seen or heard of any other person with such a wound, and injury to the sinus of the brain and to the brain itself, who lived even for an hour." Nevertheless, Dr. Leale cleared Lincoln's airway and stimulated his heart and lungs with external pressure, performing the Civil War–era equivalent of CPR. "Then a feeble action of the heart and irregular breathing followed."

Dr. Leale had no hope of saving Lincoln's life—only of buying him enough time to die with the dignity befitting his office. The floor of a theater box was no place for a president to die, especially on Good Friday, and any attempt to transfer him to the White House would likely end with Lincoln expiring in the street. And so, within minutes of the shooting, the doomed Lincoln was conveyed, on the shoulders of two doctors and four soldiers, to a brick house diagonally across Tenth Street from the theater. There he was laid crosswise upon a narrow bed. He had not shown any sign of consciousness since the instant the bullet had penetrated his skull.

The wound was so unquestionably mortal that some newspapers began reporting the president as "assassinated" while he still lived. Though visibly wearied by four grueling years of civil war, Lincoln's body still possessed an uncanny physical strength. The bullet had plowed a ten-millimeter trench from one side of the president's brain to the other, extending from behind his left ear to the orbit of his right eye, and yet all throughout that long night his great and powerful heart still beat. His lungs continued to draw breath. Nearly nine hours would pass before Lincoln succumbed. Five seconds short of 7:22 a.m., April 15, 1865, his final breath left his lips. Fifteen more seconds passed, and the president's pulse ceased forever.

CHAPTER THREE

The man who took charge of the situation was not Vice President Andrew Johnson but Edwin M. Stanton, Lincoln's mighty secretary of war. Stanton was a veritable titan, capable of working twelve-hour days standing at his high desk, a man whom Lincoln had affectionately nicknamed "Mars," after the ancient Roman god of war. Nevertheless, the sight of the president on his deathbed had reduced Edwin Stanton to tears—not just tears but sobs as thunderous as Stanton himself.

Lincoln's god of war was not overcome for long. As soon as he recovered himself, Stanton requisitioned the room nearest to the one where Lincoln lay dying and transformed it by his very presence into the de facto War Department.

His first order was to dispatch military guards to the home of every member of Lincoln's cabinet, as well as to Vice President Andrew Johnson's hotel, the Kirkwood House. A telegram was likewise dispatched to General Grant, ordering him back to the city for his safety. There was no telling how vast the conspiracy might be. As the next most powerful man in Lincoln's administration, Stanton had every reason to believe his own name was next on the assassins' death list. If he was frightened, it did not show.

At Stanton's command, Major General Christopher Augur, commander of the military district of Washington, DC, turned out his troops, doubled the guard, put forts on alert, and manned their guns. Before midnight, General Augur further ordered the city closed—anyone attempting to leave Washington would be arrested. Clearly more than one criminal had to be apprehended. But how many?

Soon after Stanton's arrival on the scene, a team of three interrogators and a stenographer were taking down testimony from witnesses. Stanton knew he needed more help than this, and he wanted the best help he could obtain. At 1:15 a.m., he wired the chief of police of New York City: "Send here immediately three or four of your best detectives to investigate the facts as to the assassination of the President and Secretary Seward."

Some clues required almost no detective work. A search of Booth's room at the National Hotel, for instance, turned up a cryptic letter containing hints and advice about an unnamed "undertaking." Fearing that the suspicions of the United States government had already been aroused, the writer cautioned, "Time more propitious will arrive yet. Do not act rashly or in haste." Most alarming of all was the recommendation that Booth "go and see how it will be taken in R——d," an indication that the Confederate government in Richmond was somehow involved in the plot. Signed simply "Sam," the letter pointed the authorities straight to Samuel Arnold as well as Michael O'Laughlen, two of Booth's Baltimore schoolmates. Both would soon be in police custody.

Another arrest came just as easily. Backstage witnesses at Ford's Theatre quickly related that upon his arrival at the back door of the theater, Booth had called out to Edman "Ned" Spangler, requesting that the sceneshifter hold his horse. Though Ned had passed off the task to a young peanut seller named Joseph Burroughs, that did not exonerate him. Jacob Ritterspaugh, a carpenter who tried to pursue Booth as he fled, reported that Ned "hit me on the face with the back of his hand, and he said, 'Don't say which way he went.'" When Ritterspaugh protested, Ned hissed back, "For God's sake, shut up!"

James O'Beirne, provost marshal of Washington, DC, took responsibility for the vice president's safety. He summoned Detective John Lee to Johnson's lodgings to examine the building, from the roof shingles to the basement floor, and determine where any "evil disposed persons" might be able to find a way in.

While Detective Lee was assessing the lax security of the Kirkwood House, the bartender there told him about a shady character he'd served just hours earlier—such a "villainous-looking fellow" that he "could be identified no matter where he was seen." This German man had checked into the hotel on Good Friday morning for a single night, paying in advance. Examination of the hotel register showed his name to be G. A. Atzerodt, occupying room 126—directly above the vice president. A search of Atzerodt's room yielded a quantity of disturbing articles: a loaded and capped Colt cavalry pistol, three packages of .44-caliber pistol cartridges, and a Perrine's map of the Southern states, for starters. Detective Lee reached into the pocket of the black coat hanging on the wall and pulled out an Ontario bankbook bearing the name of J. W. Booth. Stripping the sheets from the bed revealed a stained bowie knife, ten or twelve inches long. "My firm conviction," Lee stated, "is that this man G. A. Atzerodt came into the house to assassinate His Excellency, Andrew Johnson."

At about the same time, John Fletcher of Naylor's Stable came into police headquarters to report a stolen horse. Charley was one of Naylor's best, a black-tailed roan with a smooth gait and gentle manner that made him a popular choice among gentlemen and ladies alike. The afternoon of April 14, a young man named David Herold had rented Charley, promising to return by eight or nine o'clock. By ten that evening, Herold and Charley had still not returned. This was all of minimal concern to the police—until they heard what had happened at the stables at around ten o'clock.

That was when George Atzerodt had shown up at the stable to collect the horse he boarded at Naylor's. Atzerodt struck Fletcher as out of sorts, nervous, and itchy for a drink. Fletcher accepted his invitation to step out for a glass of ale. The alcohol seemed to go straight to Atzerodt's head. "Coming back he spoke as if he was half tight though very excitedly and said that I would hear of a present about eleven o'clock," Fletcher recalled. A present? The remark made no sense. "Your acquaintance is staying away very late," Fletcher observed, recalling that Atzerodt and Herold were friends. As Atzerodt mounted up and prepared to go, he reassured Fletcher that Herold had only been delayed. Neither horse nor rider appeared steady on their feet to Fletcher. "I would not like to ride that mare through the city in the night," he said, "for she looks so skittish-looking."

"Well," said Atzerodt, "she is good upon the retreat." That, too, seemed an odd remark. Retreat from what? Fearing "there was something wrong," Fletcher decided to follow Atzerodt. Fletcher watched him stop off at the Kirkwood House long enough to down another drink before riding off toward Tenth Street. It was about twenty minutes past ten.

Improbably, just as Fletcher turned to head back to Naylor's, he heard a familiar sound: Charley's hooves. The horse's gait was as distinctive as a human voice. Just down the block was David Herold astride Charley. "He apparently saw me, and immediately put spurs to the horse," Fletcher would tell the authorities. Fletcher called out to Herold,

"You get off that horse now! You have had that horse out long enough." Herold wheeled and galloped off.

Fletcher ran back to Naylor's, saddled up the fastest horse left in the stable, and gave chase all the way to the Navy Yard Bridge, where he was stopped by a sentry. Yes, a man on a roan horse matching Charley's description had just ridden through—followed by another fellow on a bay horse, who'd taken off just as fast once he'd crossed—but Fletcher would not be permitted across the bridge unless he was willing to remain outside the city until curfew lifted at dawn. John Fletcher had no intention of staying out all night, even for Charley.

It was after one o'clock in the morning by the time he returned to the stable and got his horse bedded down for the night. By then the horrible news was everywhere and the streets were crawling with cavalry. Fletcher stopped a sergeant, asking if they had "taken up any horse." The officer directed him to the police. Upon hearing his story, the police took him straight to General Augur.

The general wanted to know if Fletcher recognized a certain saddle and bridle. They were not Charley's, but Fletcher had indeed seen that saddle and bridle before. They belonged to George Atzerodt. The tack had come from a riderless horse—a brown mare, fifteen and a half hands high with one blind eye—that had been discovered panting and sweating near the Lincoln General Hospital. John Fletcher knew that horse as well. She, too, had belonged to George Atzerodt, until just two days before.

No one was quite sure how these details fit together yet, but Atzerodt was undoubtedly connected to Booth, and Herold to Atzerodt. Could it be a coincidence that David Herold had galloped out of the city on a stolen mount just minutes before a horse and rider matching Booth's description had crossed the Navy Yard Bridge? The authorities did not think so, and so George Atzerodt and David Herold joined John Wilkes Booth on the top of the most-wanted list.

While news of the assassination careened across the city, Metropolitan Police detective John Clarvoe was questioning Mary Surratt in the hallway outside her bedroom. She confirmed that she was indeed Mrs. Surratt, the mother of John Surratt Jr. Clarvoe informed Mrs. Surratt that he wished to see her son.

"John is not in the city, sir," she said. It had been two weeks since she had last seen twenty-one-year-old John.

"Mrs. Surratt," said Clarvoe, "I want to ask you a couple of questions, and be very particular how you answer, for a great deal depends upon it. When did you see John Wilkes Booth?"

Mrs. Surratt replied that she had seen the actor just the day before, at two o'clock in the afternoon.

"When did you see your son John last; where is he?"

"I told you, sir, I had not seen John for over two weeks."

Clarvoe wanted to know whether Mrs. Surratt could tell him where John was. The last she knew, he was in Canada.

"Gentlemen, what is the meaning of this?" she asked, then told Clarvoe that in those days there were "a great many mothers who did not know where their sons were."

The police officer turned to his colleague, Detective James McDevitt. "Mac., you tell her," Clarvoe said, and headed up the stairs to the next floor.

How the soldiers and detectives had ended up at Mary Surratt's home within a few hours of Booth's pulling his trigger is a question that remains without a firm answer to this day.

"That was a night of horrors," Detective James McDevitt would later say when he recalled the circumstances that had led him to 541 H Street. He'd been at headquarters, just one hundred yards from Ford's Theatre, when news of the assassination had broken. A swarm of detectives, McDevitt among them, was immediately unleashed in search of information. "As fast as we could find a man who had seen the shooting or had had a good look at the face of the murderer, or who knew anything whatever about the affair, we would bring him in and make him tell what he could," McDevitt said.

But a crowd was forming outside the building, "wildly excited over the murder." Every time an officer brought a witness in for debriefing, it threw the growing mass of soldiers and citizens into a frenzy of anger and grief. "They wanted to storm the building, carry off these people and hang them to the trees in the street." Emotions rose to such a pitch that the police feared they would not be able to guarantee the safety of the actors and theatergoers who had information to volunteer. Outside the theater itself, incensed citizens were threatening to hang the actors and burn the building to the ground.

Aware that the situation was on the verge of detonating, McDevitt went out onto the steps of police headquarters and appealed to the people for their cooperation.

"You are the friends of the President and so are we," he called to the mob. "You are anxious to see justice done to the perpetrators of this crime, but your anxiety is no greater than ours. If you will help instead of hindering us we shall be able to do our work. These people who are coming to headquarters with us are not criminals. They are friends of the President, too. They are coming here to tell us what they know, so that we can use the information in capturing the assassin."

That placated the crowd enough that McDevitt and his fellow officers could come and go without disturbance. As McDevitt would tell it, he was out scouring the streets for witnesses when he came across a man "whose face seemed very familiar." An actor he had seen perform before, McDevitt thought, possibly John McCullough, though it would turn out that McCullough hadn't been in Washington for nearly three weeks.

"If you want to find out all about this desperate business," the man is said to have told Detective McDevitt, "keep an eye on Mrs. Surratt's house on H Street." (Four other men would eventually claim the honor of pointing the authorities toward H Street—a foreman at a stable who had rented a horse to one of Booth's accomplices, the keeper of the saloon that adjoined Ford's Theatre, a friend and fellow actor of Booth's, and Louis Weichmann's supervisor—all of them adamant about their role in guiding the police toward Mary Surratt's house.)

"Mark you, this was the first intimation given or received by any one as to where the plot was hatched," Detective McDevitt declared. "I acted on it without delay."

And yet McDevitt could not have been the first to connect the name of Surratt with the assassination, for the Metropolitan Police blotter shows this notation, made at around eleven on the night of the assassination: "Secretary Seward and both his sons and servant were attacked at the same hour by a man supposed to be John Serrett [sic]." It is a curious entry. The big, dark-haired, clean-shaven man who had assaulted the Sewards was impossible to mistake for Mary Surratt's son. John Jr. was slight of frame and sandy-haired, with a goatee. But there is his name, recording him as a prime suspect less than an hour after the shooting and stabbing had begun.

In fact, John Surratt's name may not have been unfamiliar to the police prior to April 14, 1865. A known Confederate dispatch courier, John Jr. had spent much of the war slipping unseen through the Union lines to smuggle information in and out of Richmond.

Despite their suspicions, the officers found nothing at Mary Surratt's home that could aid in the investigation of Lincoln's murder. No sign of John Surratt, or any incriminating evidence.

It would not be their last visit.

☞

The horror at the news of Lincoln's murder was so profound, it was as though the entire nation had been struck by Booth's bullet. "A shock from heaven laying half the city in ruins would not have startled us as did the word that started out from Ford's Theatre half an hour ago, that the President had been shot," wrote the *Boston Daily Advertiser*'s Washington correspondent that night. No American president had been assassinated before; the Secret Service did not yet exist. In its eighty-nine-year existence, the United States had seen just one would-be assassin: a mentally unstable housepainter who'd tried to shoot Andrew Jackson with a pair of malfunctioning pistols on the US Capitol steps. Jackson had successfully beaten the man off with his cane until onlookers, including Congressman Davy Crockett, had been able to tackle the assailant.

Four years of bitter civil war had made Lincoln's staff more watchful of his safety, but once the Confederacy fell, one of Lincoln's guards remembered, "Washington was a little delirious. . . . Those about the president lost somewhat of the feeling, usually present, that his life was not safe. . . . It did not seem possible that, now that the war was over . . . after President Lincoln had offered himself a target for Southern bullets in the streets of Richmond and come out unscathed, that there could be danger."

Now not only was the president dead, but as news of the attack on Secretary Seward spread, coupled with rumors of an aborted attempt on Vice President Johnson's life, it became apparent that a conspiracy to upend the entire government had been unleashed. General Ulysses S.

Grant had been invited to accompany the Lincolns to the theater that night, too. Only a last-minute change of plans had removed the Union Army's commander from the path of the assassin's bullet.

In Washington itself, the ensuing terror and confusion created a panic unlike anything the capital had ever known. There was no telling how deep the conspiracy ran, or who might yet be in its crosshairs. "This is terrible, awful horrible," witness Sarah Hamlin Batchelder wrote within twenty-four hours of the attacks; "nothing can describe the intense feeling of fear & dread of more to come and none can judge in the least degree its depth save those who witnessed the horrible scenes."

The anxiety of the hours and days that followed left a fathomless mark on the memories of those who had lived through them. "No person, not present in the city, could possibly form any true conception of the horror, mixed with apprehension of threatened danger, which prevailed here," Horatio King, former postmaster general of the United States, would recall almost thirty years later.

*

And what of John Wilkes Booth?

Until the telegraph wires began to sing with the news, word of the assassination traveled only as fast as a horse could run. Booth had ridden his swift bay mare—a mount he had bragged could dash "just like a cat"—hard enough to outrun the first dispatches, galloping into southern Maryland's Prince George's County, a stronghold of Confederate sympathy where only six citizens had cast their vote for Abraham Lincoln in November 1864. But the state of Maryland as a whole was loyal to the Union. If he were to truly escape, Booth had to get into genuine Confederate territory. His goal was to cross the Potomac into Virginia. From there, he could melt into the Deep South.

But before he could go anywhere, Booth needed a doctor. His left leg was a throbbing, swelling mass of pain. History would record that his magnificent leap from the presidential box to the stage had cracked his fibula in half, straight across the top of his ankle. In reality, the injury may have been the result of Booth's horse taking a nasty tumble as they sped through the swampy countryside. By the time he reached his first known stop, where New Cut Road intersected the Marlboro-Piscataway road, the bay mare was lame and bleeding from a cut on her left front leg. Booth was no longer atop the bay. He had traded with his guide, David Herold, in favor of a smooth-gaited, black-tailed roan named Charley.

CHAPTER FOUR

Louis Weichmann was up early on April 15. Very early. By five o'clock, he was out in the streets in search of a newspaper.

Overnight the city had been transformed. Not a vestige of the postwar celebration remained. Now the city was swathed in mourning. Portraits of Abraham Lincoln were appearing on doors and windows. Festoons of black crepe draped nearly every edifice. Newspapers were gobbled up as fast as they could be printed, one edition after another, as soon as details of the president's funeral arrangements and clues in the chase for the assassin were made public.

The fallen president's image, too, was undergoing a rapid transformation. In his lifetime, Abraham Lincoln had been a controversial figure even within the states that remained loyal to the Union. He had suspended the fundamental legal right of habeas corpus. This suspension had allowed the government to arrest and detain its own citizens without showing probable cause. Despite his reputation as "the Great Emancipator," in 1863 he had freed only the people enslaved by the Confederacy, leaving those people who were enslaved in the states loyal to the Union—Missouri, Kentucky, Maryland, and Delaware—trapped in bondage until the ratification of the Thirteenth Amendment in December 1865.

"He who had for years been derided by tongue and pen as a 'clown,' a 'gorilla,' and a 'negro lover' was now transfigured and became immortal," Louis Weichmann observed. "Booth had turned the execration and hatred of many, even of Lincoln's own party, who had been his bitterest political enemies, into the most profound reverence."

Weichmann got hold of a copy of the *Washington Chronicle* and read the dispatches from Secretary Stanton. "Thank God! Thank God!" he exclaimed as he read the description of the Sewards' attacker; "that is not John Surratt." A great cloud of dread lifted from his heart, but an ominous weight still remained.

Despite his momentary relief, Weichmann had reason to be wary. He had been boarding at John's mother's house for only five and a half months, but in that time he had seen things inside the Surratt home that would surely raise investigators' eyebrows.

Those who saw him that morning could not miss Weichmann's "state of great excitement." Among the first to interact with him were the men at Naylor's Stable. "He called for whiskey," a report of his visit there noted, "and seemed to be laboring under great apprehensions." Of course he was apprehensive—workers at the stable knew Weichmann as someone who "rode out with Booth often." He shook visibly as he spoke, desperately trying to convince the stableman that John Surratt was in Canada.

There was plenty to make Louis Weichmann tremble, for there was no question that the president's assassin was John Surratt's friend. Weichmann himself had chatted with Booth in the parlor during many of his frequent visits to H Street. Before the assassination, Weichmann had "rather considered it a fine thing to be acquainted with Booth." He was famous and talented and came from a lustrous family.

Weichmann had known John Surratt for almost six years—they had been schoolmates at St. Charles College in Maryland—and yet John's friendship with Booth baffled Weichmann. "I never could understand the sympathy and affection which existed between Booth and Surratt," he said; "they were so dissimilar in their natures, education, and the social position they held in life." Booth was "familiar with the tinsel and glitter of theatrical life . . . a worldly man given to wine, women, and conviviality." As far as Weichmann could tell, John Surratt was not much more than a common farm boy by comparison. Bluntly put, Louis Weichmann could not see a reason in the world why as renowned and celebrated a man as John Wilkes Booth had bothered befriending anyone like John Surratt.

Though proud of this eminent association, John's mother had also seemed faintly puzzled by her son's association with Booth. "Mrs. Surratt some time in February did remark that Booth and John appeared to have business together and that she was bound to find it out," Weichmann recalled. "She went into the parlor and spoke to John but whether she found out their business I do not know."

Weichmann, in fact, had been present when John and Booth had first become acquainted. Weichmann and John had been walking down the street one winter day when they'd heard someone calling out to John. John recognized the fellow at once and introduced him to Weichmann as Dr. Samuel Mudd, an acquaintance from Maryland. The doctor in turn introduced both of them to his companion, who was none other than John Wilkes Booth. A hospitable man, Booth invited everyone up to his room at the National Hotel, where he ordered cigars and wine for his guests. But no sooner were they seated together in the comfortable suite than Mudd went out into the hallway, asking Booth for a private word. After they returned, Booth and John stepped out together. Then they called for Mudd, leaving Weichmann alone. For another fifteen or twenty minutes, Weichmann sat by himself while the other three discussed some private business.

Booth and Mudd both apologized to Weichmann when they returned, explaining that Booth was considering purchasing Mudd's farm. The price Booth had offered, Mudd confided, was not satisfactory. And yet immediately after begging pardon for their rudeness at excluding him, the three men clustered around a small table at the center of the room and began to confer among themselves all over again in tones that were "scarcely audible." Booth laid an envelope on the table and began marking up the back of it. From where Weichmann sat about eight feet away, the motions of the pencil did not look like writing, "but more in the direction of roads or lines." The whole thing seemed a trifle odd, but not in the least alarming.

After that, Weichmann noticed, Booth began calling "frequently" at the Surratt home. For the most part he came asking for John. When John was home, they would talk openly in the parlor for a while, but from time to time Booth would request a private chat, saying, "John, can you go up-stairs, and spare me a word?" These upstairs conversations might go on as long as two or three hours. If John was not home, Booth asked for Mrs. Surratt instead, though his chats with her never lasted as much as ten minutes.

☞

Weichmann had no hope of convincing himself that the Surratts had nothing in common with Booth's political sentiments. He knew perfectly well that the entire Surratt family was Confederate sympathizers. A month before, John had accompanied a woman named Sarah Slater to Richmond after her previous escort had been captured. Mrs. Slater, it turned out, was "either a blockade-runner or a bearer of despatches," carrying contraband or information to the Confederate capital. Mary Surratt herself had told Weichmann so, and Slater had kept her veil over her face during her entire stay at H Street. And it was certainly no secret that John Surratt himself was a Confederate operative. He'd spoken openly of traveling to Richmond and having met with Confederate president Jefferson Davis and Confederate attorney general Judah Benjamin.

It further seemed that the Surratt boardinghouse had been known for some time among Confederate blockade-runners—men and women who smuggled contraband goods and information across Union lines—as a safe lodging place. One man in particular troubled Louis Weichmann's conscience greatly. He was introduced as Mr. Spencer during his stay, but Weichmann knew that was not the man's true name. His behavior was an odd mix of careless and secretive. On the one hand, he seemed to be hiding from something. The way he skulked around the house struck Weichmann as suspicious, as did the fact that he would not go out at night. Yet despite knowing that Weichmann was employed by the United States War Department, the man took no pains to conceal that he was part of the rebel underground. He even taught Weichmann a Confederate cipher—a method for encoding secret messages. Weichmann used it to encode an entire poem by Henry Wadsworth Longfellow, in hopes of stumping a coworker who was fond of puzzles.

For three days Louis Weichmann "agitated the question" of whether to inform on this Mr. Spencer, for doing so would incriminate John and Mary Surratt for hosting him. Weichmann also asked the advice of his supervisor at the War Department, Captain Daniel Gleason.

Ultimately Weichmann decided not to imperil his friends. "I thought it would be the only time the man might be there, and let him go in God's name." Only after Mr. Spencer had departed did Weichmann learn that he was Augustus Howell, considered a "notorious rebel" by the federal government.

There were other unusual characters, too.

About two months before the assassination, Louis Weichmann answered a ring at the door to find a man asking for John. The fellow was tall, pale, and strikingly broad-shouldered, with dark hair, a black frock coat, and gray pants. Learning that John was not in, he asked for Mrs. Surratt. Weichmann ushered him into the parlor and introduced his landlady to the man, who gave his name as Wood. He had no bags, but he boarded for the night and left on the first train for Baltimore the next morning.

Three weeks or so later, he came knocking again. Weichmann opened the door, and to his chagrin could not remember the man's name. This time he introduced himself as Paine, explaining that he was a Baptist preacher from the South who had recently taken the oath of allegiance and intended "to become a good and loyal citizen." Again Weichmann ushered him into the parlor and introduced him to Mrs. Surratt, Anna Surratt, and Honora Fitzpatrick. It was not until one of the ladies called him Mr. Wood that Weichmann realized that the man had given a different name.

Since John Surratt was not at home, Reverend Paine was given John's place in the room that Weichmann shared with Mary's son. Though Paine was amiable enough as a guest—chatting in the parlor, requesting that the ladies play piano, and sitting down to a round of cards—nobody in the house thought the fellow had anything of the air of a clergyman about him. "One of the young ladies looked at him, and remarked that he was a queer-looking Baptist preacher; that he would not convert many souls," Weichmann would remember. Mary Surratt had agreed, wryly remarking that "he was a great looking Baptist preacher."

That was not the only odd thing about him. The next day, Weichmann returned to his room to find Reverend Paine's mustache lying on the table. "I thought it rather queer that a Baptist preacher should use a mustache," Weichmann said, "and I did not care about having false mustaches lying round on my table." Perturbed and puzzled, Weichmann hid the feeble disguise in his toiletries box, then moved it to a paint box in his trunk. When Paine came in and noticed his mustache was missing, Weichmann said nothing. Instead of returning it to the man who called himself Reverend Paine, Weichmann took it to work the next day and fooled around with it among the other clerks. "I put on a pair of spectacles and the mustache, and was making fun of it," he said.

When he returned to the boardinghouse that afternoon, Weichmann realized "from the appearance of things" in the bedroom that John Surratt must have come home. Rather than force a guest to relocate, John had likely taken some of his things to a room on the third floor. Weichmann went up to say hello. He strode in without knocking and found John Surratt and Reverend Paine seated on a bed, toying with a couple of bowie knives. Scattered across the bedcover were a pair of navy-issue long revolvers and four sets of brand-new spurs. "The moment the door was opened they instantly and almost unconsciously threw out their hands as if trying to conceal the articles," Weichmann recalled. Recognizing Weichmann, they relaxed a bit. Weichmann seemed not to have been disturbed by what he saw. He picked up one of the spurs for a closer look, then "took up a sword Mr. Surratt had on the mantel-piece, and commenced fencing with him."

That same evening, John teased Weichmann by showing off a ten-dollar ticket for a private box at Ford's Theatre. Booth had given it to him. Weichmann "playfully wrested" the ticket out of John's hand, announcing that he was going to see the play, too.

"No, you are not," John said, giving Weichmann a wallop in the gut and yanking the ticket back. "I don't want you to go to the theatre this evening for private reasons." John invited Paine instead, as well as Honora Fitzpatrick and another young boarder, ten-year-old Apollonia Dean.

Little Miss Dean was thrilled by the entire experience. "And, oh! Mr. Weichmann!" she said to Weichmann afterward; "what do you think; while me and Miss Fitzpatrick were sitting there Mr. Booth came to the box and called Mr. Surratt and Mr. Paine into the entry, and he was so excited." They had been seated in a box above the stage—either the very same box where Lincoln would be shot, or its mirror image on the opposite side of the theater. At the time, nothing about the occurrence had struck Weichmann as out of the ordinary. But after the assassination?

Louis Weichmann got his own chance at a free theater ticket a few days later. On March 18, John invited Weichmann and another of his mother's tenants, Mr. John Holohan, to accompany him to Ford's, where Booth was starring in *The Apostate.* On the way in they met up with a man who had boarded once at Mrs. Surratt's—a squat German fellow whose name was crowded with consonants. Rather than learn to pronounce it, Mrs. Surratt and her boarders had simply called him "Port Tobacco," after the town where he lived. Booth's friend David Herold also joined the party.

Booth's performance as the play's villain made a lasting impression on Weichmann. "Never in my life did I witness a man play with so much intensity and passion as did Booth on that occasion. The hideous, malevolent expression of his distorted countenance, the fierce glare and ugly roll of his eyes, which seemed ready to burst from their sockets as he seized his victim by the hair . . . are yet present with me," he wrote decades later. "I cannot use language forcible enough to describe Booth's actions on that night."

In and of itself, there was nothing strange about that evening, but on the morning after the assassination, the thought of having been

Booth's guest at the scene of the crime was enough to make anyone feel as though they were somehow implicated. Then there was what happened after the final curtain fell that night. The five men left the theater together, apparently headed out in search of supper. But as they turned a corner, John Surratt noticed that Port Tobacco and Herold had not followed. He sent Louis Weichmann to fetch them and invite them to go out for oysters. The two had ducked into a restaurant. Weichmann found them "talking very confidentially with Booth; and on my approaching them, they separated." Always generous, Booth asked Weichmann to join them for a drink, after which everyone but Booth went to Kloman's restaurant for oysters.

Louis Weichmann could not have been blind to the fact that Mrs. Surratt and John Wilkes Booth were on friendly terms as well. At least twice, Weichmann himself carried messages to Booth on behalf of his landlady. On April 2, 1865, Mrs. Surratt asked Weichmann to go to the National Hotel and tell Booth that she wished to see him on "private business." Booth obliged that evening.

Just over a week later, on April 11, Mrs. Surratt asked Weichmann if he would take the afternoon off to drive her to Maryland. She had business in the country—a debt to collect from a Mr. John Nothey. Weichmann agreed, and once again she sent him to speak with Booth at his hotel, to see if she might borrow Booth's buggy for the trip. Booth would have been perfectly willing to lend the buggy to Mrs. Surratt, except that he had quite recently sold it. To make up for the inconvenience, he offered Weichmann ten dollars to rent one for the afternoon.

Perhaps most unsettling of all was the coincidence that occurred on the day of the assassination itself. Louis Weichmann was released from work at ten a.m., as a courtesy from the secretary of war toward those who wished to attend Good Friday services. Weichmann attended Mass and enjoyed lunch with a few friends before returning to H Street to curl up with a book for the rest of the afternoon. Soon after he arrived at his lodgings, Mrs. Surratt rapped at his bedroom door. It was between two and two-thirty.

She needed to return to the country, she explained. Word had apparently gotten out that she had been attempting to collect from Mr. Nothey, and now a Mr. George Calvert was insisting that Mary Surratt use that money to repay a debt owed to him by John Surratt Sr.

Weichmann was agreeable, and Mrs. Surratt gave him ten dollars to go rent a buggy for the drive. As Weichmann headed out the door, he caught sight of John Wilkes Booth in the parlor, talking with Mrs. Surratt. By the time Weichmann returned, Booth had gone. As she climbed into the rented buggy, Mary Surratt carried two parcels. One was a packet of paperwork connected with a tavern she owned in Prince George's County. The other was about six inches across and looked to Louis Weichmann "like a saucer or two, or two or three saucers, wrapped in paper." Mrs. Surratt confirmed his guess, telling him it was "china dishes." They were Booth's things, to be dropped off at the tavern at his request.

Within mere hours of this seemingly benign trip, Louis Weichmann opened the door to find the police on Mary Surratt's doorstep. "I myself had a great deal to fear," Weichmann would later admit. "Being in this house where these people were, I knew that I would be brought into public notice."

There are at least two versions of what happened next. The way Louis Weichmann preferred to tell it, he promptly presented himself to Detective McDevitt, told what he knew about Booth and John Surratt, and the next day was made a "special officer" for the purpose of tracking down John Surratt in Canada. "I never considered myself under arrest," he would later assert, though he had to concede that he had been in the presence of a police officer from the moment he entered the station until he left for Canada two days later. "I considered myself as much a detective as McDevitt was on that occasion."

According to Mr. Holohan, however, Weichmann did not qualify as a civic hero. He went to police headquarters only because Holohan took him there. "I delivered him up," Holohan said. "I told McDevitt and Clarvoe that I was satisfied he knew everything about it."

Detective James McDevitt's recollections are similar to Holohan's, lending credibility to the possibility that Weichmann did not turn himself in willingly. McDevitt eventually testified that on the night of the assassination "I ordered Mr. Weichmann and Mr. Holohan to report at our office at nine o'clock next morning." Years later the detective further recalled that Louis Weichmann "proved so useful that I kept him under arrest for some time, not letting him out of my sight—even taking him home with me for his meals." This corresponds with Holohan's memory of Weichmann spending Saturday night at the station house. Weichmann himself even later admitted that he'd passed the night of April 16 "on the floor of the police station with nothing but a knapsack for my pillow." In fact, McDevitt had arrested Weichmann on the orders of Metropolitan Police superintendent A. C. Richards.

Weichmann's claim of being dubbed a "special officer," though not untrue, was perhaps not what it seemed, either. The entire nation was on high alert, and McDevitt wanted to get Weichmann and Holohan to Canada without any unnecessary complications or delays. As McDevitt explained, "I asked that we all might be designated as special officers, for fear that we might have trouble on the road with them if they were not mentioned some way in this order."

Regardless of how he arrived at headquarters, Louis Weichmann would not leave police custody for nearly three months.

While Detective McDevitt and his colleagues on Tenth Street were extracting all the information they could from Louis Weichmann, a knock sounded at the door of the Surratt tavern in Maryland between nine and ten a.m. on April 15.

A roundabout tip had led the authorities to this doorstep. Chasing the trail of a known Confederate murderer deemed capable of the assault on Secretary Seward brought a cavalry lieutenant, David Dana, and his troops fifteen miles southeast of the capital to the tiny crossroads of Surrattsville, "a rebel hotbed."

John Lloyd, Mary Surratt's tenant, answered the door. Lieutenant Dana wanted to know if he had seen anyone passing through the night before.

"I told them I had not," Lloyd later said. "Then they told me that the President had been murdered, and an attempt had been made to murder [the] Secretary."

Later that day, Detective Clarvoe—the same man who had questioned Mary Surratt just hours before—arrived with the same questions. Had John Wilkes Booth and any accomplices passed through Surrattsville during his escape the night before? According to Clarvoe's supervisor, Lloyd again "denied all knowledge of their having passed, and called God to witness to the truth of his asseverations."

John Lloyd was lying.

CHAPTER FIVE

No one seemed to have considered whether Mary Surratt had any involvement in the conspiracy until a man by the name of John Kimball went to the authorities with a tip. "Tip" is perhaps a generous description of Kimball's information. It was a story he'd heard secondhand, from a woman named Mrs. Griffin, who worked afternoons at his home on the corner of Eleventh and O Streets. According to Kimball, Mrs. Griffin had heard about suspicious goings-on at the Surratt boardinghouse from her niece Susan Mahoney, who was one of Mrs. Surratt's own servants. Neither of these women went to the police. Nor did Mr. Kimball until another man, P. M. Clark, heard the story from a third man on the evening of Monday, April 17. Clark "became convinced, within the certainty of inspiration, that Mrs. Surratt's house was a rendezvous of the conspirators" and toted Kimball straight to the police.

As Kimball told it, Miss Mahoney had confided to her aunt that on Saturday night, three strangers drove up to the Surratt boardinghouse. Miss Mahoney had been asleep on the floor of the basement kitchen when the men's talk woke her. The three of them were having a "low conversation" with Mrs. Surratt. Miss Mahoney lay still with her face covered by her blanket, lest anyone realize she was listening. Kimball reported that among other things, Miss Mahoney "heard them say that Surratt was in the theater Friday night with Booth." Then she heard Mrs. Surratt ask the men "if they had seen their friends." Indeed they had, but they had not spoken with these unnamed friends, for fear of being seen. "Afraid to let on" was the expression Miss Mahoney had used, Kimball said. After that brief and cryptic conversation, one of the visitors asked for a change of clothes. Mrs. Surratt went to fetch the clothing, and the men drove off. Once they were gone, Mrs. Surratt returned to the kitchen, leaned in close to Miss Mahoney, and listened to see if she was asleep. Miss Mahoney "breathed hard to pretend to her that she was asleep," and Mrs. Surratt was apparently satisfied. In addition, the Surratt women spent the better part of the next day burning letters and other papers.

Kimball's version was not wholly accurate, however. Kimball at first directed officers to the wrong house entirely, for instance. And the provost marshal would eventually record that Kimball's statements were "to some extent exaggerated" when compared with Miss Mahoney's statement. Unfortunately, the provost marshal did not specify which details had been stretched out of shape as the story had spread.

Nevertheless, Kimball's secondhand information, combined with other tidbits collected since the night of the president's murder, was enough for the police to take action. Shortly before ten-thirty on the night of April 17, Colonel Henry H. Wells ordered Major Henry Smith and three detectives—Ely Devoe, Charles Rosch, and William Wermerskirch—to arrest Mary Surratt and everyone else at 541 H Street. They were further ordered to establish a guard around the property, search the place, and "bring away all that seems of importance, especially pictures, letters, and other witnesses." Anyone who happened to come to the door while Smith and his men were there was also subject to arrest. Guilt or innocence was of no concern. There would be time to straighten out those details later.

Major Smith posted one man at the back door and another at the base-ment door. He and Devoe climbed the steps to the main entrance of 541 H Street. Through the window Smith could see four women seated in the parlor. He signaled for Devoe to ring the bell.

The window rose, and a female voice called out, "Is that you, Mr. Kirby?"

"No, but open the door at once if this is Mrs. Surratt's house," Smith replied. "Are you Mrs. Surratt?" he asked the plumpish, dark-haired woman who complied.

"I am Mrs. Surratt, the widow of John H. Surratt," she answered.

"And the mother of John H. Surratt Jr.?" Major Smith specified.

"I am."

"Madam, I am come to arrest you and all in your house, and take you to General Augur's headquarters for examination," Smith announced. He directed Captain Wermerskirch to lock the front door and pocket the key, then sent Devoe down to the basement kitchen to guard any servants he might find there. Rosch kept watch outside.

"Who are these ladies?" Major Smith asked as he entered the parlor.

"That one is my daughter, that one is my niece"—Mary indicated fourteen-year-old Olivia Jenkins—"and that one is Miss Fitzpatrick, who boards with me."

Just then two more men arrived—R. C. Morgan and Thomas Sampson—reinforcements sent by the provost marshal. Smith ordered one of them to the basement to relieve Devoe. "Go out and get a car-riage and bring it to within half a block of the building as I do not wish to excite suspicion," Smith instructed Devoe when he'd emerged from the basement.

"Let the women walk, it is good enough for them," Devoe retorted.

Though she was the eldest of the three young women present, Anna Surratt could not bear any of it. The shame, the fear, and the rudeness were all too much. She began to cry.

Major Smith, too, was unwilling to tolerate such blatant disrespect from Devoe. "I at once ordered him to go and get the carriage . . . and said that they should be treated kindly, as long as they were in my charge," he recalled. Turning to Mary, he said, "Madam, I will accompany you to get the necessary hats and cloaks for you all to wear to General Augur's headquarters." Captain Wermerskirch was tasked with making sure that Anna, Olivia, and Honora did not exchange any information or attempt to coordinate their stories. As Major Smith delicately put it, "Please entertain these ladies while I am gone and do not allow any communications to pass between them."

Mary gathered shawls and bonnets for everyone, taking special care, at Major Smith's urging, to get warm wraps and shoes for her distraught daughter.

Back in the parlor Anna could not take hold of herself and "broke out into loud exclamations of grief" when her mother returned. Anna's agitation was so great that Major Smith believed she was ill.

"Do not behave so, baby," Mary soothed as she fastened Anna's shoes as though she were a child, "you are already so worn out with anxiety that you will make yourself sick, and the officer who has arrested us is in uniform, and is a gentleman and will treat us kindly."

"Oh Mother! But to be taken there for such a thing," Anna protested.

"Hush!" Mary said.

When the four of them were ready, Mary said to Major Smith, "Sir, if you have no objections, I should like to ask the blessing of God upon me as I always do on all my undertakings." The major did not object, and Mary knelt beside the piano for "at least five minutes," as Smith recalled.

Long though the prayer was, the carriage had still not arrived when Mary was finished and pronounced herself ready to depart. The women were directed to take a seat in the parlor and wait.

Just then the worst stroke of luck in Mary Surratt's life occurred. Footsteps sounded on the front stairs.

Captain Wermerskirch and Detective Morgan positioned themselves behind the door, ready to lock it again as soon as the visitor was admitted. Major Smith took up a post in the parlor doorway, facing them. As soon as the bell rang, Captain Wermerskirch unlocked the door.

On the threshold stood a "remarkably powerful man with a figure that must attract the attention of any observer," with a pickaxe slung over one shoulder. His clothes were gray and black, his fine boots muddied to the knee. On his head he wore a strange makeshift hat. It looked to be the cutoff sleeve of a shirt, or perhaps the leg from a pair of drawers, pulled over his head like a stocking cap.

"I guess I have mistaken the house," the man said as Major Smith stepped into view.

"Whose house are you looking for?" Morgan asked at the same time that Major Smith told the visitor, "No you are not."

"Mrs. Surratt's," the man answered.

"This is the house," Smith said, loosening his pistol from its holster; "come in at once."

Wermerskirch locked the door, and Smith began to question the visitor, wondering what he was doing knocking at doors this time of night. The stranger said Mrs. Surratt had sent for him that morning, that she'd hired him to dig a gutter. He claimed to be itinerant, illiterate, and poor—working with his pickaxe for a dollar or a dollar and a half a day when he could get work at all. None of that explained why he would show up for work at nearly midnight. The man told Smith that he had come to find out what time to start work in the morning. Even his pickaxe aroused suspicion. It was rusty, its handle discolored on one side, as though it had lain unused for some time.

As Major Smith remembered it, he went to the parlor door and said, "Mrs. Surratt, please step here a moment." Mary came into the entry-way, to within three paces of where the self-proclaimed digger of gutters was seated. "Mrs. Surratt do you know this man and did you hire him to come and dig a gutter for you?" Smith asked.

Mary Surratt raised her right hand and declared, "Before God, sir, I do not know this man; and I have never seen him before, and did not hire him to come and dig a gutter for me."

Captain Wermerskirch, who was standing nearby, would remember it just as Major Smith did: "She held up either one or both hands,—I cannot say,—and said, 'Before God, I have never seen that man before. I have not hired him; I do not know any thing about him;' or words to that effect."

"Your story does not hang together," Smith told the man. "I arrest you as a suspicious person and shall take you to General Augur's head-quarters to be examined."

Major Henry Smith did not know it, but he had just accidentally apprehended Secretary of State Seward's assailant.

The officers spent close to five hours searching the Surratt boarding-house. Major Smith's team took possession of several cartes de visite—small photographs mounted on cardboard. The portraits of Union generals Ulysses S. Grant, George B. McClellan, and Joseph Hooker were deemed of no importance. But the images of Jefferson Davis and Alexander Stephens, the president and vice president of the Confederacy, and two of General P.G.T. Beauregard, the man who had led the attack that had launched the Civil War, were considered worthy of note. There was also a card bearing the coat of arms of the state of Virginia, with two Confederate flags and the motto "Thus will it ever be with tyrants; Virginia the mighty; *Sic Semper Tyrannis.*" That phrase—*sic semper tyrannis*—was permanently frozen into the memories of many who had witnessed Booth fleeing the scene of his crime, dagger raised in triumph. And the most incriminating photo of all was a carte de visite of John Wilkes Booth himself, tucked behind the backing of a painting, as if to protect it from prying eyes. All the other photos had been prominently displayed in albums, or on the parlor mantelpiece.

In Mary Surratt's bedroom, Captain Wermerskirch found a bullet mold on top of the wardrobe, and a number of percussion caps—necessary for firing bullets—in a bureau drawer.

CHAPTER SIX

News of the raid on the Surratt boardinghouse made its way into the papers the very next morning. Nearly all of them jumped to the conclusion that the strangely dressed man who had been arrested in Mary's front hall was John Surratt Jr. After all, word was out that William Bell, the Sewards' servant, had already identified the tall, dark-haired man as the secretary of state's assailant. Bell had trembled at the sight of him, instantly exclaiming, "That is the man, he did it. I don't want to see any more of him."

But this man was emphatically not John Surratt. They did not resemble each other in the slightest particular. And if he was not Mary's son, why had this wanted man come knocking on her door in the dead of night?

Suspicion pivoted to Mary Surratt.

The provost marshal had ordered that every occupant of the Surratt boardinghouse be taken into police custody, regardless of guilt or innocence, a fact that never entered into the initial news coverage of Mary

Surratt's arrest. Many Americans' first impression of Mary would be of a woman admitting the police into her home without a qualm, as though she had offered up her wrists to be shackled as amiably as others might shake hands. "The mother took it calmly as though she had been expecting it," the *New York Times* reported, insinuating that an innocent woman would have been shocked to find the authorities ringing her doorbell. And indeed, it was true that none of the women at 541 H Street had inquired as to what the police were doing there.

Yet this was an odd detail to single out for special attention, considering that the day after the president's murder, Americans as far away as Lewiston, Maine, had opened their newspapers to learn that John Surratt was believed to be Secretary Seward's assailant. John's name had been all over the papers ever since. A man thought to be John Surratt had even been mobbed by an "infuriated" crowd outside the Old Capitol Prison the previous afternoon. With her son the prime suspect in a vicious attempted murder, how could anyone have expected Mary Surratt to be surprised by the sight of police detectives at her door?

Everything the *New York Times* had to say about Mary cast her in a suspicious light. Not only her actions but even her facial features, clothing, and housekeeping were taken as evidence of guilt. "Mrs. Surratt is a large-sized woman, about forty years of age, and of coarse expression," the paper noted. "She was rather shabbily dressed."

Almost every word was a veiled insult, right down to the word "woman." Any female qualified as a woman. "Lady," on the other hand, indicated a paragon of femininity, a woman worthy of respect and deference, due to the refinement of her manners, breeding, and dress. Ladies were expected to be physically dainty and fragile if at all possible, though exceptions could be made. Emotional fragility, however, was an absolute must. A large woman, particularly one with a coarse (that is, masculine) expression, aroused immediate misgivings. And a shabbily dressed woman clearly took no pride in her appearance—something a lady would never dream of neglecting.

Mrs. Surratt's domestic duties likewise struck the *New York Times* as not only relevant to the investigation but worthy of raised eyebrows. "The house was found in a very disordered condition, the beds all unmade, the clothes piled on chairs, and everything in confusion, showing very plainly that the inmates had other business on hand than the usual business of housekeeping."

Anyone who read that report would come away feeling distrustful of Mary Surratt.

☞

Who was Mary Surratt, really? Few people knew the answer. Even her priest would soon have occasion to remark, "I do not remember that anybody talked about her before this last affair happened." Only a handful of words apply without question: "Widow." "Mother." "Businesswoman." "Catholic."

For the most part, Mary Surratt—born Mary Elizabeth Jenkins—had an unremarkable early childhood in southern Maryland. She was born in 1823 and grew up sandwiched between two brothers, John Zadock Jenkins and James Archibald Jenkins. Her parents were tobacco farmers who used the free labor of eleven enslaved Africans to raise their crop.

In the fall of 1825, Mary's father died, leaving his widow with three children under age five. Unlike most women who found themselves in similar straits, Mrs. Jenkins did not remarry. Instead she managed the farm herself, and ably, too, for in the years to come she added acreage to the property and never sold off any of her slaves.

Thanks to her mother's business savvy and an aunt's generosity,

Mary was granted an opportunity uncommon for nineteenth-century girls: an education. November 26, 1835, found Mary enrolled in the Academy for Young Ladies, a Catholic boarding school across the Potomac River in Alexandria, Virginia, at a cost of $25 (about $750 today) for her first three months of tuition, room, and board. Courses available at the academy ranged from scholarly pursuits, such as chemistry, arithmetic, and philosophy, to more domestic skills, like bookkeeping and plain and fancy needlework.

What Mary studied, as well as her abilities as a student, has gone unrecorded. Yet it is certain that school changed her life, for sometime during her four years at the academy, the teenage Mary Jenkins converted to Catholicism, taking "Eugenia" as her confirmation name. Until the day she died, religion would remain Mary's unwavering cornerstone.

When the academy closed in 1839, the course of Mary's life changed once again. At age sixteen, Mary met her future husband, John Surratt, a man ten years her senior.

What drew Mary to John Surratt is unknown, as is nearly everything about John's life before their marriage. By the time Mary met him, John Surratt was already looked upon as something of a ne'er-do-well. Raised by foster parents on a vast Washington, DC, farm called Pasture and Gleaning, John grew up without siblings, unaware of who his birth parents were. To this day, no one has been able to uncover the identity of John Surratt's mother or father. This apparent shroud of secrecy strongly suggests John Surratt was born out of wedlock, a stigma impossible to shake in the nineteenth century. In 1838, he fathered a child of his own with a woman named Caroline Sanderson. The two never married, and John assumed no financial responsibility for his infant son until a court order in 1840 forced him to do so.

Nevertheless, that same August, Mary Jenkins and John Surratt took out a marriage license and were subsequently married—despite the fact that John was not Catholic. Mary was just seventeen. The couple settled on a tract of land John had inherited from his foster father, where he intended to run a gristmill. Three children followed in quick succession: Isaac in June 1841, Elizabeth Susanna (called Anna) on New Year's Day 1843, and John Jr. in April 1844.

Debt began to accumulate almost immediately, and at an alarming rate. Doctors' bills. Medicine. Loans for additional acreage. By 1845, John had relinquished the mill to try his hand at planting, and moved with his family to his foster mother's home at Pasture and Gleaning. Misfortune began piling up beside the debts. John's foster mother died. The house burned to the ground, the fire possibly set by one of the seven enslaved men and women that John Surratt counted among his property.

In 1852, John purchased 187 acres of land at the intersection of Marlboro-Piscataway and New Cut in Prince George's County. There he built a nine-room tavern that could also accommodate overnight guests. Mary grandly dubbed it "Surratt's Villa." In time the building would come to serve as a polling place and post office as well, earning the tiny crossroads the name of Surrattsville. The profits from this venture eventually allowed John Sr. to invest $4,000 in a three-story town house at 541 H Street in Washington City, which he promptly rented to a succession of businesses.

This newfound prosperity, it turned out, was not without serious drawbacks. The prospect of bringing up her children in a tavern, surrounded by barrels of alcohol and the men who imbibed it day and night, gave Mary cause for grave concern. Worse, John Surratt Sr. himself drank, and drank heavily. As a tavern keeper, temptation was always close at hand, and John Sr. rarely resisted. By 1855, it had become bad enough for Mary to lament that "my husband wollars in the mire of drinkenness."

Through it all, religion remained Mary's greatest consolation. She took joy in sponsoring the baptisms of relatives (including her mother-in-law) and friends into the Catholic faith and in helping raise funds to found St. Ignatius Church. Her greatest solace appears to have come from her priest, Father Joseph Maria Finotti. He was not only her confessor but her friend. In fact, it is thanks to Father Finotti that the only known glimpses into Mary Surratt's heart and mind have been preserved. In 1852, much to Mary's dismay, Father Finotti had been transferred to Brookline, Massachusetts. What constituted a genuine tragedy for Mary proved to be a boon for history, for their separation forced Mary Surratt to commit her woes to paper rather than whisper them in the confessional.

Just six letters written in Mary Surratt's own hand are known to survive. All six of them are addressed to Father Finotti. This scanty handful of documents divulges an astonishing amount of insight into the harsh realities of Mary's life. The weight of the burdens she carried, however invisible to others, was laid bare to Finotti. "My dearest Father I keep nothing from you though I would not have any one elst to know what I under go," Mary wrote in 1855.

Her husband was by far the greatest of Mary's trials. For her children's sake, she tried her best to conceal this fact in hopes that the family might not be disgraced entirely. Mary was evidently successful, for the Washington *Evening Star* would one day characterize John Surratt Sr. as "an inoffensive, good-tempered man." The true John Surratt bore no resemblance to that description. As his drinking accelerated, he grew increasingly ill tempered. "Mr. Surratt has be come so that he is drunk on every occation and are more and more dis-agreeable evry day," Mary privately confessed to her priest. She saw no hope of his ever changing, for with Finotti gone, no one else in the neighborhood was willing or able to intervene. "I think some times I would give the world if you could come in and give him a good lecture for me," she told Finotti. "Father John calls to see us often but he is affread to say any thing to him." In the spring of 1853, John Sr. attended Mass three times, and Mary briefly allowed herself to dream "that God may releave his family by the conversion of his dear soul." Thirteen years of marriage to John Surratt had taught her time and again that such hopes were likely misplaced. "Sometimes I try to think this is a great change in him but then again he forgets all his promises and goes on as bad as ever." This time was no different from all the rest.

One at least one occasion, John Sr.'s transgressions were so serious that Mary did not speak to him for "ten or twelve days," leaving history to wonder what offense had prompted her silent censure.

Shortly after Mary resumed speaking with her husband, another incident plunged her back into despair. One Saturday night, when John had not come to bed by three o'clock in the morning, Mary ventured downstairs to see if he intended to get any sleep at all. What she found disgusted her: "His company had all left him and he was spread out at his full leanth Beastly drunk in the bar room—think what my feelings must have been when I had for a few days bean trying to prepare for *Holy* Communion this morning."

Though but a single hint exists to suggest that John Sr. was physically abusive toward his wife, it is a strong one. "Good bye perhaps these are the last lines you will ever receve from these poor feeble fingers," Mary wrote Finotti in an undated letter, "as he has sed he will take my life if I do not become what he wishes[,] and that I am determined never to be." What John Surratt wished his wife to be, Mary left unsaid. Perhaps it was something she and her priest had spoken of before. Whatever it was, Mary deemed it a fate worse than death.

Even the comfort of religion, of worshipping the God to whom she was so devoted, was denied her by John's deteriorating behavior. "I have not had the pleasure of going to church on Sunday for more than a year," she wrote in 1858. She was by then shouldering John's duties as postmaster and likely managing the tavern as well, not to mention endeavoring to keep her children on a straight and narrow path while simultaneously preventing her neighbors and customers from discovering that her husband was an indolent drunkard. All Mary asked for herself was "grace and strenth to bare it all."

Mary Surratt did not take these trials in stride. Her letters uncloak a woman deeply troubled and beaten down by her circumstances. A January 1855 letter is signed "Yours a true Childe of sorrow." Five months later, she was still suffering silently: "Beleave me my dearest Father while my poor unfortunate fingers are engaged in these few lines I am sad my poor heart are akeing & my eyes are allmoste blinded with tears of the bitterest kind."

Her correspondence with Father Finotti also reveals a profound loneliness. Though her mother and both brothers lived nearby, Mary never mentioned any of them. It will likely never be known whether this absence was due to tension in the Jenkins family or to the simple fact that so few letters remain. Judging by those half-dozen letters, Mary Surratt's priest seems to have been her only friend in the world. Indeed, a rumor would eventually emerge that their relationship was more than that of clergyman and congregant. In 1881, a *New-York Tribune* reporter would claim that a "prominent" unnamed Maryland gentleman had told him that "while her husband was yet living[,] an Italian priest who ministered in that part of the country got in such a flirtation with Mrs. Surratt that it raised a commotion, and he had to be sent to Boston to get him out of the scandal."

A story such as this, appearing in print only once and from an unnamed source, hardly seems worthy of consideration as anything more than common gossip. But in fact, there are clues in Mary Surratt's correspondence that lend credence to this rumor. In January 1855, Mary asked Father Finotti for a favor: "I pray you not object it as it would afford me so much pleasure and could not perswade my self you would refuse me so small a request and costing you nothing." Could she borrow a daguerreotype portrait of him so that she could have a copy made for herself? Mary knew perfectly well what people might make of such a request if word got out, or if the image itself were spotted in her house. "And if you would not like it known I pledge myself for no one to know it but my self," she promised, "and I feal very shure you know me well anknuf to have that much confidence in me for let the rest of your friend say what they will I still reman the same and always to the end."

Mary's words suggest that she was aware of the talk swirling around her, which indicates that the rumor was likely real. Whether it was *true*, however, remains a mystery.

Concern for her children's futures dominated Mary's correspondence with Finotti. Every one of her surviving letters mentions her desire that her children be educated—not just the boys but Anna as well. A number of factors may have been at play.

The gaps in Mary's own education are betrayed by her letters. Beautiful though her penmanship is, erratic spellings abound, and sentences often run together without punctuation or capitalization to divide them. Mary was not ignorant of these shortcomings, and she felt self-conscious about putting them on display, even to someone she trusted as much as her priest. "Please answer this cribble and look at the intention of it and not the mistakes," she implored Father Finotti at the close of one letter in May 1855. It is conceivable that she wanted to spare her children the same kind of lifelong embarrassment.

Perhaps most important to Mary Surratt was the fact that enrollment at boarding schools would also guarantee that Isaac, John Jr., and Anna would not be exposed to the shame caused by their father's drunkenness. "I have found out long ago a publick house is [no] place for children with a Fathers example," she wrote in that May 1855 letter.

The greatest hurdle was money. Mary aspired not only to an education but to a Catholic education for her children, and that was not to be had for free. "I am trying evry day to make some arrangement for Isaac to go to chool but I can not tell how it will be as yet as you know how often misfortune has visit us in the last few years," she lamented. There was no time to waste. The older Isaac grew, the more Mary worried over his prospects. "Dear Farther please write to me and tell me what you think would be best for me to do with him as he is now geting large and it is time for him to leave this publick house as you know how many temtations thire is all ways before him," she begged Finotti when Isaac was fourteen. (Any advice from the priest has apparently been lost to history.)

If Anna was to be educated, it would have to be "on as cheap a scale as possible"—hopefully without causing Anna to feel inferior—for Mary knew that any money to be set aside for tuition "will all have to come threw and by my own management."

John Jr. in particular gave her plenty to fret over. His admiration for his father worried Mary ceaselessly: "I find it nessary to try and get John some whare to chool or he will go astray. I can not get him to go to his dieutys he thinks his *Pa* aught to know what is right as well as any one elst."

In this matter as in so many others, Mary received no support from her husband. John Sr. was either indifferent or hostile to the idea of paying for schooling for Isaac, Anna, and John Jr., terming one academy "unhealthy" for his son. "But I care not for what he thinks," Mary wrote, "as it seams the hole charge of the children has fawlen on me and I must trust in *God* and do the best I can for them."

Mary did her best and was soon rewarded for her tenacity. In 1854, Anna became a student at St. Mary's Female Institute in Bryantown, sixty miles away. Before long Mary was writing proudly of her daughter's progress with French and piano. In late December that year, a chance meeting with a priest who stopped at the Surratt tavern for a meal on his way to Bryantown led to Isaac and John Jr. becoming two of twenty-one boarders at the newly established St. Thomas Manor in

Chapel Point. Isaac's improvement was so swift, Mary even dared to entertain hopes that her elder son might become a priest. Instead, he would take a job in a dry goods shop before enlisting in the Texas cavalry to fight under the Confederate banner. John Jr., however, would extend his studies to St. Charles College, renewing his mother's hopes that one of her sons might join the clergy.

On August 19, 1862, John Surratt Sr. died suddenly—so suddenly, Anna wrote to a friend a month later, "it has almost caused me to frown upon the will of a Just God."

John Sr. had been in such lively spirits the night before, talking of politics with a visitor, that his wife and children could not make themselves believe that the man lying motionless in his bed the next morning was truly dead. "We hoped at first that he was paralyzed and that reason would be restored," Anna wrote, "but the Doctors knew that he was dead and were afraid to tell us."

John Surratt Sr. left Mary saddled with a legacy of bad debts and painful memories. Another financial blow was not far behind. In 1864, Maryland drafted and ratified a new state constitution that abolished slavery. With that vote, Mary Surratt's labor force shrank while her expenses increased. The only feasible solution seemed to be to move into the city, to the three-story town house on H Street that John Sr. had purchased in 1852, and rent out some of the bedrooms. "I wanted to get a few boarders as we had two back rooms and I thought if I could get them filled I could live," Mary would later explain. She rented the Surrattsville tavern to John Lloyd, a former officer with the Metropolitan Police, for $500 a year, and arrived in Washington, DC, on October 1, 1864.

With help from a local priest, she soon had sufficient boarders—all observant Catholics—to keep her family afloat. The income was generous enough to afford her two or three Black servants to help keep up with the cooking and laundry. Then John Jr., whom for over a decade she had feared would turn into a wastrel like his father, befriended one of the nation's most prominent actors.

By the first months of 1865, Mary Surratt could finally breathe a sigh of relief. And that was when the police came knocking.

CHAPTER SEVEN

The carriage containing the four women halted at General Augur's headquarters late on the night of April 17 or in the earliest hours of April 18. There, Anna Surratt, Honora Fitzpatrick, and Olivia Jenkins were held in an anteroom while Mary was questioned. The stranger with the pickaxe soon arrived to occupy a separate corner of the room. When the police removed his makeshift skullcap, Honora Fitzpatrick suddenly realized that she had seen him before. It was the selfsame man who had called himself Mr. Wood and Reverend Paine. Authorities would soon identify him as twenty-one-year-old Lewis Paine of Florida, but his true name was Lewis Thornton Powell.

Determining just what was said during the interrogations that were carried out during the investigation of the assassination is no simple matter. Although the original handwritten transcripts were carefully preserved in the National Archives, the questions and answers themselves were recorded in a haphazard manner.

At times the witnesses' responses appear to have been taken down word for word, in a standard question-and-answer format common to courtroom transcripts. Then, abruptly—sometimes smack in the middle of a witness's reply—the answers shift from a verbatim ac-count, complete with the usual verbal stumbles and hesitations, to a terse summary. In these instances the questions are omitted, and the stenographer's notes replace both the interrogator's and the witness's voices. Take, for example, this excerpt from Anna Surratt's questioning regarding Lewis Powell's eyes:

> **Question:** But why did you dislike his eyes?
> **Answer:** I don't know.
> **Question:** Was there a wild look about them?
> **Answer:** I do not know now. I think there was. I said he
> did not look like a preacher to me. He was not dressed
> like a preacher; wore a common dark suit of clothes. Did
> not notice whether he had an overcoat or not. Do not
> know whether he wore standing or turn down collars.
> Do not know how tall he was. Do not know whether
> he was very tall or very short. He did not appear to be
> very tall or very short. I could not tell how long he was
> there. Did not notice the man much. He had black hair.
> I did not notice his whiskers. I do not know what kind
> of mustache he wore or whether he had mustache or
> whiskers.

Either Anna Surratt was swerving from detail to detail without prompting or something is missing. Anna's questioning regarding her brother's whereabouts is equally jarring, leaving us to imagine the questions that prompted this seemingly unsolicited lump of in-formation:

> I saw my brother three weeks ago last Monday night. I
> saw him at home. He came up from the country, took

his dinner & went away. He said but very few words to us. He did not tell me where he was going. I thought he was going away to Canada. I have no idea where he was going in Canada. Ma did not tell me any particular place where he was going. I did not think she knew anything about it more than I did.

Though it appears a simple enough task at first glance to fill in the missing questions, their absence nonetheless leaves significant gaps. Did Anna evade certain aspects of the questions posed to her, holding back information that might have been deemed incriminating? Or did she volunteer more than was asked? There is nothing to do but guess.

In short, the only certainty is that it's impossible to know exactly what was said. What remains in many cases is only the gist.

Honora Fitzpatrick was assessed as "a plain unassuming girl and was not one that would be trusted with any plot and evidently knows nothing of the assassination." She was apparently not questioned to any significant extent until April 28.

If Anna Surratt was also questioned on April 17, no indication of it remains. Her earliest known statement is also dated April 28. It may well be that on the night of her arrest she was too distraught to be properly interrogated. As she and Honora and Olivia waited in the anteroom for Mary to return from questioning, a soldier happened to refer to the man with the pickaxe as John Surratt. Anna erupted into a blaze of temper at the very idea. "That ugly man," she proclaimed, was absolutely not her brother, and anyone who dared call him so "was no gentleman." Anna's protests were so vehement that her mother's interrogation had to be interrupted in order for Mary to come and calm Anna.

In Mary Surratt's case, the handwritten transcript of her first interview "in the matter of the murder of the president" bears no notes revealing what time the examination occurred, or who posed the questions to her. Other documents suggest that it may have been Colonel Henry H. Wells. (Wells was one of three men, along with Lieutenant Colonel John A. Foster and Colonel Henry S. Olcott, that Secretary Stanton had appointed to manage the mountain of potential evidence that had already accumulated since the murder.) Lieutenant Colonel Foster may also have been present.

At the outset, Mary stated the names of her current boarders: Louis Weichmann, the Holohans, Honora Fitzpatrick, and Apollonia Dean. She acknowledged that her son was acquainted with John Wilkes Booth and that, as near as she could recall, Booth had been calling at her home for the last two months. Sometimes he stopped in twice during the same day. Usually he asked for John, "but not always"; he seemed just as willing to sit in the parlor and talk with the ladies. The fact that her son had forged a friendship with such a famous actor seemed perfectly unremarkable to Mary because, as she put it, "I consider him capable of forming acquaintance in the best society." As to how her son had made the acquaintance of John Wilkes Booth, Mary could offer no answer. She could only suppose that her son had done so as "any other gentleman would."

"Has not this question occurred to you since the murder?" the interrogator wanted to know.

"Yes, sir," she said, "but I could not account for it, and I think no one could be more surprised than we were that [Booth] should be guilty of such an act. We often remarked that Mr. Booth was very clear of politics; he never mentioned anything of the kind and it was a subject that we never indulged in."

"What are your political sentiments?" the interrogator asked.

"I don't pretend to express my feelings at all," Mary said. "I have often said that I thought that the South acted too hastily; that is about the amount of my feelings, and I say so again."

As for the whereabouts of John Surratt Jr. himself, Mary said that her son had left town two weeks earlier, on April 3, and that she had not seen him since Sunday, April 2.

"Did your son say where he was going when he left you?"

"He did not; when he left he was a little vexed." The draft was being enforced in Maryland, Mary explained, and John apparently had no intention of serving for the Union cause. Mary had suggested that he pay fifty dollars for an exemption, but John had dismissed her advice and "went out with Mr. Weichmann." Louis Weichmann returned alone, with the news that John had bade him farewell and gone "to call on a friend." That was the last Mary had seen of her son. Sunday, Monday, and Tuesday had passed with no word from him. He'd left with no goodbye for his mother, without telling her where he was headed. On Wednesday, April 5, Mary finally received a note from John, informing her that he'd spent half a day in Springfield, Massachusetts, before continuing on his way. Where he was headed, he did not deign to say. Mary presumed Canada "because I heard him say he would leave the country. Last fall he spoke several times of going to Europe. I supposed he had gone to Canada, but I had no particular reason for so supposing."

That curt note had perturbed Mary. "When I read it, I felt very much vexed, and pitched it on the windowsill and have not seen it since," she told her interrogator.

The man questioning her was skeptical, particularly since the note—the only evidence that John was not in Washington—had vanished. "No man on the round earth believes [John Surratt] went to Canada," he remarked.

"I believe it," Mary returned.

"No one can believe it; they would just as soon believe that a bird could fly if we cut off his wings."

His suspicion was at least in part due to the fact that on the day that John Surratt had left his mother's house, he'd swapped two twenty-dollar gold pieces with Mr. Holohan, receiving sixty dollars cash in return. No man headed to Canada would want to fill his pockets with American greenbacks instead of gold. Gold was worth two and a half times more than cash and could more readily be spent outside the United States. But a man who intended to go south would rather have the greenbacks, which were far more valuable than the nearly worthless Confederate currency.

Mary did not acknowledge this logic, or the remark about the wingless bird. "He has never been away long enough to go South and back," she said instead.

"How long does it take to go across the river?" the interrogator countered.

Mary Surratt would not say one word that might incriminate her son. Not then, not ever. "I don't know the width of the river," she replied.

"How wide do you suppose it is?"

Mary did not suppose anything at all. The Potomac's width varied, she said, depending on where you crossed. That was undeniably true. It also did not answer the question.

"You certainly could go to Fredericksburg and back in four days, to Richmond and back in a week," the interrogator informed her, adding that John was known to have made the trip "a great many times for a great while longer than that."

"I don't think he has."

"Oh yes, he has. Have I made any error in my record so far as his movements are concerned?"

"No, sir; that is all correct."

"You cannot explain how he makes the acquaintance of Booth; nor why he exchanged his gold for greenbacks. Can you explain how he makes any other acquaintance?"

She could not. According to Mary, her son brought very few visitors to the house.

"Don't you know of his making the acquaintance of Mr. Atzerodt?"

Mary acknowledged that there was a man from Port Tobacco who'd come to the house sometime in the first half of March, on a day when she'd happened to be away. Mary's boarders had found his name difficult to pronounce, so they'd all dubbed him "Port Tobacco" and told him he could stay until the landlady returned. "When I came I found him rather a rough looking man," Mary recalled. This new customer had not endeared himself to Mrs. Surratt. "He remained only part of a week," she explained, "when I found some liquor in his room; no gentleman can board with me who keeps liquor in his rooms, and I told my son that that man could not stay, that I could not board him." It is a plausible explanation. Twenty-two years of marriage to John Surratt had taught her to abhor alcohol.

Was the man stoop-shouldered? the interrogator wanted to know. Did his hair turn up under his hat? Did he use slang words? Was he clean-shaven, or did he have a mustache? Mary Surratt could not remember much except that he was German, round-shouldered, and dark-haired; he might have had a mustache and side-whiskers; and he rode a tall, dark horse.

Then there was another man, she said, tall and light-complected, whose name might have been Wood. He had spent two nights and a day at the Surratt boardinghouse around the same time as this so-called Port Tobacco.

"There was a young gentleman who used to meet your son, whose mother lives over the Navy Yard Bridge, David or Daniel Herold?" the interrogator asked.

"No such man ever visited my house, I assure you."

Next the interrogator showed Mary a photograph. She recognized the image easily. "That's Mr. Booth, ain't it?" Then he presented a photo of David Herold for her to examine. "I don't know that man," Mary said.

"He is a very intimate friend of your son's."

"Well, sir, I assure you he is not a visitor to our house, on the honor of a lady."

The time had come to probe for the information that had led investigators to arrest everyone at 541 H Street. "Speaking of visiting at your house," the interrogator said, "I will bring the thing down a little nearer. I will be happy to have you give me the names of three men who came to you on Saturday and had a private conversation with you?"

The question appears to have puzzled Mary Surratt. "Last Saturday?" she asked.

"Yes, madam."

"No three gentlemen came to my house, I assure you."

The interrogator phrased his next question to ensure that Mary was not attempting to dodge the issue: "How many did come?"

This was a key moment to observe Mary Surratt's reaction. Did her face show any indication of surprise? Confusion? Did she pause to consider before answering?

"You mean the gentlemen who came in to search the house?" she asked. Whether she spoke quickly or slowly, confidently or with uncertainty, the transcript gives no hint.

The interrogator, on the other hand, provided a clear indication of suspicion in his response: "No, you know who I mean," he said. Because of the tip the authorities had received from John Kimball regarding an incriminating conversation allegedly overheard by Susan Mahoney on the night after the assassination, the man questioning Mary Surratt had reason to believe she was now telling him bald-faced lies.

Only two gentleman had come to the house that day, Mary insisted. One was her friend Mr. Kirby, and the other was Father Bernardine Wiget. Mary was adamant about that. "I pledge you my word of honor," she declared.

"I mean the three men who come to your house and you had a private conversation with them, and supposed you were alone, but you were not," the interrogator pressed.

"Upon my word, that I do not know; upon the honor of a lady, I do not remember anybody except Mr. Wiget."

"I can tell you what you said."

"Perhaps I can remember, then."

"I can tell you what they wanted at your house, too."

"Well, sir, if you will please to tell me, if I remember it I will tell you."

"You cannot remember anything about it?"

"Don't remember of any gentlemen come to my house."

"Of the three persons, there was not a gentleman among them," he said. The interrogator's response was tinged with a sarcasm that is easy for modern readers to miss. Just as "lady" indicated a particular kind of woman, "gentleman" was a term reserved for honorable, well-bred men—the furthest thing from the suspects that the interrogator was intent on apprehending.

"I don't remember indeed."

"There were three men, though," the interrogator remarked.

Again Mary denied any knowledge of visitors to her house, not even "if it was the last word I had to say."

Her insistence appears to have left the interrogator flummoxed. "I don't know but I have misunderstood you," he said. "Do you say to me that no two or three or four men ever came to your house the last three or four days, on Friday or Saturday or Sunday?"

The only other gentlemen she was aware of had arrived Sunday morning, after Mass. "I assure you on the honor of a lady that I would not tell you any untruth," Mary said.

"I assure you on the honor of a gentleman, I shall get this information from you," the interrogator retorted.

"Whatever it is, I shall tell you."

"Now, I know they were there," he argued.

"Well, sir, if you do, I do not."

"I mean men who called at your house and wanted to change their clothes."

That, at last, brought some recognition from Mary. "Mr. Weichmann and Mr. Holohan and one of the detectives came there; that might have been Sunday morning," she offered. She'd been sitting in the parlor with Mr. Kirby when the three men had pulled up in a carriage. Louis Weichmann had gone up to his room to change his clothes. As nearly as she could recall, that had been around ten o'clock.

The similarities between these two incidents ought to have given the interrogator a moment's pause. Was it possible that two different groups of three men had come to Mary Surratt's boardinghouse in search of a change of clothes within just a few hours of each other? Or were the incidents in fact one and the same? If the details had somehow gotten confused and exaggerated as the story passed from one person to the next, then the Kimball tip—the one that had led the authorities to 541 H Street in the first place—had almost certainly been a false lead. The questioning, however, carried on with no sign of a hesitation.

"What did you say to them?" the interrogator continued.

"Nothing except to say good morning or something of the kind."

By then the interrogator was so fed up, even the dryness of the transcript cannot obscure his frustration. "Will you tell me, in the presence of Almighty God, who first mentioned the name of Mr. Booth in that party?" he demanded.

Mary's words, by contrast, give no indication of whether she was ruffled by the fury mounting before her. "I don't remember," she said simply.

"Indeed you do. I pledge you my word you do and you will admit it, and I should be very glad if you would do it at once."

"If I could, I would do so."

It is difficult to read the transcript without coming away with the impression that Mary Surratt's responses had thoroughly stymied her interrogator. "Reflect a moment," he replied, "and I will send for a glass of water for you."

The glass of water was brought, and shortly thereafter the questions began again. Mary's position had not budged during the momentary lull. No matter how many times or in how many ways the interrogator asked, she could not remember anyone mentioning John Wilkes Booth's name to her that Sunday morning. "These gentlemen came in and asked me how I felt," Mary said. "I told them I felt as well as I could expect to feel, or something similar to that; then something was said in relation to my son. I think, to the best of my knowledge, that was the conversation."

"That is getting near it," the interrogator said, encouraging her to continue in the same vein. "I want to know if you believe what was said about your son being in the theater with Booth?"

"There was nothing said about his being in the theater with Booth."

"Now, what I want to ask of you is, whether you think your son was there with Booth."

"No, sir, I do not believe he was there; if it was the last word I had to speak."

Once again, the interrogator insisted on knowing how Mary had replied to the men's remark about John's involvement with Booth.

"If it was made; I pledge you my word of honor, I did not hear it."
Louis Weichmann had returned from upstairs just as some other offend-
ing remark about John Surratt had been made, she explained, and then
Weichmann, Holohan, and the detective had left. "If I remembered it,
I assure you, if I heard it, I would tell you," Mary said. "I was too much
hurt; you can imagine a mother's feelings to hear such a thing from the
face of one she did not expect." What that cutting remark was, or who
had made it, she never said. Nor did the interrogator ask. He gave up on
sussing out the Kimball tip altogether, and instead handed Mary a letter
signed "Kate" at the bottom.

"Whose writing is that, Mrs. Surratt?"

"I don't know it, sir. My eyesight is not very good." It was written
in pencil, making it harder yet for her to see. "Don't know it," she confirmed after a second look.

The next questions were about her son's horses. He'd owned two,
Mary said, a black and a bay, but one had been sold recently.

The interrogator's interest perked up. Was John's horse blind in one
eye? he asked. Mary's answer disappointed him. The horse was still on
their farm in Surrattsville and was not blind. He'd once been a large,
fine animal, though the winter had made him thin, and a recent injury
had left him unfit to ride.

Here the interrogator abruptly changed the subject. He wanted to
know about the fellow the soldiers had arrested at her house. Had she
met that young man before, and had she been expecting his arrival?

"No, sir," Mary answered. "The ruffian that was in my door when I
came away? He was a tremendous hard fellow with a skullcap on, and
my daughter commenced crying, and said those [officers] came to save
our lives. I hope they arrested him."

"Did you have any arrangement made with [him] to do anything
about your premises?"

"I assure you I did not."

"He tells me now that he met you in the street and you engaged him to come to your house."

For the first time, Mary Surratt's apparent calm deserted her. "Oh! Oh! It is not so, sir, for I believe he would have murdered us, every one, I assure you," she exclaimed.

"Did he have anything in his hand?"

"He had some kind of a weapon."

"When did you see him first?"

"Just as the carriage drew up; he rang the doorbell, and my daughter said; 'Oh! There is a murderer.'"

"Did you ever engage a man to come and clean your yard?"

"No, sir. I engage a black man; I never have a white man."

With that, the examination ended.

CHAPTER EIGHT

Following the interrogation, all four women were conveyed to the Old Capitol Prison. Built as a temporary house of Congress after the British burned the Capitol during the War of 1812, the building had been adapted in 1861 as a prison for captured Confederates, insubordinate Union officers, spies, horse thieves, and blockade-runners. The Surratt women and their companions were assigned to room 41 on the second floor of the Carroll Annex, a building which up to that point had mainly housed "such unfortunate females as aroused either the ire or suspicion of the Government."

The ten-by-twelve-foot cells were shared, almost dormitory-style, and female prisoners could be given permission to circulate freely between them. The amenities in these rooms included a fireplace and iron bedsteads with pillows, straw mattresses, sheets, and brown blankets. A small table held a stone water jug and a tin cup. On the floor sat a tin basin and a wooden toilet bucket. A plain wooden chair or two completed the meager furnishings. Little but spiderwebs adorned the crumbling wallpaper. Roaches, ants, and mice shared the prisoners' accommodations and their food.

The women were more fortunate than they knew. The men believed to have been involved in the conspiracy had been imprisoned in the dark holds of the USS *Saugus* and the USS *Montauk,* a pair of armored iron-clad warships anchored in the Washington Navy Yard. Each man's wrists were shackled in two wide circlets of iron, somewhat like bangle brace-lets, that were joined together by a bar rather than a chain. These Lilly irons had a fat bolt at the center of the bar that clamped the bracelets shut and immobilized the hands with the palms facing each another. There were no furnishings for the men at all; to rest, they leaned against the iron bulkheads. Conditions aboard the ironclads were so abysmal that Lewis Powell would attempt suicide by trying to dash his brains out upon the wall. Thereafter, Secretary of War Stanton ordered that all prisoners' heads should be covered by padded canvas hoods, "with a hole for proper breathing and eating but not seeing." These hoods were misshapen, macabre-looking articles, stitched together like something out of Dr. Frankenstein's laboratory. Though the men were blinded and stifled at all hours, mealtime proved an especial torment, for with manacled hands it was next to impossible for prisoners to guide a spoon to the misaligned mouth hole.

In the Carroll Annex, Mary Surratt was spared these torments and subjected only to the customary indignities and limitations of prison life. It would seem that she weathered them with admirable grace. Vir-ginia Lomax, who chronicled her own experiences in the Carroll Annex in an anonymously written book called *The Old Capitol and Its Inmates,* came to know and respect Mary Surratt while incarcerated. (The thirty-four-year-old Mrs. Lomax, who had come to visit her cousin, the wife of a rebel general, found herself arrested on general suspicion.)

"There was a calm, quiet dignity about the woman," Lomax wrote of Mary, "which impressed me before I even knew who she was. She mingled very little with the other prisoners, unless they were sick or sorrowful; then, I may truly say, she was an angel of mercy."

Mrs. Lomax witnessed Mary's kindness with her own eyes when her cousin's husband was summoned by the guard. Often prisoners obeying such calls never returned, and her cousin was much disturbed—"weeping bitterly at the departure of her husband, when a lady entered the room," Mrs. Lomax remembered. "She was apparently about forty years of age, a tall commanding figure, rather stout, with brown hair, blue eyes, thin nose, and small, well-shaped mouth, denoting great firmness. This lady was Mrs. Surratt." Mrs. Lomax watched as Mary sat down beside her cousin, drew the sobbing woman's head to her shoulder, and commenced comforting her with the tenderness usually reserved for the dearest of friends.

Mary Surratt showed the same compassion toward a rebel soldier in the prison infirmary, a boy of just seventeen whose mother had been forbidden to visit him. Though his wound was not mortal, typhoid fever set in and sealed his fate. Daily, Mary mothered him as best she could, until he died in her arms. Remarkably, the profound suffering of others seemed to extract no toll from her. Rather, comforting those around her appeared to provide a sort of solace to Mary.

The tremendous load of anxiety she herself was carrying showed itself outwardly to Mrs. Lomax on only one occasion. News was important to Mary, and she read the papers each day. When an article appeared that contained "an outrageous account of herself and household," her fellow prisoners tried to keep it from her. Mary insisted upon reading it. "I watched her closely while doing so," Virginia Lomax remembered, "and for an instant a flush of womanly indignation overspread her pale countenance at the insult."

"I suppose I shall *have* to bear it," she said, clasping her hands. Never before had Mrs. Lomax heard Mary say a word about her suffering. And never would she hear another word about it.

Mary Surratt neither smiled nor complained, instead retaining a calm composure that Mrs. Lomax admired. "She rather avoided conversation, and never uttered one word of reproach or virulence against those by whose authority she was imprisoned. She always retained her self-possession, and was never in the least degree thrown off her guard."

On April 18, John Lloyd, the proprietor of the Surratt tavern, was forced to confront his lies. A cavalry detachment led by Lieutenant Alexander Lovett intercepted him as he returned from a trip to the village of Allen's Fresh. The soldiers escorted Lloyd to a nearby post office that was serving as a temporary detention center. What happened to John Lloyd while he was in police custody has been a matter of debate ever since.

"When first arrested," Detective George Cottingham reported, Lloyd "denied all knowledge of Booth, Herold, or Surratt." Soon, though, Lloyd's entire story changed. Information came pouring out of him—information he had avoided divulging since the small hours of April 15.

Several weeks prior to the assassination, John Surratt, David Herold, and George Atzerodt had stopped at the tavern. Lloyd knew all of them—they'd enjoyed rounds of whiskey and hands of cards together at least once before.

This time, John Surratt called Lloyd into the front parlor. On the sofa lay two Spencer carbine rifles, cartridge boxes of ammunition, a length of rope, and a monkey wrench. Surratt wanted Lloyd to hide the weapons and proceeded to show him exactly where. In an upstairs room that had never been plastered, some of the first-floor ceiling joists were still exposed. John Surratt carefully slid the rifles into the long, narrow space between two joists, concealing them between the dining room ceiling and the floor of the room above.

The whole thing gave John Lloyd an "uneasy" feeling that persisted for weeks. As the proprietor of a Confederate safe house, he was already shouldering a considerable risk. If the authorities searched the place and found the weapons, John Lloyd knew, he—not John Surratt—would be held immediately accountable. Yet Lloyd could not simply demand that Surratt take his rifles elsewhere. It was not Lloyd's tavern, after all. He was only renting the property, and John Surratt was his landlady's son. "I told him I did not like to receive such things into the house," Lloyd later said, "but I consented at last to do so." Surratt placated Lloyd with a promise that he would "take them away soon."

Lloyd's misgivings had finally started to fade when, on April 11, as he was driving toward the Navy Yard Bridge on his way through Uniontown, he happened to recognize Mary Surratt in an approaching carriage. It was a gray, muddy day, but Lloyd stopped his carriage and got out to speak with his landlady.

Later he could not remember precisely what Mary said, in part because she brought the topic up so indirectly—"in a manner as if she wanted to draw my attention to something so that anybody else could not understand." The two were not alone. Lloyd's sister-in-law was with him, and Mary was accompanied by a young man. Whatever she wanted to discuss seemed not to be meant for their companions' ears.

Her roundabout hints were lost on Lloyd. "Finally she came out bolder with it," he remembered. The phrase that would stick in Lloyd's mind afterward was "shooting-irons," though he would admit he was "not altogether positive" about just how she had put it. Either way, he understood at last: the carbines. She wanted to know if the rifles were still hidden at the tavern. Indeed they were, "shoved far back," Lloyd said, because he feared the house being searched.

Mary's instructions were clear enough. "Get them out ready: they would be wanted soon." She gave no indication of who would want them, or why.

Near five o'clock on April 14, Lloyd continued, he arrived at the tavern with a wagonload of fish and oysters and was met by Mary Surratt as he drove up to the woodpile.

"Talk about the Devil, and his imps will appear," she said by way of greeting.

Lloyd was not in a mood for teasing. He'd driven all the way to Marlboro that day to testify in an assault-and-battery case, only to find that the court date had been postponed. He'd then proceeded to fill his empty time with liquor—a great deal of liquor, in fact. By his own admission he had "got pretty tight."

"I was not aware that I was a devil before," he replied.

The way John Lloyd would recall the conversation, Mary Surratt then said, "Well Mr. Lloyd, I want you [to] have those shooting-irons ready: there will be parties here to-night who will call for them." He was to have two bottles of whiskey set out and waiting as well.

Even in his inebriated state, the news was a godsend for Lloyd. "I could not divine what they wanted of these carbines," he would claim, "and I was very anxious to have them taken away, and felt relieved that they were going away; but I had no idea of what was going on, more than the man in the moon."

Mrs. Surratt had also brought a small package wrapped in paper— "a little bundle rolled up." When these unnamed "parties" called for the rifles, she instructed, Lloyd was to hand it over as well. That settled, she bade him goodbye. "This matter seemed to be her whole business with me," he said of the conversation.

John Lloyd had hardly gotten into the barroom before Mrs. Surratt was back. The front spring bolts had come loose from her buggy, and she needed assistance. He did not have the equipment or the sobriety to fix the buggy properly. The best he could do was lash the spring to the axle with some cord. When Lloyd returned to the house, he unwrapped the bundle she'd left and found an expensive pair of binoculars.

Lloyd was drunk enough that he headed to bed much sooner than usual that night. Probably not long after eight o'clock, as near as he could remember. "I was pretty well in liquor & consequently wanted to retire early," he said. As his sister-in-law would later verify, he was so drunk, he felt sick when he stood up, and could not get his coat off without help. She had never seen him "more in liquor than on that occasion."

At the stroke of midnight, Lloyd awoke, unaware that anything had roused him. "Just at that time there was a rap at the door." He went down and found David Herold standing on his doorstep, and another man he did not recognize, with a pale face and mustache, sitting atop a horse. "Herold told me to hurry up and get those things, meaning, as I supposed, the carbines." Lloyd went for the guns while Herold came in and poured himself a glass of whiskey. Then Herold carried the bottle out to his companion, who took a swig so generous, it nearly finished off the bottle.

They accepted only one of the two rifles; the mounted man had broken his leg, and could not balance himself properly in the saddle with a carbine in hand.

"I will tell you some news if you want to hear it," the second man said from his perch high on the horse.

John Lloyd was none too keen to hear what this fellow had to say. Judging by the hour and the nature of the weapons they had come for, Lloyd had already concluded that whatever had happened (or was about to happen) was sure to be "of a serious nature." "I am not particular," Lloyd said; "you can tell it if you think it proper."

"We have assassinated the President and Secretary Seward," the pale man announced. Then he and David Herold galloped off into the night.

Lloyd's stunning confession might very well have been provoked by his conscience. There can be no doubt that as a former member of Washington's police force, John Lloyd understood the consequences of withholding information from an investigation of this magnitude. For the seventy-two hours he had remained silent, he had obstructed justice, as well as aided and abetted John Wilkes Booth's escape. As the pursuit of justice lengthened, though, a rumor would emerge that Lloyd had been pressured—perhaps even tortured—to fatten his story with additional incriminating details.

Intriguingly, the documentation of Lloyd's initial interrogations by police is scanty at best. The confession the authorities would come to rely on is dated April 22, a full four days after his arrest. But that was not Lloyd's first statement. What did he tell the police on April 18? And why did they neglect to record it in any significant detail?

In fact, John Lloyd had made at least two confessions prior to April 22—one to Lieutenant Lovett, and another to Detective Cottingham. Lieutenant Lovett described Lloyd's first "partial" confession as "very much confused, as he was very agitated and frightened and cried most of the time." Lovett apparently reported this "private" confession to no one for more than ten days, and then gave it the most inadequate of summaries—a mere four sentences in his April 29 account of the arrest. His report listed just three scraps of information he had gleaned: Lloyd was acquainted with Booth and Herold and had concealed their carbines in the tavern; on April 14, Mary Surratt had instructed him to have the weapons ready; Booth and Herold had arrived after midnight to collect the rifles. "He knew the whole party and that to save himself would 'come out' on all of them," Lovett wrote, "and that though he supposed he might be hung, he would not hesitate to tell all he knew of the affair."

No record of Lloyd's first conversation with Cottingham seems to exist. Instead there are only indirect references to it. "Mr. Lloyd has made an additional confession," Detective Cottingham reported on April 23, confirming that he, too, had questioned Lloyd when the tavern keeper had first been taken into custody.

Apparently the bulk of the information Lloyd shared with Cotting-ham did not come quickly. "After Lloyd's arrest I told him for the sake of his family to make a clean brest of the whole matter, as I had the proof against him." Cottingham gave Lloyd some time to mull the dilemma over, treating him "kindly." When Cottingham tried again, he reported, Lloyd exclaimed, "My God they will kill me if I implicate them."

John Lloyd had put himself in an utterly unenviable position. If he did not comply with the investigators' demands, he had every reason to believe that he would be prosecuted for his failure to report Booth's stopover in Surrattsville on the night of the assassination. As far as in-vestigators were concerned, John Lloyd had "virtually acknowledged complicity" with his second confession, giving them rock-solid grounds for trying him as a conspirator alongside Booth. In Cottingham's view, Lloyd was an "accessory to the murder of President Lincoln before and after the deed."

All the same, there was a compelling reason not to prosecute him. John Lloyd's information was as unique as it was valuable, and crimi-nal law at that time forbade anyone accused of a crime to testify at their own trial. If Lloyd's information was to be of any use against the conspirators, therefore, he could not be indicted in Lincoln's murder. Both Lloyd and the investigators, then, had an incentive to embellish the facts. The more Lloyd could be made to dread being prosecuted, the more information he was likely to volunteer. And the more he told, the more valuable he became as a witness, thereby reducing his chances of joining the accused.

Lloyd could be sure of one thing: no matter what he said, he was going to jail. Witnesses and accomplices alike were being held by the government at the Old Capitol Prison. A witness, at least, could look forward to being set free when all was said and done.

Detective Cottingham must have been persuasive. In August he would boast, "Had it not been for me . . . this confession would not have been made by Lloyd." The exact nature of Cottingham's methods of persuasion is clouded by conflicting reports. Although to his superiors Cottingham carefully detailed the "strategy" he deployed to gain Lloyd's confidence, encouraging the tavern keeper to "be relieved from a very heavy burden," another detective would document Cottingham candidly bragging, "I dragged it out of Lloyd."

Whether the information was extracted by way of patience or threats (or both), the process was an agonizing one for John Lloyd. As Detective Cottingham recalled in another, undated report, "Lloyd shed tears while making the confession, and said, 'That vile woman (Mrs. Surratt) has got him in all that trouble, and that he would be shot.'"

Whatever the cause of this apparent gap in documentation may be, the fact remains that the record of John Lloyd's encounters with police in the hours and days immediately following his arrest has been lost to history. Only the April 22 version remains. That version proved to be devastating to Mary Surratt. "I hope Mrs. Surratt is in close confinement," Cottingham advised his superiors after obtaining Lloyd's second confession.

Ultimately, it was this version of Lloyd's story that the very next day caused Colonel Wells to conclude "that the house of Mrs. Surratt was not only a stopping place for the conspirators but that she was one of them. . . . I order her to be sent to the Old [Arsenal] and she should be securely held."

CHAPTER NINE

John Wilkes Booth had confounded the authorities. Five days after his crime, he had somehow managed to evade the largest manhunt in United States history. It seemed certain that with such a colossal head start, he must have put hundreds of miles between himself and Washington, DC. In fact, Booth and David Herold were practically under the investigators' noses.

Hampered by his injury, Booth had detoured from his planned escape route to obtain treatment from Dr. Samuel Mudd, four and a half miles south of Bryantown. After setting Booth's broken bone, Mudd directed him to seek out Captain Samuel Cox, a trustworthy rebel sympathizer. Rather than conduct Booth and Herold across the Potomac as Booth had originally planned, Cox offered to hide the two fugitives in a dense pine thicket on his property. It proved to be a sly tactic. No one expected the man who'd had the audacity to commit the nation's most high-profile murder in front of a theater full of witnesses to shelter in the woods for days like a wounded animal.

Damp, cold, and aching to move, Booth and Herold hunkered among the pines while soldiers and detectives swarmed the countryside, following one false lead after another.

The effect of Booth's getaway on the nation's mood was dismal. One of the cavalry officers tasked with tracking Booth's trail recalled the strain of working under "the weight of indignant and impotent grief that was added to a Nation's sorrow for its loss, as the conviction settled upon the hearts of man that the murderer had escaped."

At the War Department, Secretary Stanton's frustration was so great, it threatened to shatter the windowpanes. Someone had to know where the assassin was. If love of justice and country was not cause enough to turn the murderer in, perhaps money would be. Reward offers of $10,000, then $30,000, brought no useful leads. Fed up, Stanton issued a broadside on April 20 that placed an unprecedented price on Booth's head.

"THE MURDERER of our late beloved President, Abraham Lincoln, IS STILL AT LARGE," the poster admonished in mammoth capital letters. Fifty thousand dollars for the capture of John Wilkes Booth, and $25,000 each for the capture of John Surratt and David Herold. It was a fortune, worth over $1.5 million today.

The notice ended on an ominous note: "All persons harboring or secreting the said persons, or either of them, or aiding or assisting their concealment or escape, will be treated as accomplices in the murder of the President and the attempted assassination of the Secretary of State, and shall be subject to trial before a Military Commission, and the punishment of DEATH."

While Mary Surratt sat in prison and the military scoured the marshes and swamps of southern Maryland for Booth, Louis Weichmann was en route to Montreal, in search of John Surratt. And contrary to the impression he later fabricated, Weichmann had no choice in the matter. He and John Holohan were both in the custody of Detective McDevitt and two other officers of the Metropolitan Police. They arrived in Montreal on April 20.

In the registry of Montreal's Saint Lawrence Hall Hotel, Louis Weichmann found three lines of handwriting he recognized. "John Harrison" (Surratt's middle name was Harrison) had registered there at ten-thirty on the morning of April 6, and checked out in time to board the three o'clock train to New York on April 12. Then he had returned at half past noon on April 18 and had departed again that same evening. The six days in between those stays would have been more than enough time for him to travel to Washington to assist in Booth's murder plot. Here the trail went cold, for the hotel records gave no indication of where he had headed on April 18.

The mission was not a complete failure, however. Weichmann's confirmation of John Surratt's presence in Montreal strengthened the police's suspicions that Surratt had been in contact with leading members of the rebel government, several of whom had taken refuge in Canada and had hence been nicknamed the Canadian Cabinet. The timing of John's stays in relation to the assassination made it look very much as though he might have been relaying instructions from the Canadian Cabinet to John Wilkes Booth. And if that was the case, the entire Confederate government was complicit in Lincoln's murder.

Meanwhile, back in Washington, Secretary of War Stanton sent word to Police Superintendent Richards that he himself wanted to speak with Louis Weichmann. Few other men had supplied as much pertinent information as the young clerk had. When Stanton got wind that one of the police's best informants had been permitted to leave the country, he was, to put it mildly, none too pleased. Not only had Weichmann left the country but Richards could not tell Stanton precisely where Weichmann was. Richards "supposed that they were at

Montreal, or Quebec, or somewhere." The secretary's orders to the police superintendent left no room for misunderstanding: Bring that man back to Washington. Immediately.

Not until April 25 did the Sixteenth New York Cavalry, commanded by Lieutenant Edward Doherty and accompanied by Detective Luther Baker and Lieutenant Colonel Everton Conger, manage to trace John Wilkes Booth and David Herold to a farm three miles south of Port Royal, Virginia, by following tips and leads about a pale, dark-haired man on crutches.

The two fugitives had spent days creeping across the marshy Maryland countryside, struggling along at an agonizingly slow pace toward the Virginia shore on the opposite side of the Potomac. Their horses were dead—shot by Herold and sunk in a swamp near the pine thicket so the bodies could not be found and used as a clue to pinpoint the criminals' whereabouts. The animals had turned out to be too large, recognizable, and hungry to keep hidden. Now the two men could move only as fast as Booth could hobble. Booth himself was in a foul temper—tormented constantly by the pain in his leg and dispirited by the newspapers he had seen, which, to his shock, condemned him as a villainous traitor rather than lauding his heroism for striking down a despot. The men's first attempt at crossing the river had ended in confusion and frustration when they'd found they had somehow rowed themselves in a circle, right back to the Maryland shore. Herold, who thus far had displayed the loyalty and devotion of a spaniel, soon began to waver, growing "sick and tired of this way of living." He wanted to go home.

Booth's carefully laid escape plan had fractured with his leg. That misfortune had scrambled his route and forced him to rely on a chain of sympathetic yet reluctant strangers to shepherd him from one temporary refuge to another. The latest link in that shaky chain was a farmer named Richard Garrett. Booth had earned a bed and a place at the Garretts' dinner table by posing as a wounded Confederate soldier in need of shelter, but by the following evening, the family had become suspicious of this heavily armed man who'd dashed into the woods upon hearing a detachment of Union cavalry galloping by. That evening, April 25, the Garretts relegated "Mr. Boyd" and his young "cousin" to the tobacco barn for the night. In fact, the two eldest Garrett brothers padlocked Booth and Herold into the barn, for fear that the pair of strangers might be horse thieves.

That was where the Sixteenth New York Cavalry found Booth and Herold when they surrounded the Garrett farm shortly after midnight.

Detective Baker issued an ultimatum: surrender all weapons, or the soldiers would set fire to the building, "and thus end the affair with a bonfire and a shooting match."

"Captain, That's rather rough," said a voice from inside the barn. "I am nothing but a cripple, I have but one leg, and you ought to give me a chance for a fair fight."

"We did not come to fight you but to capture you," Baker returned.

Baker gave Booth and Herold five minutes to decide. Inside the barn, a low argument broke out. Baker heard the words "go away from me" and "damned coward." The straw rustled. Then came a knock from inside the barn door. "Captain! Here's a man that wants to surrender mighty bad." The same voice called out, "Let him out; that young man is innocent."

Baker ordered them to surrender their weapons first.

The voice replied, "I own & have all the arms that are here, and he cannot get them."

Detective Baker unlocked the door and reached one hand across the narrow opening, bracing the door with the other so that it could not be flung wide. Lieutenant Doherty stood ready with the keys. "Put out your hands!" Doherty commanded. A pair of hands appeared in the gap, and Baker pulled David Herold out by the wrists while Doherty slammed and locked the door behind him. "The poor little wretch was dragged away, whining and crying like a child," one of the Garrett sons remembered, "and securely bound to a tree in the yard."

Baker warned Booth that he had two minutes left to surrender.

"Well, you may prepare a stretcher for me," Booth proclaimed. "Throw open your door, draw up your men in line, and let's have a fair fight."

Lieutenant Colonel Conger, meanwhile, would listen to no more wheedling: "I made up my mind that the best thing for us to do would be to close up the matter immediately," he recounted to his superiors the next day. He fished out some hay through the wide gaps between the slats at the back corner of the barn, set it alight, and shoved it back inside. "It blazed almost like powder. The whole inside of the barn was at once lighted up."

Now John Wilkes Booth was visible through the cracks in the barn walls. "Instantly his countenance changed," Conger reported. Booth's first instinct seemed to be to put the fire out, Baker noticed, "but a moments [sic] glance at its magnitude must have soon convinced him that it could not be done." Baker, cognizant that they had been ordered to take Booth alive, "sprung to the door and unlocked it." Conger watched as Booth, too, spun toward the door, a carbine in hand. Conger raced around the corner of the barn to intercept the assassin. Halfway there, he heard the shot. When he reached the doorway, Booth was dangling from Baker's grasp.

"Is he dead?" Conger demanded. "Did he shoot himself?"

He was not dead—not yet. The bullet, fired from the revolver of

Sergeant Boston Corbett, had struck John Wilkes Booth clean through the neck. He was paralyzed. The two officers dragged the assassin away from the blistering heat of the blaze and up onto the Garretts' porch.

Booth asked for water. He asked to be killed. The officers gave him a cool wet rag to suck every two minutes, bathed his wound, fetched him a mattress, and watched his lips turn purple as his neck swelled. They rigged a makeshift curtain to shade his face from the glare of the rising sun. But they would not kill him, though he asked again and again over the next two or three hours. The grief of the nation demanded that John Wilkes Booth be made to answer for his crime.

But by now Booth could hardly whisper. Paralyzed below the bullet wound, he could not even cough to relieve the choking sensation in his swelling throat. He motioned to Detective Baker that he wanted to speak. "I put my ear down, and he said, 'Tell my mother—Tell my mother that I did it for my country—that I die for my country.'"

He would speak just once more. Again Baker leaned in close, and heard the words "my hands." Baker bathed them in water and held them up for Booth to see. With an effort, the assassin said, "Useless, useless."

The officers did not record the precise time of Booth's death, only that the sun, which had just been tinging the night sky with gray when the assassin had been pulled from the barn, had risen high enough to shine in his face "before his consciousness departed."

With the help of Lieutenant Doherty, Detective Baker wrapped Booth's body in a saddle blanket and sewed it shut. "We put the body in an old, rickety one horse wagon, with some corn and fodder," Baker said, "and I went in advance with the corpse." Booth's remains would be autopsied, then buried with utmost secrecy beneath the floor of an Old Arsenal Penitentiary storeroom to prevent an enraged public from desecrating his corpse.

CHAPTER TEN

Two days after Booth's death, Mary Surratt was questioned again, this time by Colonel Henry S. Olcott, another member of Secretary Stanton's evidence team.

The authorities knew much more now than they had during Mary Surratt's first questioning on April 17. During those intervening eleven days, Lewis Powell, George Atzerodt, and John Lloyd had been arrested and questioned. Police were beginning to piece together the threads of a web that connected Mary Surratt to all these men. There were no current ties to David Herold, but investigators knew he had visited her home in Surrattsville in 1863, as a guest of her son. No links yet joined her to Arnold, O'Laughlen, or Spangler. Dr. Mudd, by now also incarcerated for failing to report that he had harbored Booth and set the assassin's broken leg on the night of the murder, had not incriminated her.

Colonel Olcott began with the 1860s equivalent of a Miranda warning: "I have been sent by the Secty to examine you among others to see what statement you are willing to make about the circumstances of this murder. You are at liberty to decline answering but you will understand any statement you make will be used on your trial." He added: "You are a woman of too good sense not to know that it is better to refuse to say anything than not to tell the truth."

The first series of questions mirrored those that Mary had been asked during her examination on April 17. When had she last seen her son? Where was he now? Mary's answers were the same. She had not seen John since Monday, April 3, almost two weeks prior to the assassination, and she still did not know where he was.

"Had he been living constantly at home before that?" Olcott wanted to know.

"We have been in Washington some three or four months," she said. "Before that time all of our business was of course in Maryland where we came from. Sometimes he was a week at home and sometimes a week in the country. I thought it better for him to be in Maryland than here where there were restaurants & bad company. I thought this was not the place for a boy."

"Up to the time when you last saw him he had not been a resident of your house?"

Again Mary explained how John would come and go—a week here, a week there. Olcott was not satisfied with that. He needed to know exactly how long John had been away before that Monday when he'd come home for dinner. Thanks to Louis Weichmann, Olcott likely knew by now that John Surratt had been in Richmond during that time, where he had met with Confederate president Jefferson Davis. Mary replied that it had been almost ten days. John had left Washington two Saturdays earlier—presumably on March 25 if she recalled correctly.

The next question was one that Mary had answered once before: "Do you know a man by the name of Atzerodt, or Port Tobacco?"

Mary Surratt had been reading the newspapers. Surely by now she knew as well as anyone else in the nation that the authorities had every reason to believe Booth had assigned George Atzerodt to murder Vice President Johnson. If she had been ignorant of the implications of her acquaintance with Atzerodt during her first examination, she could not have failed to understand them now as she sat before Colonel Olcott. "Yes, sir," she said, and then she appears to have done what she could to mitigate the damage this admission caused. Either that or Olcott's individual questions were not recorded, for here Mary's sentences switch to the short, clipped tone that hints at such omissions: "He came to my house to board. I had several rooms. I came from Maryland & I had no way of living except by renting the rooms and taking in a few boarders. I advertised in the 'Star' several times that I had rooms to rent." As before, Mary explained that Atzerodt had arrived when she was "down in the country," but she did not recall how many days he had stayed. As soon as she had discovered the liquor bottles in Atzerodt's room, she'd had John turn him out of the house. "That is all of my acquaintance with 'Port Tobacco,'" she said.

Colonel Olcott then aimed his questions in a new direction—toward a subject untouched in Mary's previous examination. "How many times did you go to the country a week or two previous to the murder?" he asked. What did he observe in Mary Surratt's face as she formed her answer? As far as Mary knew, the investigators were not aware of her drives to Surrattsville.

Mary answered honestly. "Twice," she said.

"Who went with you?"

"The gentleman who boarded with me, Mr. Weichmann; he drove me down in a buggy."

"Where did you stop?"

News of John Lloyd's arrest had not yet made the papers. Unless word of his presence had somehow leaked within the prison itself, Mary Surratt could not have known that Lloyd had spoken to investigators, much less what he had told them about their encounter on the day of the assassination. If Mary felt that she had anything to conceal, she had a choice to make, and very little time to make it.

Again, she told the truth. "At Mr. Lloyd's who rents my place down there." So far, her story aligned with Lloyd's.

"What conversation did you have with Mr. Lloyd?" Olcott asked.

Here Mary's version of the April 14 meeting departed from Lloyd's. "I do not remember any particular conversation," she said. Her tenant had arrived just as she'd been preparing to leave. All she recalled was an invitation to dinner, and an offer of some of the fresh fish and oysters that filled his wagon.

Colonel Olcott cast about for a few more peripheral details he could compare with Lloyd's version of the encounter. What time was it when the meeting took place? Who was within earshot? How long did the conversation take? Then he asked a question as direct as a punch: "What did you say about any shooting irons or carbines?"

"I said nothing about them."

"Any conversation of that kind? Did you not tell him to have those shooting irons ready, that there would be some people there that night?"

"To my knowledge, no conversation of that kind passed."

"Did you know any shooting irons were there?"

"No, sir, I did not."

Next Olcott probed Mary's connection to Lewis Powell. It was odd enough that a bizarrely dressed man with a flimsy story had knocked on her door so late at night. Now that the police knew Lewis Powell, Reverend Paine, and Mr. Wood to be one and the same man, it seemed even less likely that out of all the doorsteps in Washington, DC, he had appeared purely by chance on Mary Surratt's. "You mentioned the other day to Colonel Foster you had a man by the name of Wood, a Baptist minister, at your house," Olcott said, conflating two of Powell's false identities.

Mary acknowledged that was correct. He had arrived during the week and left on a Friday, so as to return to Baltimore in time to preach.

"How did he happen to come to your house?"

"I advertised those rooms and he came to board."

Colonel Olcott wanted to know when Wood had arrived. Was it before Inauguration Day in March?

"I think it was in February," Mary said. "I do not remember & I would not like to state it."

"You could tell by the advertisement in the paper?"

"Yes, sir. He said he saw we had rooms to rent, and he wanted to get rooms and board." This was possible in the strictest sense, though not especially probable. Mary had indeed placed an advertisement for her spare rooms in the Washington *Evening Star*. That advertisement, however, had last run in the newspaper on December 27. That did not explain why a man from out of town would come looking for lodgings at 541 H Street in the early spring of the following year. "He was a stranger to me," Mary concluded. "I had never seen him before."

"Do you recollect the man who came to your house at the time of your arrest?" Olcott asked.

"I do not. I thought he was someone calling for the gentlemen there. I never noticed him."

That was perhaps an unexpected response, considering how Major Smith had asked Mary to step into the hall and identify the visitor. At her previous examination, Mary had vividly recalled how disturbed Anna had been by the sight of "a tremendous hard fellow with a skull-cap" in their hallway. A "ruffian," Mary had termed him then, and one with every appearance of a murderer.

"You did not look to see whether it was this man Wood?" Olcott said, framing the question from an awkward angle that partially obscured his point. What Olcott wanted to know was whether Mary had ever seen that man before.

Over the weeks, months, and years to follow, Mary Surratt's reply to this question would provoke more scrutiny than any other: "I only saw a stranger. I never saw him before. I never thought it was the Wood who was at our house."

Nearly everyone who had seen Lewis Powell in the flesh would regard Mary Surratt's answer with skepticism. His physique alone was so singular, it was difficult to see how something as minimal as an alias, a false mustache, or a pickaxe and a makeshift stocking cap could disguise him beyond recognition. William Bell, the Sewards' servant, had not hesitated an instant to identify Powell as the attacker. The very sight of him had made Bell quiver with remembered trauma, and his encounter with Powell had lasted only minutes. Mrs. Surratt, by contrast, had hosted Powell in her home on two separate occasions, seated him at her dining table, and played cards with him in her parlor. Nevertheless, it was a point on which Mary Surratt would not waver in the slightest: she had taken the man with the pickaxe for a total stranger.

"When did you get acquainted with Mr. Booth?" Olcott next wanted to know.

"Some three months ago."

"Who brought him to the house?"

"He came to the house and asked whether my son was in. We always found him pleasant. His visits were short. I never knew anything about his private matters at all."

"Were his visits always visits of courtesy?"

"Yes, sir." The boardinghouse residents never discussed business or politics with Booth, Mary declared, and he never stayed over an hour.

"Did not an attachment spring up between him and your daughter?" Olcott asked. This may have been an opportunity to absolve a piece of incriminating evidence—the carte de visite of Booth, found tucked behind a painting in Anna's room. If Anna had secretly fallen for the dashing theater idol, as so many other women had, it could plausibly have accounted for why the assassin's image had been in the house, as well as why it had been hidden.

If Olcott was offering Mary an out, she did not take it. "Not particularly, I should suppose. Not that I knew of."

"He was a handsome man?"

"He was a handsome man and gentlemanly," Mary acknowledged; "that is all we know of him. I did not suppose he had the devil he certainly possessed in his heart," she added.

Finally Colonel Olcott turned to the question that had so stymied Mary Surratt's previous interrogator. "The night of the murder who was at your house?" he asked.

"No one except our own family," Mary said. Though a man had stopped and dropped off some newspapers for her niece, Mary had not seen him. She only knew he had come when the servant girl had brought the papers up for Olivia.

"Anyone else?"

"No, sir."

Colonel Olcott, like the examiner before him, did not believe a word of this. The tip from John Kimball, detailing the kitchen conversation between Mary and three unknown men on the night following the assassination, remained the most incriminating piece of evidence against her. Once again, the investigators' faith in this unverified piece of information led them to assume that Mary Surratt was lying in the boldest possible fashion.

Olcott, determined to get the information he was sure Mary Surratt was withholding, asked the question three more times, in three different ways.

"Who were there Saturday or Saturday night besides the detective police?"

"Who came there Saturday night?"

"Did three men call there on Saturday or Sunday night talking about your son & other friends who had disappeared?"

It made no difference how he worded it. Mary still did not give him the answer he was hoping for. Aside from the detectives, no one but her friend Mr. Kirby had stopped in on either of those evenings, she insisted. The only remotely similar incident she could recall happened on Sunday morning, when Louis Weichmann, accompanied by John Holohan and Detective McDevitt, had stopped in to get a change of clothes. Olcott was no more distracted by the similarity of this incident to the Kimball tip than the first interrogator had been.

"I am speaking of the visit of three or more men to your house on Saturday or Sunday evening when you had a conversation with them," he pressed yet again.

Mary Surratt did not give an inch. If she was telling the truth, she had not an inch to give. If she was lying, she was displaying remarkable resolution under pressure. "I do not remember. There was no one there but detectives."

No matter how Olcott tried to make her story fit into the shape outlined by Kimball's information, Mary would not oblige. The colonel asked one last time, forcing Mary to explicitly deny every detail of the information the Kimball tip had provided: "Did you or not, have a conversation with three men in the dining room about your son asking whether they had seen your son and his friends & receiving the information they had seen them but dare not speak to them there were so many people about."

Mary Surratt replied, "No such conversation, nothing of the kind, occurred."

The interrogation was at an end. Two blank spaces, eaten away by deterioration, mar the final page of Mary Surratt's examination. Each leaves a gap the size of two or perhaps even three words in Colonel Olcott's last question: "___ son or Mr. Booth ___ or Port Tobacco ever tell you that they had engaged in a plot to kill the President?"

"Never in the world if it was the last word I have ever to utter," Mary Surratt said.

Two days after Mary Surratt's second interrogation, Louis Weichmann found himself summoned before the secretary of war, "the man of iron and blood." Weichmann had returned to Washington, DC, on April 28 or 29 and was almost immediately questioned by Stanton on April 30.

Obviously this was not Weichmann's first examination by the authorities. But what did Stanton already know, and what did he hear for the first time from Weichmann's own mouth? This is not as simple a question as it should be, for it's unclear when Louis Weichmann's statements were first recorded.

There can be no doubt that he gave a great deal of information to the police on April 15, yet the earliest dated statement is marked April 30. Two statements by Weichmann are undated, as is one of the two reports on Weichmann by Lieutenant Colonel Foster. One especially intriguing document is an undated paper labeled "Items not brought out in the examination of Weichmann, or that he has since recalled."

These missing dates matter. Louis Weichmann's story would grow and change over time, making it critical for us to understand exactly when—and perhaps why—specific details emerged. Without those dates, tracing the metamorphosis of the evidence he gave becomes impossible.

The fact of the matter is that Louis Weichmann had gotten himself onto treacherous ground. His position was not entirely unlike

John Lloyd's. The more information he offered, the more valuable he became to the investigation, and the closer he came to becoming one of its heroes. And yet if the authorities began to get the sense that he knew *too* much about Booth's plot—if they believed that Weichmann had comprehended Booth's intentions but remained silent—then Louis Weichmann put himself at risk of being charged as a conspirator.

And the authorities did indeed have their own suspicions about Weichmann. As Lieutenant Colonel Foster reported, "It seems extremely improbable that Weichmann was ignorant of the plot, if he was not an accomplice." Foster further believed that Weichmann had tried to enlist his coworkers in the conspiracy, using hints of a foolproof money-making scheme as cover. Colonel Wells also considered him a conspirator as early as April 18, noting that Weichmann was among "the principle parties" involved in the plot. "On Tuesday it was discovered that Booth, Atzerodt, Herold, and Weichmann had been in the habit of meeting at the house of Mrs. Surratt in Washington," he reported.

There was physical evidence against Louis Weichmann, too. Stacks of envelopes, marked with the official frank of the Office of the Commissary General of Prisoners (the agency of the War Department in which Weichmann was employed), had been found in the bedroom he shared with John Surratt on H Street. This was a graver matter than simply pilfering supplies from his workplace. Any message placed in one of these envelopes could be mailed free of charge, appearing as if it had been sent by the federal government. What were those envelopes doing outside the office, in a boardinghouse that was frequented by Confederate blockade-runners? Not only that but the envelopes had been in the bedroom of John Surratt Jr., the postmaster of Surrattsville and a known rebel courier.

Colonel Wood, superintendent of the Old Capitol Prison, eventually came to view Louis Weichmann as a traitor. Weichmann's position in the Office of the Commissary General of Prisoners gave him access to sensitive information regarding Union prisons and the Confederate prisoners they housed. That kind of intelligence would be of immeasurable worth to rebel operatives like Augustus Howell, who were known to have boarded at Mary Surratt's home. "I am satisfied he has frequently purloined important papers which have been forwarded to Richmond by or through John Surratt," Wood wrote of Weichmann. "This corrupt scoundrel betrayed his official trust by compiling statistics and information in the interest of the Confederacy, and using his official connection as a cover he often went into southern Maryland with Mrs. Surratt to deliver his information." Wood viewed Weichmann as a traitor not only to his government but also to his landlady. "Directly after the arrest of Mrs. Surratt[,] Weichmann was arrested and to save his worthless carcass from imprisonment evidently gave such testimony to clear himself as implicated this unfortunate lady with the conspirators."

That accusation would stalk Louis Weichmann for the rest of his life.

On the evening of Weichmann's first recorded interrogation, a guard and a soldier entered Mary's cell. "Mrs. Surratt, you are wanted," the guard said. "You will put on your bonnet and cloak, if you please, and follow me."

Mary obeyed without a word, though she could not hide her trembling as she did so. Anna clung to her, pleading with the guard to be allowed to go with her mother, but the men paid her no mind.

"Mrs. Surratt kissed each one of us," Virginia Lomax wrote of the parting, "and when she came to me, she threw her arms around my neck, and said in an agitated voice, 'Pray for me, pray for me.'" The women waited up all night for Mary, never dreaming that they had seen her for the last time.

Anna Surratt was distraught. She was so devoted to her mother and so easily laid low by distress that she seemed far younger than her twenty-two years. Those who observed her could not help thinking of her as childish or immature. All she could do that first night was kneel beside her bed and cry, "Oh mother, mother!" After that, she could hardly keep still.

"Night after night did I hear the patter of Anna Surratt's little slippered feet, as she restlessly paced the room above me," Mrs. Lomax sorrowfully recalled. "I fancy I can see her now, her light hair brushed back from her fair face, her blue eyes turned towards heaven, her lips compressed as if in pain, and her delicate little white hands clasped tightly, as she walked up and down that room, hour after hour, seeming insensible to fatigue, and speaking to no one. Sometimes she would be quite hysterical, then again perfectly calm, except for the constant walking. We all thought she would lose her mind if the strain were not relieved."

A week passed before the women could pry any news of Mrs. Surratt from their jailers. She was confined in the pitch-black hold of a gunboat, they were told, wearing an iron collar chained to an iron ball, with a soldier standing guard day and night. There was even talk that the ship would be sunk with all the prisoners on board. Not one bit of this was true, but it was the only information Anna and her prison mates would receive.

Before hearing this, none of Mary's fellow prisoners had entertained the thought that her life might be in jeopardy. "She had endeared herself to all by her kindness and consideration, and was the last person one would suspect of a cold-blooded murder," Virginia Lomax wrote. So far as Mrs. Lomax could tell, Mary herself had never suspected such a fate, either. "That her position sorely tried her, was apparent to all; but there was never the least appearance of guilt, and not for one moment did her faith in an All-merciful Providence waver. There was no pretence about it,—you felt that the woman was deeply and sincerely religious, yet without any ostentation."

Mary Surratt would need every scrap of faith she could summon in order to endure what awaited her.

CHAPTER ELEVEN

On a narrow finger of land once known as Buzzard Point, which extended into the meeting of the Potomac and Anacostia Rivers, stood the Washington Arsenal. The time had come to separate the suspects from the witnesses and informants that had been detained at the Old Capitol Prison and isolate the suspects in a more secure location. The arsenal, with its empty prison, had been tailor-made for just such a purpose. Only eight of its more than two hundred cells would be required. A second-floor room large enough to host a trial guaranteed that the prisoners would not have to be transferred daily to and from a separate courthouse.

Mary Surratt arrived at seven o'clock on the evening of April 30. She was promptly searched by the special provost marshal of Washington, DC, General John Frederick Hartranft, who had been detailed to guard the president's accused murderers. Mary was assigned to cell 157. Thereafter, General Hartranft would refer to her by that number in his letter book.

A meticulous, scrupulously fair man, General Hartranft would do everything in his power to make his prisoners comfortable without bending the steely rules that governed their incarceration. Though the eight most hated individuals in the nation were under his direct supervision, never once would he take advantage of his position to persecute them in any way. By all accounts, he was a man beyond the reach of such temptations.

Dispassionate fairness could only go so far in a place like the Old Arsenal Penitentiary, however. Conditions were austere at best. The cells were narrow enough for Mary to touch both sidewalls at once. There were no iron bedsteads or wooden chairs here, only a corn husk mattress and a toilet bucket. Nothing but "necessary food and water" was permitted to enter the cells, and that only in "small quantities." Anything, even a spoon, might be employed as a tool for escape or self-harm.

The cells on either side of Mary's were empty. The seven men were similarly situated. This was intentional, to thwart any attempts at communication between the accused conspirators, be it verbal or by signals such as rapping or knocking. Mary was not obliged to wear the canvas hoods that six of the seven men were subjected to (Dr. Mudd was also exempted), but that was where her special treatment ended. Like the rest, she was forbidden to communicate in any way with the guards (and vice versa), the only exception being to request medical attention.

Medical inspections occurred twice daily, conducted by Major George Porter, an army surgeon. Major Porter's first report gives some indication of the conditions the prisoners had endured thus far in the Old Capitol Prison. On May 1, he recommended that they be bathed and given clean clothes and woolen slippers, and that the inside of the men's hoods be padded with cotton over the ears and eyes, to prevent the rough canvas from rubbing them raw. (The slippers may have been a precaution rather than a kindness, "to prevent the use of shoes for signal knocking.")

Mary Surratt was the only one of the eight prisoners that Major Porter singled out for a brief character sketch in his memoir of his duties at the arsenal. "Mrs. Surratt was a striking woman," he wrote in

1911, "and a handsome one despite the unavoidable imprint of prison life. She kept herself in hand, despite the seriousness of her position, and gave me but little trouble."

Though Major Porter downplayed it later, at the time this "little trouble" had been cause for grave concern.

Mary Surratt would not eat. On May 2, she refused the meat and bread offered to her in the morning and at noon. Late that afternoon, Major Porter recommended providing her with a cup of tea. That evening, she refused the nightly ration of bread and coffee. The next morning, Mary took only tea, again declining her portion of cold beef, soft bread, and coffee. That evening, she told General Hartranft, "I am a catholic, I would like to see the Priest." On May 4, General Hartranft reported, "The prisoner in 157 again refused to eat, saying she had no appetite. She drank a very little tea." Later that afternoon, she was moved to cell 200. No reason was specified—Hartranft only noted that he had been instructed by his superior to do so. Seventy-two hours had passed since Mary Surratt's last meal.

By now Mary Surratt knew she was to be tried as a conspirator in the murder of Abraham Lincoln, for Colonel Olcott had made mention of "your trial" at her last interrogation. Worse, and perhaps as yet unknown to Mary, Andrew Johnson had issued a proclamation decreeing that the conspirators would be tried not in the civil courts but before a military tribunal.

The charge was more than homicide. It was deemed an act of treason. And the accused, Attorney General James Speed reasoned, were not simply murderers but "enemy belligerents." Their ultimate goal in murdering Abraham Lincoln, Andrew Johnson, and William Seward had been to upend the federal government entirely. Thus, according to Speed's way of thinking, the assassination had been no less than an act of war. In order to meet the severity of the crime, therefore, Samuel Arnold, George Atzerodt, David Herold, Samuel Mudd, Michael O'Laughlen, Lewis Powell, Edman Spangler, and Mary Surratt would be tried before a panel of army officers.

This would be no neutral jury. Rather than using the customary selection process that allows the defense to question and reject potentially prejudiced jurors, the government would appoint a tribunal of nine high-ranking military officers to decide the prisoners' fates. In effect, the people who had accused Mary and her seven co-defendants were hand-selecting the men who would ultimately decide whether the defendants should be put to death. Neither would there be an impartial judge. Objections would be sustained or overruled by the tribunal—eight members of which had no legal experience whatsoever. When questions arose, the government-appointed prosecutors—termed "judge advocates"—would be permitted to advise them on legal matters, creating a scenario in which the courtroom equivalents of opponent and referee were playing on the same team. And the burden of proof was not on the prosecution. No one would be presumed innocent until proven guilty. Quite the opposite, in fact. As one of Mary Surratt's lawyers would later put it, "The commission was organized to convict."

The decision to try the accused in this fashion was immediately controversial, and remains so. Both the secretary of the navy and the secretary of the treasury opposed the move. Former attorney general Edward Bates went further, deeming it unconstitutional. After all, the civil courts were open, and not one of the accused was a member of the military. Those in favor of the military tribunal pointed out that the atmosphere was so malignant, the desire for revenge so feverish, that a civil court would likely return a guilty verdict out of sheer malice, no matter what the evidence showed. The city of Washington in particular had been "on the verge of a riot" ever since the assassination, a correspondent for the *New-York Examiner and Chronicle* reported. Anyone known to be a Southern sympathizer was on edge. Many blanketed their homes with triple the usual amount of black crepe ribbon, banners, and bunting in hopes that a show of respect for the slain president would discourage the angry mobs from retaliating with "unpleasant visits"—or with flames. A military commission, proponents argued, was the only chance for a fair trial.

The *Washington Chronicle* put it more bluntly. The "wretches" responsible for "this unparalleled crime" were "entitled to the extremest and severest punishment, and as only worthy to fiends and savages."

Just how much of this Mary was aware of is impossible to pinpoint. The newspapers she had insisted upon reading in the Carroll Annex were forbidden the moment she stepped into the Old Arsenal Penitentiary, and Johnson's executive order had not been announced until the day after her transfer. She had had no visitors to relay the news; the only people permitted to speak to her were General Hartranft and Major Porter. Knowing all of this about the trial would have been terrifying enough, but *not* knowing may have been worse yet. Amid such ominous uncertainty, Mary's appetite could very well have been strangled by dread and anxiety. Her refusal to eat also constituted a very real problem for General Hartranft, who was responsible for her life. Of the twenty-three rules that had been drawn up specifically for the incarceration of the accused conspirators, the eighteenth explicitly stated: "No prisoner will be allowed to escape alive, or to defeat the ends of justice by self destruction." In short, Mary Surratt was not allowed to starve.

Major Porter, having been entrusted with her health, took charge of the matter. "I had a quiet, earnest talk with her," he recalled, "pointing out that abstinence from food would make her ill; that she was under my medical care and I should be forced to adopt means of insuring that she received the proper amount of nourishing foods at regular intervals." Put more bluntly, she would be force-fed, a supremely unpleasant procedure in which she would be physically restrained while a tube was threaded through her nostrils and pushed down the length of her throat to her stomach. Afterward, she might be tied down to prevent her from vomiting deliberately.

Finally, at seven o'clock in the morning on May 5, Mary Surratt drank a cup of tea and accepted a single slice of toasted bread. General Hartranft also noted that Mary requested a visit from Father Boyle of St. Peter's Church. Over the next five days, she would subsist on two or three pieces of toast and three cups of tea a day.

In the Carroll Annex, meanwhile, Louis Weichmann's story had begun to metamorphose.

On May 5, Weichmann wrote to the newly appointed assistant judge advocate Colonel Henry Burnett. "I have the honor to call your attention to the following additional facts in my recollection," he said. "You confused and terrified me so much yesterday that I was almost unable to say anything. I am as anxious as you and the Government are that all the guilty parties should be brought to justice and meet the fate they well deserve but for God's sake do not confound the innocent with the guilty."

It is among the most tantalizing of statements that would be made during the investigation. The nature of Weichmann's terror remains unknown. As for confounding the innocent with the guilty, was he concerned about his own innocence, or that of another?

Either way, it seemed that whatever confusion and terror Burnett had subjected him to had sharpened Weichmann's memory. Now he wrote to Burnett that he could not "exactly remember whether I told you" that upon returning home from work one day in mid-March, he'd found his room unexpectedly empty. Weichmann rang for the servant, Dan, and asked where John Surratt had gone. Dan replied that the young master had gone out on horseback at around two o'clock with six other men. Among them had been Booth, Paine, and Port Tobacco.

When Weichmann went downstairs for his afternoon meal, he found his landlady "weeping bitterly." Asking what was wrong, he tried his best to console her.

"Oh, John is gone away," Mary Surratt told him. She was too distraught to see to his dinner, and instructed him to go down to the kitchen and do the best for himself that he could. Weichmann did as he was told, and retired to his room to read Dickens's *The Pickwick Papers*. Around six-thirty, John Surratt suddenly returned from his mysterious errand—"rushed into the room," Weichmann later recalled, "very much excited." In one hand he held a Sharp's revolver small enough to fit into a vest pocket. His pants were tucked into his boot tops, and a pair of spurs glinted on his heels.

"John, what is the matter? Why are you so much excited?" Weichmann asked.

"I will shoot any one that comes into this room," John Surratt declared. Without explanation he began to lament that his prospects were ruined, his hopes "blighted." He needed a job and impulsively asked Weichmann to get him a clerkship at the War Department.

"You are foolish," Weichmann said with a bewildered laugh. "Why don't you settle down and be a sensible man?"

Ten minutes after John had burst in, Reverend Paine appeared, also holding a pistol and in a similar state of agitation. Excited though they were, Surratt and Paine gave no hint of what had gotten them so riled up. "They were very guarded indeed," Weichmann would remember. Paine said not a word. Booth followed on the reverend's heels fifteen minutes after that, a whip in his hand. "Booth was so excited," Weichmann remembered, "that he walked around the room three or four times very frantically, and did not notice me." Weichmann spoke, almost startling Booth from his focus.

"I did not see you," the actor said.

Booth signaled the others to follow him up to the third floor, where, as near as Weichmann could remember, they remained for about thirty minutes before leaving the house together. John Surratt returned alone. Paine had left for Baltimore, and Booth for New York, John said.

Weichmann's suspicions died down for the most part after that. As he later put it, "To all appearances, what they had been after had been a failure." He was "glad" that John's "mysterious and incomprehensible business" had come to an unsuccessful end, and "thought Surratt would be recalled to a sense of his duties."

Nevertheless, in light of the assassination, it was an extraordinary circumstance to have suddenly recalled some three weeks after the president's murder. By now the authorities had pieced together fragments of a failed plot to kidnap Abraham Lincoln and ransom him for Confederate prisoners of war, masterminded by Booth and John Surratt. Here was further confirmation.

☞

Weichmann also claimed in the same letter that more details about the day of the assassination—the day he had driven Mary Surratt to Surrattsville—had bubbled up into his memory.

On their way to Surrattsville, he said, they had slowed when they were about three miles outside Washington so that Mrs. Surratt could ask a soldier "if the pickets remained out all night." No, the man replied, the sentries were called in at eight o'clock. According to Weichmann, Mary told the soldier that she was "glad to hear it."

And that night after tea, Weichmann said, "Mrs. Surratt was more nervous than I ever saw her." Up and down the parlor she paced, fingering her rosary. When Weichmann asked her what was wrong, she replied that she did not feel well. At one point she turned to him, Anna, and Honora Fitzpatrick and asked that they "pray for her intentions." The young people were apparently too boisterous for her, and, Weichmann told Colonel Burnett, "she chased the young ladies and myself upstairs to our room and remained alone in the parlor."

That, allegedly, was when Booth had made yet another visit to H Street. At some earlier interrogation whose record is apparently lost, Weichmann had already told the authorities that at around nine o'clock on the evening of the murder he'd heard a ring at the door, and footsteps.

The identity of the visitor had remained unknown to him until the next morning at breakfast, when, Weichmann claimed, Anna Surratt had remarked, "Think of that man Booth having called at this house not more than an hour and a half before the assassination."

All of these details cast an increasingly suspicious light upon Mary Surratt.

How much significance do these developments have?

At the very least, the timing of Weichmann's additional recollections must be weighed. By his own admission, this information was brought out as a result of an upsetting interrogation with Assistant Judge Advocate Burnett. If he was as fearful and muddled as he claimed to be, did his emotional state have any bearing on his reliability?

John T. Ford, co-owner of the theater where Lincoln had been shot, certainly thought so. Ford had also been imprisoned at the Old Capitol alongside many of the government's witnesses. During his thirty-nine days there, he had ample opportunity to observe Louis Weichmann. Terror and confusion seemed to be hallmarks of Weichmann's prison tenure. "That all this testimony was fabricated deliberately or otherwise, I do not for a moment doubt," Ford eventually revealed to the *New York World*. "So far as Weichmann's testimony was concerned, it was not entitled to credence."

In Ford's opinion, Louis Weichmann's character and demeanor spoke more convincingly than anything the young man would proclaim under oath in the courtroom. "Weichmann was a frightened witness at first, and bullied afterward," Ford recalled in 1868. "He was afraid for his own life while in prison—afraid of his shadow, scared by a threat, startled by a noise. His weak brain was hemmed round by horrors. It was not consciousness of guilt, but terror lest he might be accused and hung for nothing, that overwhelmed him."

Weichmann was as pliable as a mound of dough, Ford said, and could be led to agree or disagree with a statement simply by a change in tone. Present a scenario "coaxingly" and Weichmann would agree that it had happened just that way. Switch to asking "sternly," in a tone that implied wrongdoing, and Weichmann would deny that any such thing had occurred. If fellow prisoners could sway him this way and that for fun, Ford reasoned, a "wily and too-eager lawyer" could influence Weichmann's testimony just as easily. "He was not a cold-blooded perjurer," Ford concluded, "only a coward."

☞

Even in the spring of 1865, rumors that Weichmann had been threatened by none other than Secretary Stanton were already circulating—not only on the streets of Washington but within the thick walls of the Old Capitol Prison. Weichmann himself was aware of the talk and felt compelled to deny it. In another, undated letter to Burnett, he insisted that Stanton had "treated me kindly," adding "I never said that he threatened me. You yourself know whether he did or not." That same correspondence ends on yet another intriguing note. "I am responsible for everything I say," Weichmann wrote Burnett, "but it is not pleasant to have things perverted and turned out of shape." There is no indication of which statements Weichmann feared were being misused by the authorities, or what the consequences of such misinterpretations might be.

But consequences were unavoidable, and the stakes could not have been higher.

CHAPTER TWELVE

On May 8, General Hartranft received copies of the charges against his eight prisoners. From six to ten o'clock that evening, he proceeded from cell to cell, lantern in hand, as each was unhooded and served with the papers. Hartranft stood silently while the prisoners read the documents. In several cases, they asked him to read the allegations aloud.

Every one of the accused conspirators was charged with "maliciously, unlawfully, and traitorously, and in aid of the existing armed Rebellion against the United States of America . . . combining, confederating, and conspiring, together with one John H. Surratt, John Wilkes Booth, Jefferson Davis . . . and others unknown, to kill and murder, within the Military Department of Washington, and within the fortified and intrenched lines thereof, Abraham Lincoln."

The document went on to include "maliciously, unlawfully, and traitorously assaulting, with intent to kill and murder" William H. Seward and "lying in wait with intent maliciously, unlawfully, and traitorously to kill and murder" Vice President Andrew Johnson and General Ulysses S. Grant.

Mary Surratt's specification charged that she did "receive, entertain, harbor, and conceal, aid and assist the said John Wilkes Booth, David E.

Herold, Lewis Payne,* John H. Surratt, Michael O'Laughlen, George A. Atzerodt, Samuel Arnold, and their confederates, with knowledge of the murderous and traitorous conspiracy aforesaid, and with the intent to aid, abet, and assist them in the execution thereof, and in escaping from justice after the murder of the said Abraham Lincoln as aforesaid."

If the accused were found guilty, the punishment was death. The indisputable fact that Mary had been nowhere near Ford's Theatre at the moment the bullet struck the president was irrelevant. In the eyes of the law, it did not matter who had done the shooting in cases of conspiracy. Everyone involved in the plot was as guilty as if there had been ten different fingers crowded onto the trigger of Booth's derringer.

There is no record of Mary Surratt's reaction.

☞

Whether she was innocent or guilty, Mary's actions over the previous few months left her with plenty to worry over. She had unquestionably received, entertained, and harbored Booth, Atzerodt, and Powell—not to mention her son John, who was believed to be Booth's right-hand man. If John Lloyd's claims were true, she had also aided, abetted, and assisted Booth and Herold by instructing Lloyd to be prepared to hand over the Spencer carbine rifles on April 14, as well as by delivering Booth's binoculars to Surrattsville. The most crucial words in the charges against her, therefore, were "knowledge" and "intent." Had she been aware of Booth's plot, and been a willing participant? Or had she been merely a pawn Booth had employed to shelter his co-conspirators, relay his messages, and ferry his binoculars to Surrattsville? Upon that question rested her life.

---

* Lewis Powell would be referred to by his alias "Paine" (also spelled "Payne") in the court transcript as well as newspapers for the duration of the trial.

☞

Two days later, on May 10, the eight defendants were brought before the court. Through the corridors and up the stairs they went, iron fetters clinking all the way. Arnold, Atzerodt, Herold, O'Laughlen, Powell, and Spangler, still encased in their hoods, were tugged along like dogs on leashes. The Lilly irons around their wrists made it impossible for them even to grope for their bearings. Guards accompanied Powell and Atzerodt, to carry the fifty-pound iron balls tethered to their ankles. Mary and Dr. Mudd were spared these cruelties.

Entering from a "dungeon-like" door in one corner, the eight accused were immediately directed into the prisoners dock that ran the entire length of the wall to their left. The "headless men," as Samuel Arnold described himself and his fellow male defendants, were guided blindly toward their seats. "Nothing visible to them, neither the Court nor its surroundings, everything dark as Egypt." To Arnold, the hood was more than a physical torture. It marked him as something less than human—something dangerous and fearsome to be contained at all costs—prejudicing the military commission against him. "How the Court viewed and looked upon those hooded and headless human beings when presented before them is unknown and a matter of conjecture. A more disgusting a more revolting and satanic a spectacle could never have been drawn or conceived by the human mind," he wrote.

To at least one commissioner, Major General August Kautz, the sight was just as disturbing as Arnold imagined. "The mystery and apparent severity" of the chained and hooded men sent Kautz's thoughts reeling backward to the days of the Spanish Inquisition—a sickening pageant of "impropriety" that he never expected to witness "in this age." Only after the prisoners were seated were their hoods removed.

Without a hood, Mary had the opportunity to gain her bearings in the courtroom more quickly than the others. It was a large room—big enough to hold three hundred people—and devoid of any decoration, but so freshly whitewashed that it nearly gleamed when light shone through the four tall, barred windows. Coconut matting carpeted the floor, and newly installed gaslights stood ready to illuminate the court should the proceedings run beyond sunset. Much of the furniture was "fresh from the shop," and as plain and serviceable as it could be: wooden chairs without cushions, and square-legged tables whose angles and corners proclaimed their frugality.

At a long table in front of the windows sat the tribunal, ablaze in brass-buttoned full-dress uniforms of Union blue, their shoulders weighted with the insignia of their ranks. Brigadier General Joseph Holt, judge advocate general of the United States Army, would serve a role equivalent to that of a chief prosecutor in a civilian court, assisted by Congressman John Bingham and Colonel Henry Burnett. In lieu of a jury, nine military commissioners ranging from lieutenant colonel to major general awaited the evidence. All were distinguished combat veterans of the Civil War. None of them had an iota of professional legal expertise. As jurors, no legal experience was necessary. However, in the absence of an impartial judge, it would fall upon the nine men at this table to sustain or overrule objections.

"Judge Holt sat immovable and upon his stern and hard face not a particle of Expression could be traced," Samuel Arnold would recall. "He looked like some grim Statue, carved in stone, neither the face nor the eye emiting [sic] the slightest expression." To those outside the prisoners dock, General Holt exuded the appearance of an even-tempered elderly statesman. During the "frequent" and "spirited" clashes between lawyers, it would be Holt who quietly intervened to settle them.

Congressman John Bingham, the first of Holt's two assistant judge advocates, was Holt's opposite in temperament. Brimming with energy, this experienced criminal lawyer excelled at "watching the movements of opposing counsel, unraveling the tangled skeins of testimony, and eviscerating truth from masses of conflicting evidence."

Holt's second assistant judge advocate, Colonel Henry Burnett, had "the duty of preparing the evidence and presenting it in logical sequence." He also took on the role of managing the prosecution's courtroom logistics, such as making sure the witnesses were ready when called and "infusing into the proceedings order, industry, and promptness."

At the center of it all loomed the witness stand. Symbolically it stood in the perfect location. In practical terms it was oddly situated due to the size and shape of the room. Either the space between the stand and the commissioners' table was too narrow to accommodate the defense counsel, or the commissioners wanted an unobstructed view of the witnesses. Whatever the reason, the lawyers would be confined to the west side of the room, to the left of the witnesses. Questions came at the witnesses sideways, and many would have to be chided for forgetting to face the commissioners as they testified.

One by one, the prisoners were arraigned. All eight pleaded not guilty to the charges before being returned to their cells.

With that business accomplished, the members of the court further resolved that no one other than the judge advocates, commissioners, defendants and their legal counsel, phonographers, and prison staff would be permitted into the courtroom during the conspiracy trial. No journalists, no spectators. Rather than admit reporters to the proceedings, Judge Advocate General Holt would review each day's testimony and select excerpts that could be released to the press "without injury to the interests of the Government." The commission reasoned that as the trial unfolded, evidence would come to light implicating members of the conspiracy who had managed to remain undetected. Publishing the full testimony each day would alert any such criminals to flee before the authorities could catch up with them. The court also believed that publishing the testimony might endanger witnesses who were already reluctant to tell what they knew, for fear of retribution. "All the arrangements made, are for a fair and impartial trial, so that when publicity is given, the world will be satisfied as to the character and fairness of the whole affair," the *Daily Constitutional Union* assured its readers.

On the day of the arraignment, General Hartranft recorded that Mary was "furnished with tea, toast, and medicine." What kind of medicine, or what ailment it was intended to treat, neither Hartranft nor Dr. Porter reported.

Anxiety was as conspicuous a culprit as any physical malady. The prisoners, the Philadelphia *Press* reported, were "already undergoing a living death." Paramount among Mary's worries was the fact that although she stood accused of a capital offense, neither she nor any of her co-defendants had obtained legal counsel. "No lawyer has yet been found degraded enough to offer his services in behalf of these criminals," the *Philadelphia Inquirer* noted. With the trial set to begin before the week was out, the majority of the eight defendants had no choice but to settle for willing lawyers, regardless of skill or experience.

Mary Surratt was not the sort of woman to accept such a dire compromise without making an attempt for something better. Through General Hartranft, she first appealed to attorneys Richard T. Merrick and H. F. Zimmerman to plead her case before the tribunal. Both refused. Merrick, though willing to help, reportedly feared retribution from his father-in-law. By contrast, Zimmerman considered it disgraceful to be associated in any way with anyone named Surratt. "Our families never visited each other," he wrote to Colonel Burnett, "and I therefore decline to have anything to do with the matter."

Mary was already being made into a villain. "Treason never found a better agent than Mrs. Surratt," the *New York World* had proclaimed on May 3. Evidence was a trifling matter as far as the public was concerned—you had only to look at her to see proof of her guilt. "She is a large, masculine, self-possessed female," the *World* reported. The way she had reacted to her arrest remained as unsettling as her appearance. A "coarse, and hard, and calm" woman, "she was imperturbable, and rebuked her girls for weeping, and would have gone to jail like a statue."

Although Booth was acknowledged as "the head and heart of the plot," the *New York World* further asserted that "Mrs. Surratt was his anchor, and the rest of the boys were disciples to Iscariot and Jezebel," comparing the pair to two of the Bible's most hated evildoers. "She is bold and cruel, and deserves to die."

Had the journalists known all that the authorities had learned from Louis Weichmann and John Lloyd, these melodramatic statements might have been understandable. The climate of fear and fury that had enveloped Washington and the nation in the days since the assassination had made such harsh judgments against the suspects all but inevitable. But the papers were not privy to that evidence. There had not been a peep about Weichmann, and only fragments of John Lloyd's story had leaked out. The vast majority of what the papers had to say about Mary Surratt was based on supposition, prejudice, and the most blatant of sexism.

A lawyer who accepted the case could expect to feel the sting of public opinion as well—perhaps not overtly with insults in the papers, but the risk of watching profits dwindle as former and potential clients took their business elsewhere remained very real.

Nevertheless, Mary Surratt had "displayed considerable force of character" since she was a child—at least according to an article in the Washington *Evening Star.* That character and her "strong will" combined to ensure that "she seldom fail[ed] in anything she undertook." Neither of these qualities was considered complimentary to a woman in 1865. However, if the *Star*'s report was correct, these very traits may have been what led to Mary securing the aid of Reverdy Johnson. Not only was the esteemed Maryland lawyer a sitting United States senator and former United States attorney general but he had also served as one of President Lincoln's pallbearers. Despite his personal feelings about the crime, Johnson decided to help Mary Surratt "because I deemed it right, I deemed it due to the character of the profession to which I belong." The Sixth Amendment to the Constitution declares that every American citizen has a right to legal representation, and Reverdy Johnson saw it as his duty to ensure that Mary Surratt's rights were not violated.

The *Philadelphia Inquirer* interpreted Mary's desire for competent legal counsel as evidence of her "impudence." Mrs. Surratt, the paper said, "evinces her boldness in sending for Hon. Reverdy Johnson." The implication could not be missed: Mary Surratt was guilty, and a guilty woman should not have the audacity to hire one of the most respected lawyers in the state.

Even with an eminent attorney at her service, Mary's disadvantages towered like a cliff before her. According to General Hartranft's records, she did not meet with Senator Johnson until the afternoon of May 12—the first day of the trial. There would be little time and even less opportunity for Reverdy Johnson and his two young co-counsel, Frederick Aiken and John Clampitt, to prepare an adequate defense. "The prosecution had had a month assisted by the whole war power of the Government, its railroads, telegraphs, detectives, and military bureau to get its evidence into shape," Lewis Powell's lawyer, who was in an identical bind, lamented.

Discovery, the process of obtaining evidence from the opposing side, would not be granted in this case, rendering the statements and confessions previously collected by the government inaccessible.

Determining what evidence the government held against Mary would be mostly guesswork, aided by little more than newspaper reports. In many instances, Johnson and his team would learn of that evidence only at the moment when it was spoken aloud in court by the prosecution's witnesses. Likewise, the identity of many of the witnesses against Mary remained a mystery until they were called to testify. There was hardly sufficient time for Johnson's team to confer with Mary herself, much less recruit potential witnesses who might be willing to testify publicly on her behalf. As Powell's lawyer would put it, "This was a contest in which a few lawyers were on one side, and the whole United States on the other."

Nevertheless, just two days after her arraignment, Mary Surratt returned to the courtroom to stand trial for her life.

CHAPTER THIRTEEN

The iron-studded door swung open, and once again the line of prisoners shuffled, clanking, onto the raised platform behind the rail. Mary was the last.

Nearly twice as many chairs as prisoners awaited in the dock—enough to place a guard between each of the defendants. Samuel Arnold received the most coveted seat, in the corner beside a window that afforded him fresh air and a view of the outside. Mary's habitual seat would be at the opposite end of the dock, nearest the door that led back to her cell.

That first day, however, Mary was seated alongside her lawyers at one of the two tables for counsel. Dr. Mudd was also directed to a chair beside his counsel. As usual, neither she nor the doctor was hooded like the others. It appeared that the two were receiving special privileges—one due to her sex, and the other thanks to his profession. That was not the case, as General Hartranft would later explain, or at least not so far as the chairs were concerned. Someone had miscounted them, and there had simply not been enough seats to accommodate all the prisoners and guards in the dock. Mrs. Surratt and Dr. Mudd, being the last in line, had nowhere to sit but outside the rail.

Despite the absence of reporters, unfamiliar faces peered up at the prisoners, pencils poised in their hands. A team of six phonographers led by Benn Pitman sat ready to take down every syllable of the testimony via the newly developed Pitman shorthand method. At the close of each day, these men would labor into the smallest hours of the night, transcribing their swiftly penciled swooshes and slashes into full-fledged longhand, which would then be read aloud in court each morning to assure its complete accuracy.

To those eager for news of the proceedings, Mary Surratt was as much a spectacle as the trial itself. The entire nation itched to know how a woman on trial for the murder of the president looked and how she acted. Only the scantiest droplets of information trickled out. It was said in the *Philadelphia Inquirer* that Mary had been "very slovenly dressed" the day before and seemed "very much broken down and humbled" as well as visibly fearful. "Mrs. Surratt, yesterday, for the first time, showed signs of contrition, and completely abandoned the stoical indifference she has maintained heretofore," the Philadelphia *Age* agreed. But how had this information leaked to the press? No source was named, and the *Inquirer* itself had lamented two days earlier that "all attempts of interfering newspaper correspondents to obtain ingress to the court room are so far useless." The prisoners were not even permitted to speak to their guards. And yet on the first day of the trial the *Inquirer* once again reported on Mary's appearance, stating that she "appeared in clean clothes today, and was rather more tidy than on yesterday." All of these reports were little more than finger-wagging, for a woman was expected to keep up her appearance no matter whether she lived in a mansion or a prison cell.

Regardless of how she looked, there was little for Mary to do but worry and try to keep her ragged nerves from betraying her fears. The day's testimony would have nothing to do with her, or with her codefendants, for that matter. Instead the commissioners listened to half a dozen witnesses testify about John Wilkes Booth's involvement with the Confederacy. The prosecution was determined to show that the conspiracy to murder Abraham Lincoln had been conceived not in the mind of a single white supremacist but within the heart of the Confederate government itself.

So while the phonographers scribbled and the commissioners sat with grave faces, the prisoners waited to see who among them would be implicated first, and how severely. Of the eight, George Atzerodt, David Herold, and Lewis Powell faced the most daunting odds.

Herold stood no chance of exoneration. He had been inside the burning tobacco barn with Booth the night the assassin had been captured. Though he had surrendered himself, he had unquestionably aided and abetted Booth's escape through the marshes of Maryland and Virginia for twelve days.

Atzerodt's case was just as hopeless. He'd already confessed that Booth had put him up to the killing of the vice president. The assignment had not sat well with Atzerodt, despite Booth's assurance that "it would be the greatest thing in the world." Kidnapping and ransom had been one thing; this new plot had been something else altogether. "I said that I did not come for that and was not willing to murder a person," Atzerodt told the authorities. Misgivings alone were not enough, however. Though he had defied Booth and drawn the line at shooting Andrew Johnson, Atzerodt's failure to report the conspiracy and save Lincoln's life had earned him a seat in the prisoners dock and a fifty-pound iron ball chained to his ankle.

Powell's prospects were only infinitesimally less dismal. The muddied boots he had worn to Mrs. Surratt's house had belonged to John Wilkes Booth, erasing any shadow of a doubt that his attack at the Seward home on the night of Lincoln's murder had been mere coincidence.

The remaining defendants had glimmers of hope to cling to.

Rumor had it that Booth had assigned Michael O'Laughlen to murder General Ulysses S. Grant. But no attempt on Grant's life had been made. Due to a last-minute change of plans, the general and his wife had not accompanied the Lincolns to the theater. If the prosecution could not prove that O'Laughlen had participated in the plotting, there was no crime to pin on him.

The letter from Samuel Arnold that had been found among Booth's things proved that Arnold had known of Booth's plot to ransom the president for Confederate prisoners of war. However, it remained to be seen whether Arnold had known that Booth had later shifted his aims from kidnapping to murder.

Some thought that in addition to holding the stage door open for Booth, Edman Spangler had also arranged the flats—the long, thin slabs of wood painted with background scenery—to make a clear path backstage for the assassin's escape from the theater. If that was not true, it was possible that Booth had simply used Spangler as a spur-of-the-moment convenience without making him privy to the plot.

Mudd's case was sketchiest of all. His fate hung entirely on the question of whether or not he had recognized that the broken-legged man who'd knocked at his door in the wee hours of April 15 was John Wilkes Booth.

The evidence against Mary Surratt fell somewhere in between. As with Mudd, her actions had aided Booth, and as with Mudd, it remained to be seen whether either side could prove that the motive behind those actions had been malevolent or benign.

By the end of that day, it seemed that John Wilkes Booth and Jefferson Davis were on trial. Not one sentence of evidence had been offered against the prisoners.

The ban on the press lasted just one day. "The secrecy which was at first attempted to be thrown over the commission's proceedings, aroused a feeling so strong, and a protest so unanimous, that Secretary

Stanton was compelled to throw open its doors," the *New York World* reported. Resisting further would only cast additional suspicion on what was happening behind the courtroom's closed doors.

On Saturday, May 13, a table furnished with "some exceedingly hard-bottomed chairs" appeared behind the witness stand to accommodate the press. Because the men and women being called to testify were required to face the commissioners, their backs would always be turned to the reporters.

The court opened itself to spectators, too, though only those holding official passes bearing the signature of General Hartranft would be admitted. Anyone who knew a military officer or a judge, governor, senator, or member of Congress had the best chance of securing entry. Some without such contacts posed as reporters, much to the consternation of the authentic members of the press. Connections alone were not enough, however. "Under no circumstances could anyone gain entrance to the arsenal grounds, much less to the court room, without evidence of loyalty free from doubt," one of Hartranft's assistants recalled. The only Confederate sympathizers permitted would be in the prisoners dock or the witness stand.

Citizens fortunate enough to lay hands on a coveted pass crowded into the courtroom, eager for glimpses of the eight prisoners. One *New York Times* reporter found himself surprised to discover that he could not immediately identify the defendants based on the descriptions he had read in the newspapers. In fact, everyone who scanned the row of faces in the prisoners dock found themselves surprised in one way or another.

Booth's band of conspirators looked like a motley crew. It hardly seemed possible that these eight people possessed the mettle to unseat the most powerful men in the federal government. As the *New York World* put it, "A more clumsy set of knaves scarce ever were set about such a deed of blood."

Yet in reality Booth had possessed a shrewd eye. He had chosen individuals uniquely suited to the tasks required of them. David Herold, for instance. For all his appearance as a "trifling boy," Herold was intimately acquainted with the landscape Booth had planned to flee through. "Passionately fond of partridge shooting," Herold had spent two or three months a year tramping the southern counties, where he knew "nearly every one in Maryland." Each of the prisoners possessed similarly specialized skills or connections that had furthered Booth's ends.

For those who came eager to see dastardly criminals, Lewis Powell best fit the bill. His physique alone captured ceaseless attention. Few could look at his broad neck, shoulders, and chest without being reminded of the gladiators of ancient Rome. Even more fascinating and bewildering was his detached, indifferent expression. There he sat, gazing straight ahead, with his manacled hands in his lap and his head propped upon the wall behind him. How could a man on trial for his life—the man the entire country already knew was the least likely of the eight to escape the gallows—appear so patently unruffled?

David Herold, on the other hand, manifested a wholly different kind of indifference. His demeanor was more that of a fidgety schoolboy at a tedious lesson. He leaned forward, eagerly returning the curious gazes as though the spectators were on trial, and by turns rested his feet on the rail, laughed, and cast rakish glances at the ladies. None of it endeared him to the public. He had helped the president's assassin evade capture for almost two weeks, and appeared no more concerned than if he had disobeyed a stuffy schoolmaster.

For the most part George Atzerodt pleased his audience by looking just as they'd imagined he should. "His whole bearing indicates the craven coward, and the great wonder is that he was ever entrusted to do a deed of blood that could not be done in the dark," said the *Philadelphia Inquirer.* He himself was small and dark—so very much the image of a skulking villain that he might have been lifted from the pages of a mystery novel. His appearance made it easy to pigeonhole him in the role of a minion slinking away from his master's deadly instructions, though in fact it had taken a great deal of courage to defy Booth's instructions.

The rest of the male defendants garnered far less attention. Their crimes were not so bloodcurdling, their appearance for the most part shockingly unremarkable. Mary Surratt, on the other hand, aroused curiosity like no other.

"Whether she was guilty or innocent, it was easy to perceive that she desired to make a favorable impression upon the court, and to inspire feelings of pity," the head of the phonographic team observed—as though anyone who wished to be acquitted of a crime would do differently. Veiled, and draped head to toe in black, her clothing signaled first and foremost that she was a widow. Social convention demanded that a woman should signify the loss of a husband by wearing this "deep mourning" for a year, but Mary Surratt's husband had died over two and a half years earlier, leaving some to wonder if her black clothing was indeed only a ploy for pity. It is impossible to say. Some women chose to wear mourning indefinitely, and no photos of Mary between 1862 and 1865 are known to exist.

What is certain is that Mary Surratt did everything she could to shield herself from the onlookers' incessant stares. Her dark veil always hung before her face. Often she propped her chin in one hand, at times holding a handkerchief in her fist to further obscure her features. As the days passed and the temperature rose, she employed a large palm-leaf fan that she could peek over while concealing her expression. Her efforts made the reporters and spectators all the more keen to catch a glimpse of her.

That day, however, there was plenty to divert everyone's attention.

The court had barely opened for business when the president of the nine-man tribunal stood up at the commissioners' table and announced, "In relation to Mr. Johnson appearing here as counsel for Mrs. Surratt, or either of the prisoners, I have a note from one of the members of the Court."

The note stated that another of the commissioners, Brigadier General T. M. Harris, objected to the presence of Reverdy Johnson "on the ground that he does not recognize the moral obligation of an oath that is designed as a test of loyalty, or to enforce the obligation of loyalty to the Government of the United States."

Almost soundlessly Reverdy Johnson drew himself up and took a single step forward. Put tactfully, his outward appearance was distinctive. A more blunt description painted him as a man with "a very repellent, dishonest face . . . though it may be slander to say so. He is short, stout, round-shouldered, has white hair, a long head, pursed out lips, and a 'cockeye,' as the vulgar have it." Though his "dignified bearing" did not falter, his displeasure at the accusation could not be mistaken.

The issue harked back to late 1864, when Maryland had been preparing to ratify a new constitution that would abolish slavery within its borders. A decree had gone out declaring that citizens of the state must take an oath of loyalty to the Union before they would be permitted to vote for or against the proposed constitution. The ploy seemed designed to put Confederate sympathizers (who were presumably also pro-slavery) in an impossible position: swear loyalty to the hated Union, or forfeit your chance to vote against abolition. The fewer Confederates who voted, the better the chances of ending slavery in Maryland. Though the goal of abolishing slavery was noble, this method was fatally flawed. Senator Johnson knew that no one had the authority to place any such conditions on a man's right to vote. Therefore, he had told his constituents that since the state government had no right to demand, much less enforce, such an oath, there was no harm in taking the oath of loyalty to the Union in order to cast their vote—regardless of where their loyalties truly lay.

Now General Harris was making it sound as though Senator Johnson—a man who had served as attorney general and taken the oath of loyalty before the Supreme Court as well as on the Senate floor—was opposed to the very idea of loyalty oaths.

The weight of this insinuation sent a wave of disquietude through the courtroom. Even the other commissioners squirmed, for they were not in agreement with Harris. All eyes turned to see how Reverdy Johnson would react. Only a thin veil of composure held back what looked to be a "towering rage."

"I have lived too long, gone through too many trials, rendered the country such services as my abilities enabled me . . . to tolerate for a moment—come from whom it may—such an aspersion upon my moral character," the sixty-nine-year-old senator replied, his tone as grave as the insult. As Johnson spoke, one member of the tribunal remembered, "his indignation was very manifest in his flushed face, but his remarks were quiet and dignified and full of irony."

"I am here no volunteer, gentlemen," Johnson declared. "I am here to do whatever the evidence will justify me in doing in protecting this lady from the charge upon which she is now being tried for her life," he said, indicating Mary Surratt. "I am here detesting from the very bottom of my heart every one concerned in this nefarious plot, carried out with such fiendish malice, so much as any member of this Court; and I am not here to protest any one whom, when the evidence is offered, I shall deem to have been guilty, even her." As Senator Johnson reminded the court, he was a member of the legislature, "whose law creates armies, and creates judges and courts-martial." If he was not qualified to be present, who on earth was?

"I have always considered his reply as a magnificent exhibition of moral courage against physical force," Powell's lawyer wrote later. "The walls were lined with soldiers and bayonets; he stood inside of the penitentiary and before an excited military commission of generals, with a determined and excitable president at its head."

"The senator and General Harris glared at each other," a member of General Hartranft's prison staff remembered, "with such threatening looks that it seemed there might be immediate trouble." Outside, shells being fired in practice maneuvers went shrieking through the air and detonated as if expressing the explosive emotions the two men struggled to hold at bay.

After "considerable sparring," General Harris formally withdrew his objection. But the damage had been done. Reverdy Johnson would leave the courtroom before the close of business that afternoon and return only twice more before the conspiracy trial ended. His continued presence before the commissioners, he later said, would have been a detriment to Mary Surratt's case, prejudicing the tribunal against her. Powell's lawyer disagreed: "I cannot help believing that Johnson's absence during the rest of the trial had a bad effect on his client's cause, on account of the conclusion drawn by many, that he had given up her case."

Reverdy Johnson did all that he could from his office—advising the junior members of the defense team and composing the closing argument—but there can be no doubt that Mary's case suffered from his absence. General Harris's objection cost her a lawyer whose "memory was so sure that he could easily refute careless statements; his acuteness was so great that he saw the real point at issue and aimed directly at it." Such keenness of mind, such rapid grasp of details were vital talents in a case that allowed no time to study the evidence.

The departure of Senator Johnson left Mary to be defended by Frederick Aiken and John Clampitt. Though they would go on to have distinguished careers, in 1865 both men were under thirty, their litigation skills largely untried. History would come to view them as too young and inexperienced and consequently too inept to handle such a momentous trial. But the greatest hindrance the two men faced was one that Senator Johnson himself shared: lack of information. Deprived of access to the evidence, Aiken and Clampitt had no option but to grope their way forward like the hooded prisoners themselves, stumbling over evidence and asking questions that made them sound like the greenest of amateurs. Defending an accused conspirator, Powell's lawyer said, was as daunting as "firing pistol shots against siege guns—two men in irons against a dozen major-generals, with a swarm of detectives within the penitentiary and a division of infantry outside."

CHAPTER FOURTEEN

If Mary Surratt could have picked a single day for Reverdy Johnson to represent her in court, there was no better day than May 13. General Holt had chosen to open the prosecution's case before the public with a barrage of evidence against her. The first witness he called to testify had the potential to leave the impact of a lightning strike.

Up stepped twenty-two-year-old Louis Weichmann. "He was seemingly not only a willing witness, but a 'swift witness,'" General Hartranft's assistant adjutant later recalled, by which he meant that Weichmann testified with an exaggerated zeal and an eagerness to volunteer information, in a way that smacked of bias. There seemed to be no end to the information he had to share.

Weichmann told of how the winter before, he and John Surratt had met John Wilkes Booth and Dr. Mudd on the street and accepted Booth's invitation for cigars and drinks at his hotel room. He told of the muffled conversations that he'd been excluded from that afternoon and of how afterward Booth had become a frequent caller at the Surratt boardinghouse. Weichmann described how Booth often took John Surratt aside for private conversations that went on for two or three hours at a time, and he revealed that on occasion the actor also conferred alone with Mary if her son was not at home.

He told of Powell's and Atzerodt's stays at the Surratt boarding-house, too, of Powell's aliases and his false mustache. He told of walking into the third-floor bedroom one afternoon in March to find John Surratt and "Reverend Paine" fooling with bowie knives, revolvers, and spurs. And he told of driving Mary to the tavern at Surrattsville on April 11, as well as on the very day of the assassination.

Hour after hour passed as the young War Department clerk held the court in thrall. It was almost as if the conspiracy were a detective story and he its all-knowing narrator, for by the time Holt's questions had ceased, Louis Weichmann's testimony had woven a web whose crisscrossing threads joined John Wilkes Booth, John Surratt, Dr. Mudd, David Herold, Lewis Powell, and George Atzerodt from a variety of angles.

Mary Surratt had a place in that web, too. Where at first she might have appeared to be a fly unwittingly stuck in Booth's web, now Mary seemed more like one of its central threads. The assassin had met with the most highly suspect accomplices under her roof. She had made two spontaneous trips to the first stop on Booth's escape route just before the crime, and on the second of those trips she had carried a package belonging to the murderer himself.

The steady buildup of evidence weighed heavily on Mary. "During the first days of her appearance she exhibited great stolidity and defiance," the New-York Tribune's curiously well-informed correspondent noted, "but to-day for the first time she shed tears and was quite agitated when the testimony regarding herself was being taken."

There was little the defense could do to offset the damage. Mary had indeed done everything Weichmann had said she'd done. The vital question was why. For that, Mary's lawyers could offer no answer. Mary herself was prohibited from testifying.

Mr. Clampitt did manage to get Weichmann to clarify that Booth's private conversations with Mary Surratt occupied "not more than five or eight minutes," in contrast to the several hours the assassin had routinely spent conferring with her son. In an effort to prove that Mary's trip to Surrattsville on April 14 was not solely at Booth's behest, Aiken brought out the fact that while she and Weichmann were at the tavern, he had written, at her request, a threatening letter to Mr. Nothey, the man whose debt Mary had said she intended to collect. Reverdy Johnson also succeeded in getting Weichmann to acknowledge that he had never seen the slightest indication of anything overtly wicked or immoral about his landlady. "Her character," Weichmann freely admitted, "was exemplary and ladylike in every particular." She was a devout Catholic and a regular churchgoer; Weichmann himself had accompanied her to Mass virtually every Sunday. That was all the three men could do for Mary defensively.

Offensively, chances were slightly better. If Mary's legal team could call Weichmann's innocence or loyalty into question, his testimony would not carry the same weight. Reverdy Johnson took up the task of undermining the young man's credibility.

"Were you in the habit of seeing John H. Surratt almost every day when he was at home, at his mother's?" Senator Johnson asked.

"Yes, sir: he would be seated at the same table."

"Was he frequently in your room, and you in his?"

"He partook of the same room, shared my bed with me, slept with me," Weichmann answered matter-of-factly.

"And during the whole of that period you never heard him intimate that it was his purpose, or that there was a purpose, to assassinate the President?"

"No, sir. At one time he mentioned to me that he was going on the stage with Booth; that he was going to be an actor; and that they were going to play in Richmond."

With these questions, Reverdy Johnson was forming a silent suggestion: If Louis Weichmann could be so close to John Surratt and know nothing of his murderous plans, was it not possible for Mary Surratt to have been similarly ignorant?

The senator also needled Weichmann about his apparent failure to find Mr. Wood, aka Reverend Paine, suspicious. In the midst of a civil war, a man with two names and a false mustache had come to stay at the house where Weichmann boarded—a house Weichmann knew to be hospitable to rebels—and Weichmann's suspicions had not been aroused enough to report him. Rather, he had filched the man's disguise, hidden it from him, and then worn it at work as a joke.

"Your only reason for not giving it to him, when he said it was his, was, that you thought it was singular that a Baptist preacher should be fooling with a mustache?" Johnson asked.

"Yes, sir; and I did not want a false mustache about my room."

"It would not have been about your room if you had given it to him, would it?" Johnson pointed out.

"No, sir."

"That would have taken it out of your room; but, to keep it out of your room, you locked it up in a box, and kept the box with you?"

"Then, again, I thought no honest person had any reason to wear a false mustache," Weichmann retorted.

The defense could not ask about the stacks of envelopes that had been found in Weichmann's room—the franked envelopes that he had evidently purloined from the Office of the Commissary General of Prisoners—because Mary's lawyers likely had no knowledge of them, nor of anything else that had led one of the top investigators to conclude that Weichmann was one of "the principle parties" in Booth's plot.

In both breadth and length, no one else's testimony would come close to equaling Louis Weichmann's. Nearly seventy defense witnesses would be required to rebut him.

But was it possible for a young man to have stood in the midst of this whirl of conspiracy and remain so blessedly ignorant of the details that might have saved the president's life? Few newspapers raised the question at all. Those that did, such as the *Daily Constitutional Evening Union,* were willing to give him the benefit of the doubt: "From the tenor of this young man's evidence . . . he appears to have known that something was going on, but he could not get the right hang of it, and the whole party used him as a go-between."

Nevertheless, the list of missed opportunities for thwarting the plot was considerable. He had shared a house, a room, and even a bed with John Surratt, yet claimed he had never suspected that any kind of plot was afoot. He had been present at what had all the appearances of a meeting of three of the conspirators in Booth's room at the National Hotel, yet had not heard a single word of their conversation, much less an incriminating one. He had shared his room for three nights with a man who'd used a false name and a false mustache, and had seen him and John Surratt toying with a cache of weapons, yet had apparently experienced not the least twinge of unease. He had sat alongside Mrs. Surratt in Uniontown as she'd leaned out of the buggy to speak to John Lloyd, yet had heard none of the conversation, much less anything odd. He had driven Mrs. Surratt to Surrattsville on the very day of the murder, yet once again had not heard anything of what she said to John Lloyd.

In Weichmann's case, ignorance equated with innocence in the public mind—as though he had been placed into these scenes for the express purpose of reporting on the conspirators later.

The feeling toward Mary Surratt was entirely the opposite. Yet no evidence had been given to show that she had known what her son and his compatriots had been plotting. All the prosecution had shown was that there was ample opportunity for her to have been aware.

Sometime after Louis Weichmann stepped down from the witness stand, Reverdy Johnson "picked up his hat, bowed to the commission, and retired."

More than just the personal insult from General Harris had rankled Reverdy Johnson. The *Boston Daily Advertiser* noted that he "seems more than any of his colleagues to chafe at the arbitrary rulings of the court, and often has hard work to keep his temper." On the verge of entering his eighth decade, he had no tolerance for the type of unorthodox proceedings he was witnessing at the hands of the government.

"Too much latitude is given in the examination of witnesses, and especially in the matter of asking irrelevant and pointless questions and repeating interrogatories in slightly different form," the *New York Times* complained. "In this particular the Commission is indulgent to a fault." Leading questions abounded as well, particularly from the prosecution.

In addition, Assistant Judge Advocate Bingham was personally grating. He objected incessantly. A member of Hartranft's staff recalled how the congressman never failed to jump at the chance to "rake the whole Confederacy, from Jeff Davis all down the line to the prisoners at the bar." Always during these tirades he turned to the defense counsel, as if berating them personally. Being mostly Southern men, the prisoners' lawyers "were often forced to exercise much self-restraint" in the face of Bingham's abuse of the South.

All day long Reverdy Johnson had walked up and down the courtroom, unable to contain his impatience while the opposition indulged in "tiresome" examinations. Even a layperson could see that this courtroom did not abide by the typical rules of evidence. "In the mass of testimony against the conspirators presented to the Washington court our readers may have noticed a great deal which is technically illegal," the *New York Herald* wrote, "that is to say, which would not be regarded as admissible under the rules of practice in our civil courts." Anything John Surratt had allegedly said, for instance, should not have been admissible, since he was not on trial. Neither was anything one defendant had said about another, unless both defendants had been present at the time. And yet such evidence routinely found its way into the record. This "great latitude," the paper explained, was "given to the witnesses so that the whole matter, unrestricted by the limitations of civil courts, may be clearly placed before the public."

Reverdy Johnson knew better. As far as he was concerned, the whole proceeding reeked of violations of the prisoners' rights, as well as flagrant diversions from courtroom protocol. "The first day disgusted him," one reporter succinctly put it, "as he is a practitioner of *law*."

With the defense lawyers still reeling from the damage of Weichmann's testimony, General Holt readied himself to land another devastating blow to Mary Surratt by calling tavern keeper John Lloyd to the stand.

By now Frederick Aiken knew what evidence Lloyd was likely to give, and knew that he and Clampitt alone were not up to the task of deflecting it. He asked the commissioners to delay Lloyd's examination until Monday, when Reverdy Johnson would return, because "the testimony of the witness now called would be of the gravest importance as affecting Mary E. Surratt."

General Holt objected. Mrs. Surratt had two lawyers present, he argued. The commission ruled in Holt's favor, and John Lloyd was sworn.

First, Holt directed Lloyd to tell the court how David Herold, George Atzerodt, and John Surratt had frequented the tavern that winter—simultaneously cementing the connections between two defendants and establishing Mary Surratt's tavern as a meeting place of the accused. Next came the carbines. One day in March, Lloyd testified, all three of the men had come to Surrattsville, and John had called Lloyd aside and instructed him to hide the pair of rifles between the tavern's joists. Surratt had also demanded that Lloyd hide ammunition, a rope coiled into "a right smart bundle," and a monkey wrench, saying that "he would call for them in a few days."

"Will you state whether or not, on the Monday or Tuesday preceding the assassination of the President, Mrs. Surratt came to your home?" asked Holt.

Lloyd told the court that he had crossed paths with his landlady on the road at Uniontown that day. He recalled that she had drawn his attention to the carbines in a roundabout way, though he could not be sure exactly how she had put it. "When she first broached the subject to me, I did not know what she had reference to," Lloyd said; "then she came out plainer; and I am quite positive she asked me about the 'shooting-irons.' I am quite positive about that, but not altogether positive." Lloyd would provide no more definite an answer than that.

Holt asked, "Was her question to you, first, whether they were still there? Or was it?"

"Really, I cannot recollect the first question she put to me," Lloyd said. "I could not do it to save my life."

More lives than his own were at stake. Being more specific might have saved him, while imperiling Mary Surratt. Unlike Louis Weichmann, John Lloyd was willing to go on record as being uncertain even when it did not benefit him. He was also not nearly so keen to offer information without prompting.

"And said they would be wanted soon?" Holt asked. A better example of a leading question is hard to come by. General Holt was putting words into Mary Surratt's mouth and asking Lloyd to simply verify them.

"Yes, sir."

"Will you state now, whether or not, on the evening of the night on which the President was assassinated, Mrs. Surratt came to your house with Mr. Weichmann?"

She had, Lloyd confirmed. He'd returned from his trip to the court at Marlboro somewhere around five o'clock that evening, and Mrs. Surratt had stridden up to him as he arrived.

"What did she say to you?"

"She met me out by the wood-pile, as I drove in, having fish and oysters in the buggy; and she told me to have those shooting-irons ready that night,—there would be some parties [to] call for them."

"Did she ask you to get any thing else ready for those parties besides the shooting-irons?"

"She gave me something wrapped up in a piece of paper. I did not know what it was till I took it up stairs; and then I found it to be a field-glass."

"Did she ask you to have any whiskey prepared for them?" Holt asked, leading Lloyd yet again.

"She did."

"What did she say about that?"

"She said to get two bottles of whiskey also."

"And said they were to be called for that night?"

"Yes; they were to be called for that night."

And indeed they had been. As everyone in the country now knew, Booth and Herold had arrived near midnight to arm themselves with a carbine, swig some whiskey, and brag of having committed the country's greatest act of homicide before hastening south to Dr. Mudd's farm.

"Did he not seem, from the manner of his language, to suppose that you already understood what he called for?" Holt asked.

"From the way he spoke, he must have been apprised that I already knew what I was to give him." As the tavern keeper remembered it, David Herold had cried out, "Lloyd, for God's sake, make haste and get those things!"

"Those things." Not "Get the carbines and whiskey!" Only "those things." No single sentence of testimony more damning than this would be given against Mary Surratt. Nothing cast her in the light of an active participant more than her instructions to Lloyd, coupled with Herold's confident assumption that the things he and Booth needed to make their escape would be ready and waiting.

Judging by the timing of Booth's visit to Mary's boardinghouse on the afternoon of the murder, it is reasonable to assume that the message Mary delivered to Lloyd had come from the assassin himself. But Mary had not specified who would call for the weapons and liquor, or why. And General Holt could not show any evidence that she had known, for one simple reason: there was none.

As with Louis Weichmann, cross-examining John Lloyd provided few opportunities for the defense. Lloyd's one point of hesitancy had been about the phrasing Mary had used to refer to the carbines, and on that point Frederick Aiken concentrated his efforts. Again and again Aiken asked Lloyd whether he was sure Mary Surratt had said "shooting-irons." Pressed this way to swear to a hazy detail, witnesses will often backtrack to avoid the possibility of being proven wrong later. John Lloyd did just the opposite. By the time Aiken had finished with his questions, he had succeeded only in causing Lloyd to repeat the incriminating phrase more than half a dozen times, sinking "shooting-irons" firmly into the commissioners' memory.

Aiken managed just one small point in Mary's favor. When he asked, "Did she ever have any conversation with you in reference to any conspiracy?" Lloyd answered, "Never."

All told, Mary Surratt had just endured the single most devastating day of the trial.

CHAPTER FIFTEEN

Two days later, Louis Weichmann and John Lloyd returned to the witness stand.

Mary Surratt had not yet recovered from the damage they had already inflicted upon her case. The Washington *Evening Star* noted that she "tottered visibly" as she was guided to her seat. Once in the prisoners dock, she dropped her head into her hand "and did not once raise it." It looked as though she did not have the strength to hear what more these two men might say about her.

By luck or design, it was Mary's good fortune to have Reverdy Johnson in the courtroom again. When Edman Spangler's lawyer finished with Weichmann, Senator Johnson took the opportunity for a second cross-examination. This time he wanted to know more about the conversation between Mary and John Lloyd that Weichmann had witnessed early in the week of the assassination—the one outside Uniontown, in which Lloyd said Mary had first mentioned shooting-irons.

"Do you recollect seeing him by the buggy at any time on your way between Washington and Surrattsville on that Tuesday?" Senator Johnson asked.

"Yes, sir: we met his carriage," Weichmann answered. Mary had called out to Lloyd as his carriage had passed theirs. The tavern keeper had stopped his buggy, stepped out, and walked over. "Mrs. Surratt put her head out, and had a conversation with him," Weichmann said.

"From the buggy?"

"Yes, sir."

"Did you hear it?"

"No, sir."

"Did you hear any thing that was said?"

"No, sir."

"Any thing about shooting-irons?"

"There was nothing mentioned at all about shooting-irons."

A curious answer—not "I heard nothing mentioned" but "There was nothing mentioned." A moment before, he'd claimed to have heard nothing at all. All Weichmann acknowledged overhearing was an exchange between Mary and Lloyd's sister-in-law, Mrs. Emma Offutt, who'd still been sitting in Lloyd's buggy some two or three yards away.

"How long was the interview between Mr. Lloyd and Mrs. Surratt on that occasion?"

"That I could not say exactly: I do not think it was over five or eight minutes. I do not carry a watch myself, and I had no precise means of judging."

General Holt cut in. "I understood you to say at first that you did not hear the whole of this conversation?"

"I did not hear the conversation between Mr. Lloyd and Mrs. Surratt," Weichmann clarified, "but between Mrs. Surratt and Mrs. Offutt, who was at some distance in the carriage."

"It is the conversation between Mrs. Surratt and Mr. Lloyd that we are talking of," Holt said. "You could not hear that?"

"I could not hear it."

If Weichmann was to be believed, he had sat next to Mary Surratt for whole minutes as she and John Lloyd had arranged a critical element of Booth's escape plan, and yet he had heard none of it. He did not say that his attention had wandered, or that their conversation had seemed of no importance, or even that he had deliberately tried to tune out their talk to give them privacy, but simply that he'd heard nothing at all. Not one solitary word.

John Lloyd's turn came next. General Holt presented him with a pair of carbine rifles, asking whether he could identify them as the ones John Surratt had hidden in the tavern. After confirming that they were the same firearms, Lloyd added, "I desire to make a statement, if the Court will permit me." He wished to clarify two things. First, that he had incorrectly stated the date of his meeting with Mrs. Surratt on the road at Uniontown. Upon reflection he realized that it had occurred on Tuesday, April 11, not Saturday, April 8, as he'd originally testified. The second point had to do with the bundle Mrs. Surratt had handed to him on the afternoon of April 14. He'd previously told the court that he had taken the package containing Booth's binoculars upstairs, but Lloyd was no longer sure that testimony was accurate. "I cannot say now that I am positive," he admitted. "The whole thing was very hurried; and I had liquor at the time, so that I cannot distinctly recollect; but I think it is likely that I laid it upon a sofa in the dining-room, and that is my impression."

Frederick Aiken jumped at the opportunity to cast doubt on Lloyd's prior testimony. "I do not know that I fully understand the witness," he said, "and I should like to ask one question. Do I understand you as stating that you were in liquor at the time you had the conversation with Mrs. Surratt?"

"I was somewhat in liquor at the time that I was in conversation with Mrs. Surratt, as I said on Saturday," Lloyd answered.

"On that account, you do not feel able to give clear testimony?" Aiken pressed. "Is that the explanation you want to make?"

John Lloyd was not willing to directly acknowledge that possibility. He dodged the question, confining his answer solely to the location of the package. "I wanted to explain that I was not positive whether the package was carried up stairs or not. It was a hurried piece of business with me, and, consequently, I did not reflect over it," he said. Nevertheless, logic dictated that if intoxication had blurred Lloyd's memory of what he'd done immediately after Mary's departure, his testimony regarding what had happened a few minutes prior—when he and Mary Surratt had been in the yard, allegedly discussing the "shooting-irons"— ought to be considered similarly murky.

◆

Mary reacted to the additional testimony almost as though it were a physical blow. "Mrs. Surratt has lost all her confidence," the *New York Evening Express* reported. "She is so weak from excess of emotion that she is obliged to be partially supported to and from Court." And still it was not over.

May 18 saw Louis Weichmann on the witness stand one last time. Recalling Weichmann was a risky venture on the prosecution's part. The more he told, the more the press began to wonder if he was truly as heroic as he appeared. "The witness himself was evidently quite intimate with Booth and Mrs. Surratt, and it is singular that, knowing so much as he does, he does not know more," Lincoln's hometown paper, the *Springfield Republican,* noted.

Little illustrated that point better than a telegram sent from New York and addressed "To WEICHMANN, Esq., No. 541, H Street, Washington," which was brought into evidence that day. Its cryptic message read, "Tell John, telegraph number and street at once." Dated March 23, it bore the signature "J. BOOTH."

"Who is the person referred to there as John?" General Holt asked Weichmann.

"John Surratt," Weichmann replied. "He was in the habit of being called John."

"Did you or not deliver to him the message contained in the despatch?"

"I delivered it to him the same day." It was a bewildering admission. The government's star witness freely acknowledging that he had served as a go-between for the president's assassin and a suspected conspirator?

"What did he say?" Holt continued.

"I asked him what particular and street was meant," Weichmann replied, "and he said, 'Don't be so damned inquisitive!'"

No one asked Louis Weichmann why Booth had chosen to use him as a messenger. No one asked him if he'd had any suspicions about the message he'd relayed to John Surratt without hesitation. Louis Weichmann was presumed innocent, as Mary Surratt should have been until proven otherwise. That is the sacred foundation of the United States justice system. Anyone who believed that Louis Weichmann had been oblivious to the meaning of the message he'd transmitted to John Surratt through Booth's telegram ought to have granted the benefit of the same doubt to Mary Surratt for allegedly carrying a message from Booth to John Lloyd. The reverse was also true: anyone who believed that Mary Surratt's conversation with John Lloyd proved her guilt ought to have been equally suspicious of Louis Weichmann. But any parallels between the two incidents were shrugged off without comment.

Next Weichmann told the court the story of John Surratt, Lewis Powell, and John Wilkes Booth bursting into his room lamenting some failed mission. Weichmann detailed how he had come home to find John Surratt gone and Mary crying over her son's absence. He also told of Mrs. Slater, the lady blockade-runner the Surratts had hosted for a night while aiding her return to Richmond. To hear Weichmann tell it, there could be little doubt that *something* had been going on in that house.

But as he heaped up more and more evidence against Mary Surratt, it became increasingly difficult to ignore how much had happened before Louis Weichmann's very eyes. "Probably all readers of the evidence have been somewhat puzzled by the testimony of the important witness Weichmann, and have wondered how a clerk in the War Department could see so much at the Surratt's [*sic*] and not suspect more, and how he could leave his office for such frequent drives into the country with his landlady," the *Boston Evening Transcript* pointed out. The newspaper boldly theorized that Weichmann had indeed reported his suspicions to the War Department, and that Secretary Stanton himself had enlisted Weichmann as a secret agent. "This story furnishes the only plausible explanation for the mystery about Weichmann's relations with the Surratts," the article surmised. The *Boston Evening Transcript*'s logic made no sense. If Weichmann had been Stanton's secret agent, and if he had reported all these strange goings-on directly to the secretary of war, then why on earth had the assassination not been averted?

That was the point Mary Surratt's lawyers strove with all their might to make. An honest, loyal man who had seen what Weichmann claimed to have seen would have done something. Anything. Especially a man employed by the War Department.

"Do I understand you as stating to the Court, that, in all your conversation with them, you never learned of any intended treasonable purpose or act or conspiracy of theirs?" Aiken asked.

"No, sir."

"You never did?"

"No, sir."

"And you were not suspicious of any thing of the sort?"

"I would have been the last man in the world to suspect John Surratt, my schoolmate, of the murder of the President of the United States."

"You state that your suspicions were aroused at one time by something you saw at Mrs. Surratt's?"

"My suspicions were aroused by John Surratt and this man Payne and Booth coming to the house. My suspicions again were aroused by their frequent private conversations. My suspicions were aroused by seeing Payne and Surratt playing on the bed with bowie-knives. My suspicions were again aroused by finding a false mustache in my room."

For once, Weichmann had said exactly what Aiken wanted him to. "Then, if your suspicions were aroused on all these [different] occasions which you have mentioned, and you had reason to believe that something was in the wind that was improper, did you communicate any of them to the War Department?" the lawyer asked.

"My suspicions were not of a fixed or settled character," Weichmann explained. "I did not know what they intended to do." Weichmann told the court that in fact he had confided in his supervisor, Captain Gleason, and the two had speculated about what sort of mischief Booth and his compatriots might have been up to. Neither of them had suspected anything worse than blockade-running or smuggling dispatches. When Weichmann had asked his superior whether it might be possible for anyone to capture the president, Captain Gleason had "laughed and hooted" at the idea.

Yet again, Weichmann had thwarted Mary Surratt's team with his frankness. The New York World noted that the young clerk "gave his testimony with much pertness, as if he was determined not to be baffled by the lawyers." Louis Weichmann succeeded. None of the defense lawyers could shake his certainty. They could not so much as make him wobble, no matter how they tried to cast suspicion on his motives for informing on his landlady. "I have never seen anything like his steadfastness," one of the nine commissioners later marveled. "There he stood, a young man only twenty-three years of age, strikingly handsome, intelligent, self-possessed, under the most searching cross-examination I have ever heard." Louis Weichmann was just so forthcoming, so relentlessly steady and consistent. In short, he was the sort of witness that juries instinctively believe—regardless of whether their testimony is true.

CHAPTER SIXTEEN

Every square foot of floor space in the courtroom was occupied on May 19. An unprecedented number of spectators had come in anticipation of the testimony against Powell, eager to hear firsthand the grim details of the assault upon Secretary Seward.

The chance for a look at the prisoners remained one of the main attractions. The massive corner door, with its abundance of heavy bolts, swung open, and the daily procession began. "As the prisoners are brought in there is a general buzz throughout the room of 'That's Mrs. Surratt!' 'That's Mudd!' 'That's Payne, sure!' 'That's Arnold—no! that's O'Laughlen!' &c., &c.," the Washington *Evening Star* reported.

Before the witnesses against Powell were called to the stand, Captain Wermerskirch, then Detective Morgan, and then Major Smith testified as to how they had arrested Mary Surratt and searched her house. They told of the peculiar arrival of Powell at 541 H Street, and how Mary Surratt had sworn "before God" that she did not recognize him. The commission knew now what the arresting officers had not known on April 17: that Lewis Powell had stayed at Mary's home on two prior occasions.

This fact seemed to point toward a simple conclusion: the Surratt boardinghouse had been Booth's headquarters, and therefore Powell had known that Mary Surratt could be trusted to shelter him from the authorities. It was a logical guess that ultimately would never be proven true or false. Nevertheless, it was a difficult notion for Aiken and Clampitt to dislodge. Following his arrest, Powell had said nothing to the authorities that incriminated Mary, but Mary and her lawyers were not privy to that fact.

Trying to convince the government's witnesses that Powell's disguise had rendered him unrecognizable also turned out to be a dead-end strategy. No matter how thick the mud, how disheveled his clothing, or how outlandish his underwear-sleeve hat, the three officers would not acknowledge the possibility that Powell the gutter digger looked any different from Reverend Paine or Mr. Wood.

"How was Payne dressed at that time?" Aiken asked Major Smith on cross-examination.

Smith described the gray coat, the black pants with one leg tucked into "rather a fine pair of boots," and the dangling gray cutoff shirt-sleeve Powell had worn as a hat.

Aiken made the major repeat the details about the makeshift hat and rumpled pant legs before asking, "He did not strike you at that time as being a gentleman from his looks and appearance?"

"Not particularly so."

"His appearance was in no wise genteel?" Aiken asked, guiding the witness closer to the point he needed to make.

Major Smith seemed to oblige. "Not at all," he said.

"Is it your opinion that any one would recognize a person in that garb, in that dress, who had seen him, if he ever did see him, well dressed, with such a thing as that on his head?"

The major avoided the question, instead remarking upon Powell's hat.

"Do you think you would recognize a person fixed up in that way, with that shirt-sleeve on his head, and a pickaxe?" Aiken pressed.

"I most certainly should," Major Smith said.

"A person you had been in the habit of seeing dressed genteelly?"

"Certainly." The major was not going to give an inch on this point. He had seen the man with his own eyes—as had everyone in the courtroom—and believed Powell's appearance so singular that he could be neither forgotten nor mistaken for anyone else.

There was also the sticky matter of the images of John Wilkes Booth, Jefferson Davis, Alexander Stephens, and General Beauregard that had been found in Mary Surratt's house. Aiken was determined to prove that it was commonplace for loyal US citizens to have photographs of famous people such as actors as well as military personnel on both sides of the conflict, and that such photographs were easily found in the city. None of the men who had searched the Surratt boardinghouse would agree that they were familiar with any such practice, however.

"Have you not been in the habit of seeing exhibited in the windows of bookstores, about the streets, photographs of Booth for sale?" Aiken asked Detective Morgan.

"I never had seen any of them before he assassinated the President," Morgan replied.

Aiken could not let well enough alone. His determination to ask the same question and re-ask only gave Morgan more chances to disagree. "Do you not know, from your own knowledge, that such pictures have been offered for sale in different bookstores, and that it is a common thing for people to have them?"

"I have not seen people have them since the Rebellion. They might have had them before."

"Since the assassination of President Lincoln, has it not been a common thing to see the photograph of Booth about?"

"If it has, I never have seen it."

By the time Aiken gave up, Morgan had effectively answered not once but five times, emphasizing exactly the opposite of the point Aiken had wished to make. Aiken was only marginally more successful with Major Smith.

"Are you aware or not that it is a common thing for newspaper-dealers, and keepers of bookshops, to advertise for sale, and to sell, photographs of the leaders of the Rebellion?"

"I am not," the major replied. "I have never given such things my attention." That was the crux of the problem. Such photos were every bit as prevalent as Aiken said they were; he was merely asking the wrong kind of person. Few soldiers and police officers had been in the habit of collecting souvenir photos of matinee idols or enemy generals since the war had begun. But again Aiken hammered away at the point like a man forever doomed to strike his thumb instead of the nail.

"Have you never seen them exposed for sale?"

"I cannot say that I have."

"Have you seen the photograph of Booth in the possession of people supposed to be loyal?"

By now Major Smith had grown weary enough of the topic to inject his response with a lethal dose of scorn. "Yes, sir: a great many of them, but only those to whom they have been given since this trial," he said, making it clear that in his opinion, anyone who'd paid money for a photo of Booth before or since the assassination was perhaps unworthy of being called loyal.

Still, Aiken doggedly persisted. "Are you aware or not that it is a very common thing for photographs of eminent actors to be published, and scattered broadcast for sale over the country?"

"I am, of *eminent* actors," Smith replied with an emphasis so snide, the word was italicized in the official transcript.

While the lawyers fired questions about the photographs and the witnesses parried them, Mary was growing noticeably agitated. For days she had appeared uninterested, intent only on making herself as invisible as possible behind her palm-leaf fan. Occasionally she rested her head on the rail before her "as if weeping." Now she leaned over that rail several times to prompt her lawyers to ask questions on her behalf.

Perhaps this was how Mary's reaction—or perceived lack thereof— to her arrest came up in court, as it had in the newspapers. In a puzzling move, one of her own lawyers interrupted General Holt's questioning to broach the topic. "Did Mrs. Surratt express any surprise or deep feeling at the moment of her arrest?" Mr. Clampitt asked Major Smith.

If Mary had prompted the question, she'd surely expected a different answer than Smith gave. "No, sir: she did not ask even for what she was arrested; expressed no surprise and no feeling at all," the major said, reinforcing the prevailing notion that an innocent woman ought to have been simultaneously confused, shocked, and horrified.

With that question gone awry, Mary endeavored to make the court aware that the last thing she had done before being escorted from her home in police custody was to kneel down to pray. At Mary's urging, Frederick Aiken put the question to Captain Wermerskirch, who confirmed that she had indeed done so. "We had sent for a carriage to take her to the Provost Marshal's office; and [Major Smith] informed her that the carriage was there, and ready to take her. Her reply was, that she requested a minute or so to kneel down first to pray."

"Then she did kneel and pray before she left the house?" Mr. Aiken asked.

"She knelt down," Wermerskirch answered slyly. "Whether she prayed or not, I cannot tell."

Sniggers rippled through the court. The captain might as well have stabbed Mary Surratt, such was the effect of his casting doubt upon her piety in public. Recoiling from the insult, she spun her face toward the wall so sharply that "for an instant her veil was thrown aside, displaying a pair of flashing eyes." There were no tears in those eyes, the *Philadelphia Inquirer* reported from halfway across the long room, only a shimmer of ire. "The incident was a trifling one," the paper said, "but the spirit of the prisoner was displayed more strongly in this little action than at any other time since she has been on trial."

***

The officers' stories were not ironclad, however. Nor did they fully corroborate one another. Both Morgan and Smith claimed to have been the one who questioned Powell in Mary Surratt's entryway, for instance. There were also more significant discrepancies regarding her encounter with Powell.

To hear Detective Morgan tell it, Mary Surratt had not been asked to identify Powell at all—a fact General Holt brought out inadvertently. "Had Mrs. Surratt left before he came in, or afterwards?" the judge advocate general asked Morgan.

"No," Morgan said, "they were all prepared to leave, in the parlor. Mrs. Surratt was directed to get the bonnets and shawls of the rest of the persons in the house, so that they could not communicate with each other. She did so; and they were just ready to go, and had started, as we opened the door, and heard the knock; and we passed them out at the time we left him within. He just got in before they stepped out." This was remarkably similar to what Mary Surratt had told her interrogator on the night of her arrest. "Just as the carriage drew up; he rang the doorbell," she'd said.

Here Holt plummeted into the very trap that Aiken had fallen prey to—trying to get his witness to correct what seemed to be a mistake, only to have Morgan repeat the damaging information over and over again.

"I understand you to say that Mrs. Surratt was not in his presence in the house?" Holt said.

"No more than passing out: she must have seen him."

"No conversation occurred?"

"No, sir." He had been standing mere steps away from Smith and Wermerskirch while Powell had been interrogated. If Mary had been brought forward to identify Powell, Morgan had to have seen it.

Even the two men who had testified to Mary Surratt's disavowal of Powell did not fully agree on the particulars. When Aiken asked Major Smith whether the hallway had been well lit when he'd called Mary in from the parlor, he replied, "Yes, sir: very light. The gas was turned on at full head."

Captain Wermerskirch's testimony on the same detail could not have been more at odds with the major's. Asked to identify the coat Powell had been wearing that night, Wermerskirch hesitated. It was difficult to be certain, he explained, because "the hall was not lit up very well: we had dimmed the gaslight purposely."

Though Wermerskirch insisted that the place where Mary had stood had been illuminated by light from the lamps in the hall as well as the parlor—each turned up to "a full head" of gas—all he could be confident of was that the color and shape of the coat were "as near . . . as can be" to Powell's.

Aiken did not ask Wermerskirch why any of the gaslights had been turned down in the first place, which of them had been dimmed, nor why all of them had not been turned back up at the moment when Mary was asked to identify Powell. Any of this information might have been as promising as a glint of gold in a mine shaft, yet inexplicably Aiken dug no further. Instead he doubled back to the same question that had served him so poorly when he'd posed it to Major Smith: "Do you think you would be able to recognize a person in such a garb in dim gaslight, when you had been in the habit of meeting the same person before genteelly dressed?"

"If I was asked to identify him, and look at him, and say if he was the same man or not, I think I would," the captain said. "The prisoner had not taken any particular pains to disguise himself: his face looked just the same as it does now: the only difference that ever existed was the clothes."

"You have not the least doubt in your mind that you would be able to recognize a man in those different garbs under these circumstances?"

Wermerskirch stuck to his story without swerving an inch, just as Smith had done. "I think I would recognize him, even if he put on another coat, and besmeared himself with mud," the captain replied.

Powell's coat proved even more troublesome to Major Smith. Handed a light gray coat by General Holt, he said at once, "That is the coat, to the best of my belief."

At that, Powell's lawyer, Mr. Doster, leapt into action. "How do you know that coat to be the one Payne had on?" he interrupted.

"How would you know any thing you had seen before but from memory?" Major Smith retorted.

"I am simply asking you how do you know?" Doster insisted.

"By the way anybody would recognize a thing after having seen it once,—by the impression that was made on the memory at the time."

Assistant Judge Advocate Bingham handed the major a darker gray coat. "Select now, between this coat and the one you have just had in your hands, which is the nearest the color," he instructed.

Smith realized his mistake as soon as he saw the buttons on the dark gray coat. "The coat now shown me is the one," he admitted.

Aiken pounced on the opportunity Major Smith had unwittingly opened. Despite the major's relentless insistence that he would recognize a man like Powell no matter how he was dressed, Aiken pressed, "you could not recollect a coat that you had only seen within a short time, but confounded it with one that was a[s] different in appearance as those two coats here?"

"It is hard to remember the particular color of a coat, as any one will very well know, that you see at night-time, if they saw it by gas-light," Smith said.

Only moments before, the major had claimed that the hall was "very light," the gas flame turned up as far as it would go. The officers seemed to want it both ways: bright when Mary Surratt identified Lewis Powell, and dim when they observed him. Yet all of the men had been standing in the very same hallway throughout the encounter. Was it reasonable to expect Mary Surratt to identify Powell under the same conditions that had stymied both Wermerskirch and Smith?

CHAPTER SEVENTEEN

As the prosecution brought its case to a close, a sudden change came over Mary Surratt. "We read in unmistakable letters upon her still features the record of some ineffable woe," the *Washington Chronicle* reported on Tuesday, May 23. "It is not fear, not the excitement of a mighty doubt, but withering, blasting woe." Despair seemed to have descended upon her like a curtain after the triple blow of the testimony of Morgan, Wermerskirch, and Smith. "Either from within or without, during the murky hours of the past Sabbath, there has flashed upon that woman some awful vision, either of future woes or some new-lighted memory of a past tragedy," the *Washington Chronicle* continued.

No veil could hide Mary's plummeting mood now. The bleak prison regime, combined with the dread of what lay ahead, formed a mental burden at least as heavy as the iron balls chained to Powell and Atzerodt. A new, nervous motion accompanied the waving of Mary's palm-leaf fan; again and again, she who had formerly been so still reached up to smooth the parting of hair over her forehead. "It is said that she suffers nightly from frightful apparitions in her dreams," the *New York World* reported.

Unrelenting scrutiny suffused her days in court. People stared at her.

Not only stared but crowded in close to peer at her, straining to penetrate the black veil she never lifted despite the mounting heat. At times the audience was so large, the defense lawyers could not see the nine men seated at the commissioners' table.

Few spectators stayed for more than ten or fifteen minutes. Some clutched copies of the *Philadelphia Inquirer,* hoping to compare the eight prisoners in the dock with the likenesses the paper had printed. A constant rustling of silk accompanied the testimony, as women in hoop-skirts passed in and out and crowded together on the benches behind the reporters. Morbid fascination rarely failed to draw each new crop of onlookers toward the cabinet full of the prisoners' weapons.

One reporter, the *New-York Tribune*'s Jane Swisshelm, went to witness the spectacle and left appalled by the behavior of her fellow citizens. Due to the immensity of the crowd that day, Mrs. Swisshelm found herself seated "so near to Mrs. Surratt that I could have easily shaken hands with her"—near enough that Swisshelm could and did touch the railing that separated her from the woman everyone was clamoring to see.

It appeared to Mrs. Swisshelm that Mary was humiliated by everything that marked her as a prisoner. From where the reporter sat, she could hear the links of the chain that bound Mary's ankles. The sound was not the bright clink of a wagon chain but the dull clatter of a hefty log chain. "She seemed to avoid moving, so as not to attract attention to the chain," Mrs. Swisshelm later recalled, "for every time they clanked she blushed, painfully, blushed so that I could see it through the heavy crape veil she wore over her face."

But that was not what lodged most firmly in Mrs. Swisshelm's memory. To her horror, people leaned in close to the rail and announced their opinions about the prisoners in no uncertain terms. With mounting disgust, Mrs. Swisshelm listened as Mary was "grossly insulted by spectators, men and women, or things that looked like men and women."

One of "these creatures" declared, "I hope they'll hang her! Just look at her! She looks like a devil!"

Mary blanched white at the insult, and an indignant Mrs. Swisshelm burst out, "She does not look like a devil! She looks like a good, kindhearted woman, and you are a mean coward for insulting a prisoner."

"She's a Rebel," a man retorted.

"Coward!" Mrs. Swisshelm shamed him; "coward."

Mary looked up at her defender. "The expression of her face will haunt me to the grave," Mrs. Swisshelm wrote years afterward, "and I thank God for the look of gratitude it wore."

The same open vitriol permeated the newspapers. The press plainly betrayed its opinions in their headlines, tacitly encouraging the public to do the same. Properly phrased, this was a conspiracy trial. More often, though, it was trumpeted as "The Trial of the Conspirators," as though the eight defendants had already been found guilty. Rarely were they referred to in neutral terms such as "the accused." The most objective label that Mary and her fellow defendants could hope for was "the prisoners." To the papers and the public, they were already "the conspirators" or, worse, "the assassins."

With Booth dead and unable to answer for his crimes, the nation needed a new target for its anger and grief. Mary Surratt became that target.

"The first feeling which the visitor experiences on entering the room is one of amazement at the conspicuous meanness, coarseness, and vulgarity of the prisoners," reported the *New-York Tribune*. "There is not one of them perhaps, excepting Mudd and Mrs. Surratt, who has sufficient character to enter into any such a conspiracy as this, from any motive less base than money. None of the rest have apparently enough personal independence and moral purpose, for even treason to fasten energetically upon."

Lewis Powell was "but an animal, ferocious, brutal, and evidently possessing but little mind or heart." Everything about him proclaimed him a criminal—especially his low, narrow forehead, prominent jaw, and disagreeably small corneas—but "not one capable of planning a deed of cunning."

With his "dingy and sallow" complexion and pathetically small tufts of beard, the boyish David Herold struck the *Boston Daily Advertiser* as having "no sense of mental or moral force, and has every appearance of abject cowardice." According to the Washington *Evening Star,* he was nothing better than a "shallow-pated blab-mouth."

Michael O'Laughlen, whose silky black hair and mustache lent him an "eminently Spanish" appearance, was deemed "dark and vindictive" but only "tolerably intelligent."

Of Edman Spangler the *New York Times* concluded, "The poor man seems to have left only enough sensibility to understand that he has got into a very uncomfortable situation somehow or other."

George Atzerodt had the misfortune to be born with the low brow, short neck, "sallow complexion," and "dull, dark" eyes that consigned a man to a life of constant mistrust. Peering across the forty-foot room at him, the *New York Times* reporter decided that Atzerodt "at no time evinces a high sensibility of his almost inevitable doom."

Samuel Arnold's appearance did not fit the criminal mold. He was "a young man of decent and respectable appearance." So decent and respectable, in fact, that the *New York Times* reporter could not understand what Arnold was doing there, for his expression showed "no evidence or capacity of guilt."

Only Dr. Mudd was regarded as having more brains than his dullwitted co-defendants. "The full forehead and rather reflective cast of the face of Dr. Mudd seemed much out of place among the low type of countenance of his fellows," the Washington *Evening Star* reflected.

The *New York Times* likewise remarked upon the doctor's high forehead, a feature widely considered to be a marker of intellect. Thus, Mudd's refined, gentlemanly appearance exempted him from the public's suspicion solely by virtue of the shape of his head. The *Boston Daily Advertiser* agreed that the doctor's face and demeanor alone "would go far toward acquitting him of a very deep participation in the conspiracy."

"The general impression of the whole set is of lack of brain," concluded a reporter for the *Springfield Republican*.

That left no one but Mary Surratt to carry the weight of the conspiracy. The Philadelphia *Press* dubbed her the mother of the conspiracy, writing that "with a cold clear, devilish gray pair of eyes, she would make a good stage landlady, ready to look after her own interests and to get all the money that she could from her customers."

The *New York Times* informed its readers that Mary was "a large, Amazonian class of woman, square built, masculine hands, rather full face, dark gray, lifeless eye, hair not decidedly dark, complexion swarthy; altogether, her face denotes more than usual intelligence." This was a remarkably thorough description of a woman who wore a bonnet, gloves, and veil every day of the trial. Nevertheless, by her silhouette alone the *New York Times* judged her "a woman of undaunted metal [*sic*]" who appeared "too strong to be weighed down by the crushing testimony against her."

The journalists' notions about Mary's looks further betrayed their biases in their daily reports of the evidence. "Mrs. Surratt appears to have been cognizant of the intended crime almost from its inception," the *New York Times* announced, "and became an active participant in overt acts." The paper asserted that she was "a general manager" and had "long confidential talks" with Booth.

None of these claims had any basis in the evidence. Louis Weichmann had testified that Mary's talks with Booth had never lasted as much as ten minutes, in contrast to the two or three hours at a time that Booth conferred with John Surratt. And no witness had given any hint as to when Mary might have been recruited by Booth. "In all the pages of the record of that trial," Mary's lawyer John Clampitt pointed out afterward, "there can be found no testimony to show that Mrs. Surratt was cognizant of the [plot], or even participated in a single meeting."

The public saw the evidence differently. In a sense, they were not seeing the same evidence at all. In the *Boston Daily Advertiser*'s estimation, the concise daily summaries the public relied upon were not "complete or always trustworthy." Even the Associated Press was guilty of "unintentionally slurring over the most important facts" and "omitting . . . indispensable links in the grand chain of circumstantial evidence."

Nor was reading the endless pages of testimony in the papers a worthy substitute for listening to the witnesses in the courtroom. "But the perusal of testimony at best is not like hearing it," the *Boston Daily Advertiser* would observe, "and when one loses the hesitations, the emphasis, the gestures of the witness, and has to judge of his credibility by what he says without the aid of knowing how he says it, the process of following the course of the trial becomes much like groping in the dark."

Nevertheless, the idea that Mary Surratt was guilty had sunk its roots deep into the public consciousness. "Women are rarely hanged in this country, and this fact may save her," said the *Daily Evening Traveler*. "Certainly nothing else can."

CHAPTER EIGHTEEN

Every day, the crowd grew. Lines of carriages stood parked outside the arsenal. "From these dismount major-generals' wives, in rustling silks; daughters of congressmen, attired like the lilies of the milliner; little girls who hope to be young ladies and have come with 'Pa,' to look at the assassins; even brides are here, in the fresh blush of their nuptials," wrote George Alfred Townsend of the *New York World*. "These tender creatures have a weakness for the ring of manacles, the sight of folks to be suspended in the air, the face of a woman confederate in blood."

May 25, the day the defense opened its case, drew swarms of spectators like flies to a corpse. In they crammed, avid to see how Mary Surratt's lawyers would defend her.

Aiken and Clampitt could not demolish the prosecution's case with a few deft blows. None of their evidence had that kind of crushing weight. Instead they had to chip away at the opposing evidence, forming a concentration of hairline cracks that might in the end leave the case against Mary Surratt too fragile to stand.

The two young lawyers had no illusions about the odds they faced. Both believed her innocent, but the way the plot had unfolded around her left little room for persuasion. "The chain of circumstances seemed to array itself against the unhappy woman," John Clampitt later wrote. More daunting yet, Mary Surratt's lawyers could not simply show the tribunal why it was *possible* for her to be innocent.

In a civil trial, they would have been required to prove nothing. The burden of proof—the burden of demonstrating a defendant's guilt so thoroughly that no juror can reasonably doubt it—rests on the prosecution. Under those circumstances, the gaps in Louis Weichmann's and John Lloyd's testimony might well have been just wide enough for Mary to slip through unscathed. Even the testimony of Weichmann, John Clampitt noted, "nowhere reveals the fact that she ever participated in any plot, or was privy to the knowledge that in her house were planned the abduction and final assassination." But Mary's defense team had a different task altogether—to prove conclusively that it was impossible for Mary to have been involved in or aware of Booth's plan.

To that end, the single greatest fact Aiken and Clampitt could hope to establish was that Booth had not abandoned his kidnapping plans in favor of murder until late in the day on April 14—*after* Mary Surratt and Louis Weichmann had departed for Surrattsville. "They will have hard work to persuade the court or the public to this belief," the *Boston Daily Advertiser* predicted. The prosecution had amply shown that Booth's plot had been simmering for months—some of it within Mary's own walls. Even if she had set out for Surrattsville before Booth had committed himself to assassinating the president, that did not mean Mary was ignorant of the fact that Booth intended some sort of malice toward Abraham Lincoln.

If Aiken and Clampitt could instead convince the tribunal of three lesser points—that Mary Surratt had turned George Atzerodt out of her boardinghouse, that she had gone to Surrattsville on April 14 solely to transact business, and that she had not recognized Lewis Powell on the night of her arrest—it might shift the weight of the evidence against her just enough for them to slip the noose from her neck.

⟿

Aiken and Clampitt aimed to open their defense of Mary Surratt as strongly as Holt had begun his case against her, with a phalanx of witnesses no one would dare to doubt.

Over the next two days, Aiken and Clampitt called five clergymen to testify on Mary's behalf. Not one of them did her case an appreciable bit of good. The very fact that they were priests and presumably incapable of deceit ought to have worked in Mary's favor. Instead, the combination of their scrupulous honesty and Aiken's scattershot questions undermined her case at nearly every turn.

Only one of them, Father Bernardine Wiget, claimed that he knew Mary well—they had been acquainted for over a decade. In the previous six months he had sometimes called at her home as often as once a week.

"During all this acquaintance, has any thing ever come to your knowledge respecting the lady that would be called of an unchristian character?" Mr. Aiken asked.

"No: never."

Yet in that ten- or eleven-year acquaintance, Father Wiget had also never heard anything about Mary's eyesight being "defective," thereby hobbling Aiken's new strategy to explain why she had failed to recognize Powell. And when General Holt put him on the spot regarding Mary's loyalty to the Union, Father Wiget had no choice but to admit that he could not remember hearing her "utter one loyal sentiment."

Reverend Francis Boyle came across as even less convincing. Though they had met "some eight or nine years ago," he could recall crossing paths with Mary Surratt just three or four times since then. Father

Boyle, too, knew her by reputation as "an estimable lady" but could nei-ther prove nor disprove her loyalty, for such matters had never entered into their brief conversations.

Reverend Charles Stonestreet's twenty-year acquaintance with Mary seemed more promising, until Aiken asked, "Have you lately, within a year or two past, been more intimate with her?"

"I have not," the priest answered. "I have scarcely seen her."

"Have you, in all your intercourse with her, ever heard her utter disloyal sentiments?"

"Never," Father Stonestreet said. "There was no question of it at the time I was acquainted with her." When General Holt got his chance at cross-examination, he quickly brought out the reason why: Father Stonestreet could not remember having seen Mary Surratt since the war had begun. "You have no knowledge then, whatever, of her charac-ter for loyalty since the Rebellion started?" Holt asked.

"Nothing but what I read in the papers," Father Stonestreet answered.

When all was said and done, five different priests would swear that they knew nothing of Mary having poor eyesight. Even Father Lani-han, who had stayed at Mary's house, could not recall witnessing her struggle to recognize anyone she knew. They might just as well have testified that Mary Surratt had lied about not knowing Lewis Powell, for the effect was identical.

The same complication came into play regarding the question of her loyalty. Not one of the five clergymen could swear under oath that Mary had ever displayed any sympathy or fidelity to the Union, and that was troubling. No matter that she had never praised the Confederacy. Absence of disloyalty was not sufficient. To be convincing, there had to be solid evidence of devotion to the Union cause. Mary had kept her allegiances quiet. With one son fighting for the rebels in Texas, an-other running Confederate intelligence across the blockade lines, and the majority of her boardinghouse's earnings coming from pro-Union boarders, an appearance of neutrality had served her well during the war. In the charged atmosphere that followed the president's assassination, however, her careful avoidance looked more calculated than diplomatic.

Oddly enough, if every one of the priests called to testify had sworn under oath that Mary Surratt was as blind as a bat and as loyal as a hound, they might not have been believed. Even clergymen were not immune from suspicion—or at least those of a certain denomination. The fact that these five men were Catholics carried its own whiff of distrust, for there were rumors afloat that Booth and all of his accomplices were Catholics. It was far from true, but in the weeks following Lincoln's murder, the truth was no match for suspicion.

☞

Next in Aiken and Clampitt's line of defense came two of Mary's boarders, Eliza Holohan and Honora Fitzpatrick. Unlike the priests, who had seen Mary at Mass and visited her home only briefly, these two women had lived alongside Mary Surratt for months. Who better to observe her relations with her boarders than the women who'd eaten at her table, sipped tea and chatted in her parlor, and, in Honora Fitzpatrick's case, slept in her bed?

Aiken turned to a topic the women were uniquely suited to address: George Atzerodt's expulsion from 541 H Street. "Were any objections made on the part of any member of the family to his being there?" he asked Mrs. Holohan.

"Yes," she answered, "I heard Mrs. Surratt say she objected to Mr. Atzerodt; she did not like him."

"And did not wish him to come there?" With this question Aiken hoped to break a link in the chain of conspirators, for surely a woman plotting to murder the president would not turn one of her accomplices out into the street.

"I do not know about his coming there," Mrs. Holohan said, "but she would not board him. I heard her say at the table that she would rather he would not come there to board." Another answer that hindered almost as much as it helped. Even if Atzerodt had not been welcome overnight or at the Surratt table, that still left an opening for him to call during the day, when Booth paid his visits.

"Did you learn any thing, while you were boarding with Mrs. Surratt, of defective eyesight on her part?"

"I have heard Mrs. Surratt state—"

"You need not say what she stated," Bingham interrupted.

"I never saw her read or sew after candle-light," Mrs. Holohan offered.

Sewing and reading were one thing. But Lewis Powell's face was larger than a line of print or the eye of a needle, which Holt quickly pointed out on cross-examination. "You say you never saw Mrs. Surratt sew or read after dark?" he asked.

"No, sir: I never saw her sew or read after dark."

"Have you not often met her in the parlor by gaslight?"

"Yes, sir."

"Did she ever seem to have any difficulty in recognizing you?" Holt asked.

"No, sir."

"Nor anybody else in the house with whom she was acquainted?"

"I never heard of it."

In the space of a few seconds, Holt had unraveled what little progress Aiken had made. Then again, General Holt's comparison was not wholly fair. Mrs. Holohan had boarded with Mary Surratt for months, and was not in the habit of wearing disguises or changing her name.

After Mrs. Holohan came seventeen-year-old Honora Fitzpatrick. The prosecution had already used her to confirm Atzerodt's and Powell's presence in the Surratt boardinghouse. Now Aiken sought to temper that damage, specifically concerning Atzerodt.

"Did you learn whether he was welcome at Mrs. Surratt's or not, or whether he was disagreeable?" Aiken asked her.

Bingham objected, as usual, and Aiken asked the question from another angle.

"Are you acquainted with the fact of his being sent away at any time, or that he was to be sent away—"

Again Bingham interrupted to object "to any question of the sort." With every objection he backed Mary's defense further into a corner, forcing Aiken further away from the fact he wanted to draw out.

Aiken began afresh. "How long did Atzerodt stay there?"

"He only staid there for a short time," Miss Fitzpatrick said.

"Can you state any of the circumstances of his leaving, or under what circumstances he left?"

"I suppose that Mrs. Surratt sent him away."

"You need not state suppositions," Bingham cut in.

Aiken rephrased again. "Do you know any thing of the circumstances of his going away?"

"No: I do not know any thing about his leaving."

"Are you aware that he got drunk in the house, and made a disturbance?"

"No, sir: I heard that he had bottles up there; but I do not know any thing about his getting drunk."

Exchanges like these constantly made Aiken and Clampitt look like bungling amateurs. They just could not seem to ask the right questions.

Bingham and his incessant objections were only half the problem. The breakneck speed with which the defense attorneys been had recruited was the other.

Where the government had spent a month amassing evidence and interrogating and re-interrogating witnesses to sift out the finest details, the defense had come on board with mere days or hours to prepare. Without similar access to the evidence, Aiken and Clampitt had no chance of hewing out questions sharp enough to pinpoint a specific detail, or penetrate the heart of an issue.

"While you were in the house, did you learn any thing of defective eyesight on the part of Mrs. Surratt?" Aiken asked Miss Fitzpatrick.

"I heard Mrs. Surratt talking about it herself."

"Do not state what Mrs. Surratt stated, but what you know."

"I know she could not read at nights, or sew, on account of her sight." Just as Mrs. Holohan had testified.

"Have you ever known Mrs. Surratt to be unable to recognize persons at once in the street,—people of her acquaintance?"

"I remember once passing Mrs. Kirby," Miss Fitzpatrick said, "and [Mrs. Surratt] did not see her at all." Finally, a glimmer of possibility. If Mary could walk right past a friend on the street in broad daylight, it followed that she might not recognize a man who changed his appearance every time she encountered him.

At the press table that day, reporters strained to hear the testimony. "Ceaseless and senseless chatter" buzzed behind them for hours, forcing the Washington *Evening Star* at one point to print a single line— "Remainder of the testimony unintelligible from the gabble of the women"—in lieu of one witness's testimony. "Lively comments upon the looks of the prisoners" dominated the conversations. No evidence commanded as much attention as the eight faces behind the rail.

"What should be the most solemn and simple, as it is the most important, trial of the age, is degenerating into a most undignified exhibition of a half-dozen criminals to an unmannerly populace," the *Boston Daily Advertiser* scolded, "and if no restriction is put on the daily issue of fresh tickets of admission, the court may as well give up its operations altogether, and place the whole matter in the hands of the people."

As the spectators jabbered over the way the men in the prisoners dock combed their hair, Mary leaned her head listlessly against the wall. She, too, seemed disengaged from the trial, despite a few incremental improvements in her case.

While reporters, lawyers, and commissioners alike struggled against the noise, George Calvert testified that he had written a letter to Mary Surratt on April 12. The court did not permit Calvert to state the contents of the letter, but the fact that it existed at all aligned precisely with what Mary had told Louis Weichmann when she'd asked him to drive her to Surrattsville on the afternoon of April 14.

After Calvert came Bennett Gwynn, a former Maryland neighbor of Mary Surratt's, who stepped onto the witness stand to inform the court that he had driven through Surrattsville on the afternoon of the assassination. "As I was passing in my buggy, some one hailed me and said Mrs. Surratt wanted to see me. I stopped to see her in the tavern."

"Have you been in the habit of transacting business for her?" Aiken asked.

"Yes, sir," Gwynn said, "I have transacted some business for her relative to the sale of some lands her husband had sold to Mr. Nothe [*sic*]."

"Did you transact any business for her that day?"

"No, sir. She gave me a letter to give to Mr. Nothe [*sic*]."

Again, this testimony dovetailed with Louis Weichmann's information regarding Mary's trip to Surrattsville: "She said, when she rapped at my room on that afternoon, that she had received a letter from [George] Calvert with regard to this money that was due her by Mr. Nothe [*sic*]."

Mr. Gwynn further stated for the record that he had seen John Lloyd in Marlboro that same day, probably at around four or four-thirty.

"What was his condition at that time?" Aiken asked.

"He had been drinking right smartly," Gwynn replied.

Aiken ought to have stopped right there. He'd made his point and made it squarely. As usual, he pushed for more and came away with less. "Would you call him very drunk?"

"He was not very drunk," said Mr. Gwynn, though "he had been drinking right smartly."

"Did he seem to be considerably intoxicated?"

"Well, I could hardly tell that. He acted like a man that had drunk some." So Lloyd had been noticeably drunk, yet "not very drunk"—at least not according to Gwynn's standards. The question of just how much faith to put in John Lloyd's memory of that afternoon remained as murky as ever. And Lloyd's credibility was about to turn muddier yet.

Detective George Cottingham took the stand and faced the commissioners. For once, Frederick Aiken could approach his witness with confidence, for he knew exactly what Cottingham would say. The two men had spoken over the past weekend, and the detective had divulged a sterling piece of information: tavern keeper John Lloyd had *not* implicated Mary Surratt in his first confession. This was the witness that could turn the entire case around.

With a few preliminary questions Aiken established that John Lloyd had been put under Cottingham's supervision immediately following his arrest. Then Aiken asked, "What information did Mr. Lloyd give you at that time?"

"He denied knowing any thing about it first," Cottingham testified. "He was there, I think, two days, denying it every day. I finally told him that my mind was made up; that I was perfectly satisfied he was into it; that he had a heavy load on his mind, and the sooner he got rid of it the better. He said to me then, 'O my God! If I should make a confession, they would murder me.'" Once Cottingham consigned Lloyd to a guardhouse and sent a lieutenant back to the city for reinforcements, Lloyd started to offer up information. "Lloyd stated to me that Mrs. Surratt had come down to his place on Friday, betwixt four and five o'clock," Detective Cottingham testified, "that she told him to have the fire-arms ready; that two men would call for them at twelve o'clock; and the two men did call."

What Aiken was hearing made no sense. It was precisely the opposite of what the detective had confided to him just a few days earlier.

Aiken tried every which way to steer the detective toward the information he was seeking—information he had heard straight from Cottingham with his own ears. Yet every question Aiken asked only brought out more incriminating details instead.

"What information did he give you about the fire-arms himself?" he asked.

Cottingham began to describe what had happened when the cavalry brought Lloyd to the tavern to locate the carbine Booth had declined to take. When Lloyd arrived, the detective was there and witnessed the frightful scene the panicked man made. "He commenced crying, and hallooing out, 'Oh! Mrs. Surratt, the vile woman! she has ruined me!'"

The more specific Aiken's questions, the more specific Cottingham's answers became—always to Mary Surratt's detriment.

"During these two days, when Mr. Lloyd was denying all knowledge of these parties, did he mention the name of Mrs. Surratt then?"

"No, not when he was denying; but, after he confessed, he did."

Finally Aiken gave up. It seemed that his own witness had handed

Mary Surratt to the government on a silver platter. It was an opportunity General Holt did not waste.

"What was the precise language which he used in reference to Mrs. Surratt, as to her having got him into the difficulty?" the judge advocate general asked on cross-examination, the better to impress Lloyd's most damning statement onto the commissioners' memories. "Give the precise words, if you can."

"He said, in the last interview in his house, 'Mrs. Surratt, that vile woman! she has ruined me: I am to be shot; I am to be shot!'"

Aiken sat, "astonished beyond measure," as Cottingham stepped down and a witness was called for Michael O'Laughlen. How could such a promising witness as Detective Cottingham have gone so disastrously awry? Aiken decided to recall the detective to the stand and challenge him directly.

"Will you state again the precise language that Lloyd used in his confession to you with reference to Mrs. Surratt?" he asked.

Once again, the detective took Aiken's questioning off the rails. Cottingham wanted to testify not about Lloyd's confession, but instead regarding the recent chat he'd had with Aiken. "If the Court will allow me," he said, "I should like to tell the whole conversation." To Aiken's despair, General Holt assented. Cottingham proceeded to explain that he and Mr. Aiken had met at the Metropolitan Hotel on Saturday. Aiken had invited him to take a drink, and Cottingham had accepted the offer. That was when the detective had learned that Aiken intended to call him as a witness for Mrs. Surratt. Cottingham agreed to talk, but not in the hotel. It "would not look well" for a special officer of the provost marshal's staff to be seen conferring privately on a hotel sofa with a defense lawyer, he'd thought. Instead he proposed that the two of them take a walk outside.

"We walked along," Cottingham testified, "and he said, 'Lloyd has made a confession to you.' Said I, 'Yes.' He then said, 'Will you not state that confession to me?'" Cottingham refused to divulge the full confession. He was proud of the strategy he had used to extract it from Lloyd, and was not willing to hand over such valuable information to anyone so easily. So Cottingham made a counteroffer: if Aiken wanted to ask specific questions about Lloyd's confession, he would answer them. Aiken did indeed have a very specific question. When John Lloyd had first confessed, Aiken asked, had the tavern keeper told the detective "that Mrs. Surratt had come down there, and told him to have the firearms ready"? Then Detective Cottingham made a startling revelation to the court: "I said not."

He had stated one thing to Aiken in the street and then contradicted himself on the witness stand. There he sat in open court—a government detective—exposing himself as a liar. More astonishing yet, Cottingham "gloried in the fact," the *Boston Daily Advertiser* reported, as he "unblushingly" told the court that he had deliberately misled Aiken, feeding the lawyer exactly what he wanted to hear. With that lie, Detective Cottingham had cunningly guaranteed that he would be called to the stand, where he could reveal the story he wanted to tell before the military commission. "I am now on my oath," Cottingham assured the commissioners, "and when I have been put on oath I have spoken the truth."

Frederick Aiken stood flabbergasted before the court. "Then you gave me to understand, and you are ready now to swear to it, that you told me a lie?"

"Undoubtedly I told you a lie there," Cottingham said, "for I thought you had no business to ask me."

Aiken could not conceal his incredulity. "No business?" he blustered. "As my witness, had I not a right to have the truth from you?"

"I told you you might call me into Court," said the triumphant detective, "and I state here that I did lie to you; but, when put on my oath, I told the truth."

In "the most striking and extraordinary event of the proceedings," Frederick Aiken had been tricked into disclosing testimony that directly harmed his client.

All in all, it was a disastrous day. After listening to the defense's best attempts to show that Mary Surratt had been unaware of Booth's plot, the *Boston Recorder* pronounced that she had been "thoroughly cognizant of all the details."

CHAPTER NINETEEN

The next days passed with only an occasional witness on Mary's behalf. John Nothey confirmed for the court that he did owe money to Mary Surratt for the purchase of seventy-five acres of land, and that Mr. Gwynn had indeed delivered a letter from Mary regarding that debt on April 14. Augustus Howell told the court that during his visit to Mary's house, she had requested that he read the newspaper aloud to her, and that on another occasion in late February he had arrived at her house and she "did not recognize me at first, until I made myself known."

These points in Mary's favor did little to sway the press toward sympathy. On the contrary, as Aiken and Clampitt labored to prove her innocence, the public's view of Mary Surratt continued to sink. Her perpetually covered face was at least partly to blame. Rather than shielding her from unwanted attention, Mary's veil inflamed curiosity. People simply had to know what was happening behind that thin black curtain—so much so that the *Daily National Republican* resorted to using opera glasses or binoculars to scrutinize her face. "Mrs. Surratt sits veiled, but a powerful glass to-day disclosed the fact that she was not weeping, as many suppose, but was active with her eyes gazing about

One of only two known images of Mary Surratt, taken around 1852.

James O. Hall Research Center at the Surratt House Museum

A photograph of Mary Surratt, likely taken about ten years later. Her appearance here is similar to how she would have looked at the time of her trial.

James O. Hall Research Center at the Surratt House Museum

Mary's younger son, John Surratt Jr. Within an hour of the assassination, John had become a prime suspect in the assault on the Seward household, despite bearing no resemblance to the perpetrator.

Brady-Handy photograph collection, Library of Congress, Prints and Photographs Division

Anna Surratt.

National Archives

Louis Weichmann, star witness in the government's case against Mary Surratt.

James O. Hall Research Center at the Surratt House Museum

Mary Surratt's boardinghouse at 541 H Street, as it looked in the nineteenth century. (H Street was later renumbered, changing the address to 604.)

Brady-Handy photograph collection, Library of Congress, Prints and Photographs Division

SURRATTSVILLE, THE HOME OF JOHN H. SURRATT.—[Sketched by A. M'Callum.]

An 1867 *Harper's Magazine* sketch of the crossroads at Surrattsville, with the Surratt family's tavern at left.

James O. Hall Research Center at the Surratt House Museum

ABRAHAM LINCOLN, Pres't U. S.

Entered according to Act of Congress, by Alex. Gardner, in the year 1865, in the Clerk's Office of the District Court for the District of Columbia.

President Abraham Lincoln, just two months before his murder.

Library of Congress

John Wilkes Booth, white supremacist and matinee idol turned assassin.

Library of Congress, Prints and Photographs Division

The box in Ford's Theatre where Lincoln was fatally shot. The president occupied the rocking chair in the right-hand arch.

Civil War photographs, 1861–1865, Library of Congress, Prints and Photographs Division

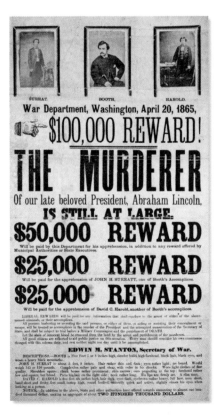

The first wanted poster issued by the War Department mistakenly featured a photograph of Mary's elder son, Isaac (upper left), rather than John Surratt Jr.

Library of Congress Rare Book and Special Collections Division

Mary Surratt was incarcerated in the Carroll Annex of the Old Capitol Prison following her arrest and interrogation.

Collection of the author

George Atzerodt, who defied Booth's order to murder Vice President Andrew Johnson.

Civil War photographs, 1861–1865, Library of Congress, Prints and Photographs Division

Lewis Powell (also known as Reverend Paine and Mr. Wood) photographed against the iron bulkhead of the USS *Montauk*. His manacles, called Lilly irons, rest in his lap.

Civil War photographs, 1861–1865, Library of Congress, Prints and Photographs Division

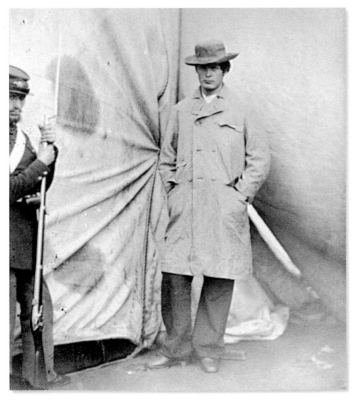

Lewis Powell under guard in the Washington Navy Yard, posed to illustrate his appearance during his assassination attempt on Secretary of State Seward.

Civil War photographs, 1861–1865, Library of Congress, Prints and Photographs Division

Twenty-three-year-old David E. Herold, Booth's guide through the swamps of Maryland and Virginia.

Civil War photographs, 1861–1865, Library of Congress, Prints and Photographs Division

Samuel Arnold, a schoolmate of John Wilkes Booth, dropped out of Booth's earlier plot to kidnap the president.

Civil War photographs, 1861–1865, Library of Congress, Prints and Photographs Division

Dr. Samuel Mudd. Unlike his six male co-defendants, a mug shot–style photograph of Mudd was never taken.

Collection of the author

Michael O'Laughlen, Booth's childhood friend.

Civil War photographs, 1861–1865, Library of Congress, Prints and Photographs Division

Edman "Ned" Spangler, accused of aiding Booth's escape from Ford's Theatre.

Civil War photographs, 1861–1865, Library of Congress, Prints and Photographs Division

One of the canvas hoods worn by six of the eight accused conspirators in prison. Mary Surratt and Dr. Mudd were spared this torture.

Division of Political and Military History, National Museum of American History, Smithsonian Institution

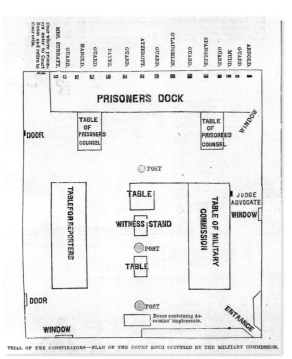

Layout of the courtroom. After the first day, Mary Surratt was seated in the corner nearest to the door the prisoners used to enter and exit the room.

Library of Congress

A sketch of the courtroom scene that appeared in the June 3, 1865, issue of *Frank Leslie's Illustrated Magazine*. The veiled figure of Mary Surratt is visible in the left rear corner.

Library of Congress

Bird's-eye view of the prison yard on the afternoon of the hanging.

Civil War photographs, 1861–1865, Library of Congress, Prints and Photographs Division

Three pine boxes lie alongside the open graves in the prison yard, awaiting the bodies of the condemned.

Civil War photographs, 1861–1865, Library of Congress, Prints and Photographs Division

General Hartranft reads the order of execution. Mary Surratt is seated at the far left, with Father Walter and Father Wiget leaning over her. To the right, only Lewis Powell's legs and feet are visible behind the center beam. David Herold and George Atzerodt are seated at the far right of the scaffold.

Civil War photographs, 1861–1865, Library of Congress, Prints and Photographs Division

A close-up shows Mary Surratt's face, barely visible through her veil, as she leans against the arm of her priest for support.

Civil War photographs, 1861–1865, Library of Congress, Prints and Photographs Division

Captain Rath (in white) places the noose around David Herold's neck while others attend to Mary Surratt, Lewis Powell, and George Atzerodt.

Civil War photographs, 1861–1865, Library of Congress, Prints and Photographs Division

Crowds disperse as the bodies dangle.

Civil War photographs, 1861–1865, Library of Congress, Prints and Photographs Division

John Surratt (aka John Watson) photographed in Rome in his papal Zouaves uniform during the nineteen months he evaded American authorities.

Brady-Handy photograph collection, Library of Congress, Prints and Photographs Division

The Surratt house as it appears today. Now in the midst of Washington, D.C.'s Chinatown, it has served the capital's Chinese community as a restaurant for decades.

The George F. Landegger Collection of District of Columbia Photographs in Carol M. Highsmith's America, Library of Congress, Prints and Photographs Division

The Surratt tavern, now the Surratt House Museum, in Clinton, Maryland.

Courtesy of Christopher W. Czajka

Mary Surratt's original gravestone in Mount Olivet Cemetery.

National Photo Company Collection, Library of Congress

Mary Surratt's gravestone as it appears today. The damaged original marker is now in the collection of the Surratt House Museum.

Courtesy of Jerry Zaetta

the court-room with the same heartless indifference to her wretched condition displayed by the male criminals." The reporters who could not see her invented descriptions of her that were based more on their own frustration than on any kind of measurable evidence. The *Boston Recorder* judged her "a good hater, but one incapable of love. Did her children ever love her, I wonder!"

On May 30, one of the three people on earth who could answer that question entered the courtroom.

Once again, curious men and women had wedged themselves into every available sliver of space. In came Miss Anna Surratt, wearing a black alpaca dress, a black silk sacque jacket, and a white straw jockey hat. Like her mother, she wore a black veil, though Anna's was made of lace rather than crape. Every eye in the court turned toward her. The month and a half she had spent in prison had made their mark upon her face, leaving a "weary, anxious look." For once, the spectators' incessant chatter ceased, and a "death-like silence prevailed" in Anna's presence. As she made her way to the stand, the *New-York Tribune* noticed, she took especial care to keep her skirts from brushing the trousers of the Yankee officers.

Anna, it seemed, was one of the few people in Washington, DC, who had not studied a newspaper diagram of the courtroom and committed the location of each prisoner in the dock to memory. Exactly a month had passed since Anna had watched the soldiers escort Mary from their cell in the Carroll Annex, and she had no notion of where to look to find her mother. Upon reaching her place on the witness stand, Anna could not see Mary without doing an about-face, for Mary was seated well behind Anna's left shoulder, in her habitual corner near the door to the prison cells.

Had she known where to look, Anna still would have been disappointed. The man who checked the credentials of all who entered the courtroom, Captain Christian Rath, fearing that Anna would run toward her mother and make "a scene," had ordered a soldier to stand in front of Mary, obscuring her from view. The usual throng of women was crowded around Mary that afternoon, too, making it nearly impossible for Anna to glimpse her.

Anna took her seat in the pivoting wooden armchair on the witness stand. Here at last was a witness Frederick Aiken could trust to provide the answers he expected. Without a qualm, he tackled the issue of Mary's eyesight. "State whether or not you are aware of frequent instances where your mother has failed to recognize her friends," he said.

"Yes, sir: her eyesight is very bad," Anna said, "and has been for some time past; and she often fails to recognize those whom she knows well."

At first Anna's testimony "was quite haughty and had an air of insulted dignity." Everyone in the room could hear her, her answers ringing out "in a clear, distinct tone."

"Is she able to read or sew by gaslight?" Aiken asked.

"No, sir; not for some time past."

Between questions Anna turned this way and that, searching every face in the audience, oblivious to the dozens of eyes staring back at her. Her foot tapped nervously on the stand, and her gaze roved over the clock.

"Have you often plagued her about getting spectacles?" Aiken continued.

"Yes, sir," Anna said, shouldering the blame for her mother's lack of eyeglasses. "I told her she was too young-looking to wear spectacles just yet. She said she could not do without them, that she could not sew or read, and very often she could not recognize those she knew best."

"Could she read or sew on a dark morning?"

"No, sir: she made out to read some, but she very seldom sewed, on a dark day."

For the first time the prosecution did not object incessantly, treating

Anna with "marked consideration and delicacy . . . allowing her to tell her story in her own way."

"Are you acquainted with Louis J. Weichmann?" Aiken asked next.

Anna's contempt for the very name of "Weichmann" reared up. "Yes, sir; I have seen him and heard of him," she said in a tone that made the *Philadelphia Inquirer* note that "her animus was unmistakable."

"Was he a boarder at your mother's house?"

"Yes, sir."

"How was he treated there?"

"He was treated too kindly."

"Was it or not your mother's habit to sit up for him when he was out of the house at night?"

"Yes, sir: whenever he was out, she would sit up and wait for him the same as she would for my brother."

Likely Aiken intended to convey the notion that Weichmann had callously betrayed a woman who had shown him nothing but warmth and consideration. This reasoning contained a significant flaw. If Mary Surratt had treated Weichmann so well and he had still felt compelled to inform on her, couldn't that just as easily suggest that her actions had been so troubling that Weichmann had been forced to put country over friendship?

Anna's feelings about Weichmann were only a secondary concern. Her primary task was to demonstrate her ignorance of her brother's plans against the president. If John had deliberately kept his sister in the dark, it would then stand to reason that his mother could have been similarly uninformed.

When Weichmann had brought Powell into the parlor at the time of his second visit, Anna testified, "I recognized him as the one who had been there before under the name of Wood. I did not know him by the name of Payne at all. I went down stairs to tell ma that he was there. She was in the dining-room. She said she did not understand why strange persons should call there; but she supposed their object was to see my brother, and she would treat them politely, as she was always in the habit of treating every one."

According to Anna's testimony, her brother John had been disturbed to discover that she and Honora Fitzpatrick had bought cartes de visite of John Wilkes Booth. "When my brother saw them, he told me to tear them up and throw them in the fire," she said, "and that, if I did not, he would take them from me; and I hid them." Unwilling to do as her brother advised, Anna had secreted her photograph of Booth behind a painting, where detectives found it on April 17. Perhaps, her testimony implied, John Surratt had wanted to protect his family from the consequences of associating with Booth.

Anna further claimed responsibility for the Confederate images found in the house. "My father gave them to me before his death," she explained, "and I prized them on his account, if on nobody else's."

"Did you own any photographs in the house at that time, of Union generals?" Aiken asked.

"Yes, sir."

"Who were they?"

"General McClellan, General Grant, and General Joe Hooker."

Anna even testified that her brother had had misgivings about Booth. "I never asked him what his friendship was to Booth," she said. "One day, when we were sitting in the parlor, Booth came up the steps, and my brother said he believed that man was crazy, and he wished he would attend to his own business and let him [John] stay at home."

Anna's nerves had grown so taut that the entire courtroom could feel their thrumming. Her foot tapped and tapped; her eyes swept from one side of the room to the other, searching for the one face she cherished above all others.

Aiken kept at it. There was still one critical point to make. "Did you at any time, at your mother's house, on any occasion, ever hear a word breathed as to any plot or plan or conspiracy in existence to assassinate the President of the United States?"

"No, sir."

"Did you ever hear any remarks made with reference to the assassination of any member of the Government?"

"No, sir."

"Did you ever hear discussed by any member of the family, at any time or in any place, any plan or conspiracy to capture the President of the United States?"

"No, sir; I did not."

Anna could stand it no longer. "Where is mama?" she asked. "Where is she—where is my mother?" she cried out, her composure crumbling with each instant.

Wisely sensing that Anna could not hold up under cross-examination, the prosecution asked no questions. Frederick Aiken took her by the elbow and steered her toward the door as the crowd of lady spectators surged toward her "with eager faces and devouring eyes." As she passed before the commissioners' table, a member of the court handed Anna a white handkerchief she had dropped during her testimony. "She snatched it from him quickly and rudely," the *New-York Tribune* observed, "without a word of thanks." Aiken continued to propel Anna forward, guiding her through the narrow passage left by the wide hoopskirts of the women who had crowded so close to Mary Surratt's seat. In a blur of movement and confusion, Anna passed within three feet of her mother.

Mary's emotions bent her double. Covering her face with her hands, she lowered her head to the rail and "wept like a child," loudly enough for more than one reporter to hear. Outside the courtroom, Anna, too, "burst into a violent paroxysm of grief."

"I didn't see my mother," she said to Captain Rath. "Was she there?"

When Rath confessed to what he had done, Anna sank to the floor as if she'd been knocked down. She was out cold. "I was nonplussed," Rath remembered, "for, though I had fought in twenty battles, had heard the shot and shell, and had faced death a score of times, I had never seen anyone faint." A splash of water revived her, and as soon as she regained consciousness, Anna unleashed a tirade of anger on Rath. "She gave me the worst tongue lashing I had ever had," he recalled, "but all I can remember of what she said was 'You mean old Yankees.'"

Two days later, Secretary of War Stanton granted Mary the privilege of a visit with her daughter.

The task of escorting Anna Surratt in and chaperoning the meeting fell to none other than Captain Rath. Rath's instructions were to remain in the room and monitor their conversation, but after witnessing how Anna Surratt reacted to the reunion, Rath had not the heart to do it. "When Annie saw her mother, she threw herself on her neck, and such a torrent of weeping I have never seen," he would remember. For a full ten minutes, Anna sobbed in her mother's arms. Rath could not even make himself watch. "I will let you have your visit alone," he told Mary and Anna. "Do as you like."

Two hours later, Rath forced himself to inform Anna that her time was up. "She didn't say a word, but bade her mother good-by, weeping all the time." Mary's composure in the face of this tide of emotion left Rath stupefied. In his presence she showed not one hint of distress. Rather than offer any tender words, she told Anna to "keep up."

"That woman is like a rock," Rath marveled to General Hartranft later that day. "When she saw her daughter, she acted as though she hadn't any heart."

"You think so?" Hartranft replied. "Then you have to have been there when I went to take her to her cell. She collapsed, cried terribly, and we had to carry her bodily from the room."

Moments like these imbued Rath with a certain respect and sympathy for his sole female prisoner. "Mrs. Surratt was a woman of unusual nerve," he said. "She bore her imprisonment without complaint and was stoical." Every time Anna visited, the captain found himself wishing that Anna would take her mother's fate into her own hands. Just a few drops of "something she could administer to her mother so that the dreadful hangman's noose would not have to be placed about her neck."

On June 3, Anna Surratt returned to court. Not to testify this time, but simply to sit as near to her mother as the authorities would allow. An officer stood between them to ensure they would not communicate. Words were not necessary. Both Anna and Mary took strength from the other's nearness. "The presence of her daughter and the affectionate glances mutually exchanged between the two seemed to have a cheering effect upon the mother," the *Philadelphia Inquirer* noticed, "for she seemed more hopeful and in better spirits than for several days previous." Mary could hardly take her eyes from her daughter, gazing at her "with a look of indescribable yearning."

CHAPTER TWENTY

Every day, the temperature rose. Ladies' fans and gentlemen's hats flapped back and forth all day long, battering the hot air as the people stood shoulder to shoulder and sweated beneath layers of silk and wool. The reporters soon abandoned any attempt at hiding the smell behind lofty prose. "The extreme heat of the weather makes the atmosphere of the court room by no means as agreeable to the olfactories as otto of roses or the spicy gales of Araby," the *Philadelphia Inquirer* observed. "Indeed, not to put too fine a point upon it, the air of the room during these hot summer days is positively sickening." Even the officers and the tribunal exhibited "a most uncomfortable appearance" in their buttoned-up wool uniforms.

With Louis Weichmann's testimony seemingly impermeable, Aiken and Clampitt took aim at John Lloyd. His claim that Mary Surratt had told him to have two rifles and two bottles of whiskey ready on the night of the assassination remained the single most incriminating piece of evidence in the entire case against her. But by his own admission, Lloyd had been drinking that day. Aiken and Clampitt made it their mission to show the tribunal that John Lloyd had been not just a little tipsy but falling-down drunk when he'd spoken with Mary that afternoon.

James Lusby, who had known Lloyd for several months and frequented the tavern at Surrattsville, took the stand. He had been in Marlboro with Lloyd on April 14, and the two had left for Surrattsville almost at the same time. Lusby had pulled up to the barroom door about a minute and a half before Lloyd had driven into the yard.

"You are satisfied that Mr. Lloyd was drunk on that day?" Aiken asked.

"Yes, sir: he was drunk, I am sure," Lusby said.

Colonel Burnett was skeptical. If Lloyd had been so intoxicated, Burnett wanted to know, how had he managed to drive home and aim his wagon into his yard?

"A man might be drunk, and his horse might carry him there," Lusby explained.

"He drove his own horse?"

"Yes, sir: I believe he did." Burnett could not counter that. Anyone who owned a horse and a stable knew how readily a horse would head home to a comfortable stall and a hay box.

Next came Joseph Nott, the tavern's bartender. Who better to testify to Lloyd's habitual drunkenness than the man who usually poured his liquor?

"Has Mr. Lloyd been in the habit, for weeks past, of drinking a great deal?" Aiken asked.

"Yes, sir," Mr. Nott answered. "Mr. Lloyd drank a great deal."

"Has he been drunk for almost every day for some time past?"

"Yes, sir."

"State how that was."

"He was pretty tight nearly every day, and night too," Nott said.

"Did he or not really have the appearance of an insane man from drink?"

"He had at times."

The trouble with this tactic was twofold. The people John Lloyd associated with tended to be drinking men themselves. To make matters worse, they also hailed from southern Maryland, "a noxious and pestilential place for patriotism," which left them vulnerable to the ticklish question of loyalty to the Union.

☞

Allegiance to the Union was as much on trial as the eight defendants. Though it was never said outright, the judge advocates' repeated questions on the topic left no room for doubt. The prosecution believed that any witness who was known to have favored the South or sympathized with the Confederacy could not be relied upon to tell the truth. As far as the prosecution was concerned, even those who had simply never been heard professing loyalty to the Union must have tacitly approved of the assassination. There was no easier way to discredit a witness's testimony. Why bother asking tedious questions to undermine accuracy and reliability when calling a witness's neighbor to the stand to declare that he or she had never said a word in favor of the Union would accomplish that in half the time?

One by one, witnesses called to defend Mary Surratt fell victim to this tactic. Her brother Zadock Jenkins. Her boarder Augustus Howell. Her business agent, Mr. Gwynn. All Southern sympathizers, the prosecution insinuated, were double-crossing liars with the stain of Abraham Lincoln's blood on their hands—every last one of them.

It was a technique that might have backfired royally had Mary's defense team been better informed. During John Lloyd's tenure on the Metropolitan Police, for instance, he'd been a member of the so-called Berret Police, a group of officers known for following the example of ousted Washington mayor James Berret in refusing to swear the loyalty oath. Yet the prosecution expected the nine commissioners who sat in judgment to trust Lloyd at his word.

By the second week in June, Mary's case, feeble from the start, was eroding. No evidence worse than what had already been heard would enter into the record. Nor would any significantly helpful testimony bolster her case.

The defense's fixation on Mary's eyesight was growing tiresome. The persistence with which Aiken and Clampitt kept returning to the issue after five priests had sworn to know nothing of her trouble reading and sewing was enough to make any spectator wince, or roll their own eyes heavenward. The only thing weaker than her sight, it seemed, was the evidence to prove it so. No matter what Anna said about her mother needing spectacles, straining to read by gaslight was one thing. Recognizing a great hulking fellow like Powell was quite another. Early on, the *New-York Tribune* had proclaimed that anyone meeting Powell on the street "would turn around with a shudder to look at him, and a stranger meeting him face to face would remember him for ten years." And then, on June 9, Honora Fitzpatrick returned to the witness stand.

"State whether or not you were present at the time the arrest of Payne was made at Mrs. Surratt's house that evening," Mr. Aiken said.

"Yes, sir; I was," Honora replied.

"You had seen Payne at Mrs. Surratt's house under the name of Wood, had you not?"

"Yes, sir."

"Did you recognize him at that time as being the person whom you had seen there before?"

"I did not recognize him until we were taken to General Augur's office," she said. "Then I recognized him when the skull-cap was removed from his head."

Here, at last, was a boon. A seventeen-year-old with perfectly good eyesight, who had seen Lewis Powell on all the same occasions and in all the same guises that Mary Surratt had, had not recognized him as he'd stood in Mary Surratt's hallway on the night of April 17.

Colonel Burnett next stepped forward to temper the effects of this revelation. "At the time Payne was arrested, were you in the hall at any time when Mrs. Surratt came out there to Payne in the hall?" he asked Miss Fitzpatrick, intending to show that Honora had been given little opportunity to observe Powell.

"No, sir," she answered, just as he had hoped. "I was sitting in the parlor on the sofa."

"You did not see her when she was called out of the parlor to see Payne?" Burnett asked.

Her answer dumbfounded him: "No: I did not know that she was called out."

"You did not hear what passed in the hall at that time?"

"No, sir."

She had been confined to the parlor the whole time, watched by an officer, and prohibited from speaking. With the possible exception of her own roiling thoughts, no distractions had existed to draw Honora's attention from her surroundings. Was it possible that Mary could have left the room to identify Powell without Honora noticing?

Here was an intriguing similarity to Detective Morgan's testimony. Morgan had been stationed in the hallway with Powell, just as Honora had been in the parlor with Mary. And yet neither of them had seen Mary's encounter with Powell.

Aiken and Clampitt probed the matter no further. Perhaps they understood that Honora's testimony, helpful though it was, did not address the most troublesome question of all, the question they had not dared touch in almost a month in the courtroom: Why had Powell come to 541 H Street that night in the first place? No one could—or would—offer a satisfactory answer. According to a 1915 account by

Powell's own lawyer, he had emerged from hiding after three days "because he could not stand hunger any longer. Came to Mrs. Surratt's, because she was the only person he knew in Washington, to get something to eat." But with Powell forbidden to testify, there was no way to put this information before the court.

CHAPTER TWENTY-ONE

As the weeks passed and the trial dragged on with no end in sight, Major Porter, the doctor who inspected the prisoners each morning, grew more and more unsettled by the toll that the severe prison conditions might be taking on the prisoners' mental and physical health. Guilty or innocent, the nervous strain of undergoing a trial for a capital offense was tremendous. Mary and the others existed in a constant state of anxiety. "These are they who are living not by years, not by weeks, but by breaths," observed the *New York World*'s George Alfred Townsend. The daily regimen included no outlets to relieve their inevitable tension. Mary and her fellow defendants could not read. They could not exercise. They had no fresh air. Caged and chained, with nothing to occupy their minds or their bodies, the accused conspirators might well descend into madness before justice could be properly served.

Most concerning of all were the canvas hoods that Arnold, Atzerodt, Herold, O'Laughlen, Powell, and Spangler were obliged to wear in their cells. It was unpleasant enough to sit in the crowded courtroom all day as spring gave way to summer. But to be shrouded all night in canvas that blotted out light and air—how could any man tolerate that?

General Hartranft, too, had concerns about the hoods. Noting that the men "are suffering very much," he submitted a request on June 6 that all but Powell's be removed, as "there may be some necessity for his wearing it, but I do not think there is for any of the others."

That week, Major Porter also relayed his concerns to Secretary Stanton, who enlisted the service of Dr. Gray of the New York State Lunatic Asylum at Utica, "one of the most noted insanity experts in the country." Stanton's orders to Porter directed him "to adopt such measures as may be deemed proper for their health and regimen."

Dr. Gray "unhesitatingly" agreed with Major Porter—the hoods were likely to drive the men insane. Thanks to Major Porter and Dr. Gray, Stanton ordered that the suffocating canvas hoods be removed from the six men. Secretary Stanton also agreed to permit all the prisoners to exercise outdoors "under heavy guard" and to read—so long as the books had been published prior to 1835. The men had to make do with "a small box . . . for a seat," but upon Dr. Gray's recommendation, Mary Surratt was granted the singular luxury of an armchair.

Though Mary had not been subjected to the cruelty of a hood, her health gave Major Porter plenty of reason for concern. When Clampitt had first come to know her, Mary "was still a woman of fine presence and form" after nearly a month in prison. But now even those without medical training could see that she was beginning to look as shaky as her case. When she entered the courtroom, she leaned heavily on the arm of her attendant, "apparently almost prostrated," reported the Washington *Evening Star.* Other papers noticed, too. "Mrs. Surratt's Health Failing" announced a subhead in the *Philadelphia Inquirer* for an article that judged her "very feeble."

The courtroom came with its own set of torments, for which the press expressed a rare measure of sympathy. "The lady visitors show very little consideration for her feelings, crowding around her closely and making many impudent remarks in her hearing, which by no means add to her serenity of mind," the *Philadelphia Inquirer* scolded. "Then, too, she is so thickly veiled as to threaten herself with asphyxia and being seated in a corner where scarcely a breeze can reach her, her situation is by no means pleasant."

🖛

For another string of days Mary simply sat and endured the looks and the remarks and the heat as the lawyers for Mudd and Powell defended their clients. When Aiken and Clampitt gained the floor again, they returned to the issue of John Lloyd's drinking. In particular, they needed to address a sticky question that Colonel Burnett had brought up on cross-examination a few days earlier. How could a man arrive home drunk after a two-and-a-half-hour drive from Marlboro? Wouldn't he have sobered up at least a little on the road? The defense called another of Lloyd's acquaintances, Richard Sweeny, to explain. Sweeny offered a simple enough answer: Lloyd had been "considerably under the influence" when he'd started for home and had swigged from a bottle of liquor as he'd driven.

However, that testimony was not as convincing as it might have been, since Sweeny had been not only riding alongside Lloyd but also imbibing from the same bottle.

🖛

Nearly every witness that Mary's defense called came with a weakness for the prosecution to exploit. Her clergymen were Catholics. Her relatives and business associates were Southerners. Lloyd's companions were fond of the bottle. Perhaps, though, a sampling of the men and women who had once been enslaved by the Surratts could be made to appear above reproach.

To that end, Frederick Aiken called Henry Hawkins to the stand. Mr. Hawkins was as familiar with the Surratts as anyone could be—he had been enslaved by them for almost eleven years.

"What was her treatment towards her servants?" Aiken asked.

"Very good, sir."

"Did she, or not, always treat you kindly?"

"Yes, sir." Though kindness was seen as a feminine virtue and therefore helpful to Mary's image, it was not strictly relevant. The real issue Aiken needed Mr. Hawkins to address was the question of Mary's loyalty to the Union. Like the priests whose testimony had opened Mary's defense, Hawkins could not remember ever hearing Mary speak in favor of the South. Nor could he relate any instances of disloyal remarks toward the Union on Mary's part. Moreover, he did recall an incident that spoke louder than words.

When a number of the federal government's horses had broken loose from the cavalry depot at Giesboro, Hawkins said, seven of them were caught and put up in Mary's stables. For the two weeks that passed before the government collected them, Mary stabled those horses, feeding them grain and hay from her own supplies. So far as Mr. Hawkins knew, the army had not reimbursed her for the expense.

Nor was this an isolated act of mercy toward the Union, according to Hawkins.

"Can you state to the Court whether it was, or was not, her habit, to feed, at her own expense, Union soldiers that passed her house?" Aiken asked.

"Yes, sir: she has done so frequently."

When prompted, Mr. Hawkins described how Mary had always given the soldiers the best fare her pantry could provide. To his knowledge, she had never been paid for any of that food, either.

Aiken could not resist touching on another troublesome issue. "Do you recollect any occasion of bad eyesight on the part of Mrs. Surratt?"

"Yes, sir," Hawkins said. "I heard she could not see some time back, and that she had to wear specs." Once again, Aiken had muddied the issue with his extra questions. According to Anna Surratt, Mary needed eyeglasses but did *not* wear them. Who were the commissioners to believe?

Next, Rachel Semus, a woman formerly enslaved by Mary's neighbor, stepped up to testify. Mrs. Semus explained that the Surratts had rented her from her own enslaver for six years. Like Mr. Hawkins, she declared that "servants" were treated "very well" in the Surratt household.

"Did you, or not, ever have any reason to complain of any hardship?"

"No, indeed: I never had any reason to complain at all," she told Mr. Aiken.

"Do you recollect any instances since the war broke out, of Union soldiers having been fed at Mrs. Surratt's?"

"Yes, sir: they have."

"What was her habit in regard to that?" (That was the sort of open-ended question lawyers on both sides of the case should have been asking all along, allowing witnesses to answer without steering them in any direction.)

"I know she always tried to do the best she could for them," Mrs. Semus said, "because I always cooked in the kitchen."

Aiken wanted to know if Mary had served meals to many Union soldiers, and whether she had offered them the best she had.

"Yes, sir; she did so," Mrs. Semus confirmed. "She always gave them the best she had; and very often, indeed, she would give them all she had in the house, because so many of them came."

"Do you, or not, recollect on one occasion of her cutting up the last ham in the house to give it to the soldiers?"

Indeed she had, Mrs. Semus said—even though it had meant doing without until Mary could get more from the city, for the nearest stores had none to sell.

"Do you know whether or not Mrs. Surratt was in the habit of taking pay for such things?" Aiken asked.

"If she took any pay, I never saw her. She always said she never took any thing."

Bingham cut in. "You need not state what she said."

"I never knew of her taking any," Mrs. Semus clarified.

"But the soldiers would come and eat and go away without paying anything?"

"Yes sir."

"While you have been in Mrs. Surratt's employment, have you ever heard disloyal expressions from her?"

"No sir."

"Do you know what 'disloyal' means?" he asked—a question he had put to none of the white witnesses.

Rachel Semus was not ignorant of politics; the last four years had altered the course of her life. "Some say it is in favor of the South."

"You have never heard her make use of expressions in favor of the South?" Aiken asked.

"No sir; if she made them I never heard them."

One more time, Aiken asked the too-familiar set of questions regarding Mary's sight. "Can you state to the Court of your own knowledge whether you know anything of defective eyesight on the part of Mrs. Surratt?"

"Yes sir; her eyesight has been failing for a long time, because very often I would have to go upstairs and thread a needle for her; she could not see."

"Was that in the daytime?"

"Yes sir, in the noon daytime. I have had to stop washing to go upstairs and thread her needle."

"Do you recollect any other instance?"

"Yes sir, I know that when the priest came to her house, Father

Lanihan, I told her he was coming, and she said 'No, that is not him, it was little Johnny,' meaning her son. She said it was not [Father Lanihan] at all."

On June 13, Aiken and Clampitt reached their last line of defense. They had found two witnesses to refute the testimony of the double-crossing detective, George Cottingham, who had lied to Aiken about John Lloyd's confession.

First came Emma Offutt, John Lloyd's sister-in-law. She had been present when Lloyd had spoken with Detective Cottingham.

"Did Mr. Lloyd on that occasion say, referring to Mrs. Surratt, 'that vile woman, she has ruined me'?" Aiken asked.

"No, sir, he did not," Mrs. Offutt replied. "I didn't hear him say it, and I was in there all the time while he was there."

Then Andrew Kallenbach stepped up to corroborate Mrs. Offutt's testimony. Kallenbach, who had been present when the newly arrested John Lloyd had been delivered to Detective Cottingham, told the court that he, too, had never heard Lloyd utter the words "Mrs. Surratt, that vile woman, she has ruined me."

Colonel Burnett interrupted. "Was Mrs. Surratt's name mentioned in all that conversation?" he asked Kallenbach. This was the sort of mistake the court had come to associate with Frederick Aiken rather than Burnett—asking a question without any assurance that the answer would help his case.

"I do not think it was," Mr. Kallenbach answered.

By the end of that day, all the evidence in Mary Surratt's case was in.

CHAPTER TWENTY-TWO

Despite Frederick Aiken and John Clampittt's efforts to prove her innocent, Mary Surratt received almost no sympathy in the press. The papers had made up their minds at the start and were not about to be swayed.

Even sitting in the courtroom with Mary before their eyes, observers sometimes had to bend what they saw to fit the molds they'd already cast for her. Reverend Bernard Harrison Nadal, writing for the New York *Methodist,* had to admit that, contrary to other reports, Mary Surratt was not unpleasant-looking. "Indeed, if there were nothing the matter, and we were called on at this distance of ten feet, to give an opinion, we should pronounce her, for a woman of her age, handsome." Reverend Nadal further allowed that her hair was "a beautiful dark brown, well polished with the brush," and her eyes were "bright, clear, calm, resolute, but not unkind." But there his compliments ended, and his observations took a sharp turn.

"Her expression, for the several hours she was under our eye, was that of deeply sombre gentleness, which still bore a look of being partly produced by the will, and for the occasion," Nadal continued. "Immersed as she is in crime, she does not forget a woman's art. She does her best to make a favorable impression, by dress and aspect, upon her judges."

Mary Surratt could satisfy no one. When she was "very slovenly dressed" or her house was in disarray, it signaled that she was likely a criminal who had no time or use for womanly cares. Yet when she presented herself in the way a lady was expected to, deceit suddenly became the only plausible explanation—even to a minister.

No one outside the courtroom stood up for Mary Surratt until June 16, when an anonymous pamphlet began appearing across Washington, DC. "Profusely strewn" in hotel lobbies and other public gathering places, its four pages raged against the treatment of Mary Surratt at the hands of the government, the public, and most especially the press.

Flowery and fiery in equal measure, the pamphlet did what no one else had yet dared to do—pity and praise Mary Surratt. According to her unnamed defender, Mary was a lady whose true character had gone overlooked by the press. "Her temper was never ruffled," the author declared. "No person in need ever passed her door without partaking freely and gratuitously of her hospitality." Clergymen, no matter which church they came from, always received the finest food and best rooms Mary had to offer, free of charge. She was also "of an extraordinary forgiving disposition."

Her reward for these kindnesses and sacrifices was undeserved suspicion. Although Booth and his accomplices had frequented a number of hotels and boardinghouses in the months leading up to the assassination, the pamphlet pointed out, "the proprietors of those establishments are not indicted for conspiracy; and justly so." What made Mary Surratt more guilty than the others who had hosted the men in the prisoners dock?

The pamphlet declined to dignify "the witnesses who blacken the name and jeopard the life of this poor lady" by mentioning their names.

Their character, conduct, and testimony, the author insinuated, had already said enough. "Future developments" would prove as much, the text confidently predicted.

The *Washington Chronicle*'s report that Mary's feet were shackled was, to her defender, too horrifying to be credible. "For the honor of modern civilization and of the country in which we live, we trust that this is a mistake." (It was likely not a mistake. Debate would rage in the papers years later—during which General Hartranft would formally deny that Mary's wrists or ankles had been manacled. However, over the course of the trial the *Boston Daily Advertiser*, Boston *Daily Evening Traveler*, *New York Times*, *New-York Tribune*, *New York World*, and *Philadelphia Inquirer* all mentioned Mary's ankle fetters.)

Sparing no spectator's feelings, the pamphlet turned loose unmitigated disgust for the public's behavior toward Mary within the courtroom. "Like a herd of deer gathering around a wounded companion to gore it to death in its disabled state, some of these people feast their eyes . . . and unfeelingly heap upon the prisoner's head and heart, the fiercest denunciation and most opprobrious terms!" Many journalists had described the crush of gawkers around Mary, but few had acknowledged the people's cruelty, much less openly shamed them for it.

But worse yet was the press, Mary's defender emphasized, which "has hunted and maligned this unfortunate woman with the unrelenting ferocity of the sleuth-hound and the venom of asps. Prejudged, condemned, sentenced in advance by every scribbler who can pen a sensation paragraph and stab a defenseless female with impunity." Words such as "murderess," "she-devil," and "traitress" were unwarranted, offensive, and undeserved, it declared, for Mary Surratt had been only accused—not convicted—of conspiracy.

In sum, the common decency owed to every citizen of the United States had been denied to Mary Surratt at nearly every juncture of the investigation and trial. "What has she to ask of her fellow-citizens and fellow-Christians?" the author demanded. Just three simple things: "Charity, forbearance, suspension of judgement."

The pamphlet was signed only "Amator Justitiae"—Lover of Justice.

The press took offense, as might have been expected after such a tirade. The Washington *Evening Star* branded it "An Injudicious Publication," predicting that with its florid style and dramatic fervor it "cannot fail of working a contrary effect on the public mind to that intended by the writer." The Bath *Daily Times and Sentinel* remarked that "certain parties are trying to make it out that Mrs. Surratt is a model of Christian excellence. Few will believe it."

What effect Amator Justitiae's diatribe ultimately had on public opinion, the press did not deign to mention. Nor is Mary Surratt's reaction known. The nine minds that mattered most to Mary sat at the commissioners' table in the courtroom.

CHAPTER TWENTY-THREE

The evidence was all in. Mary's last hope of convincing the nine-man tribunal to acquit her lay in her lawyers' closing arguments.

On June 19, the words of Reverdy Johnson were once again heard in the courtroom on behalf of Mary Surratt. But Senator Johnson did not deliver his argument in person. Instead, Mr. Clampitt read it aloud to the court.

The entire argument focused on a single issue: jurisdiction. Did the tribunal have the legal authority to try the accused conspirators before a military court? "That question in all courts, Civil, Criminal and Military, must be considered and answered affirmatively before judgment can be pronounced," Johnson had written. "And it must be answered correctly or the Judgment pronounced is void."

Point by point, Reverdy Johnson dissected the reasoning that the president and attorney general had used to justify a military trial.

First and foremost, Senator Johnson argued, the president of the United States did not have the power to decree that a citizen be tried outside the civil courts. The framers of the Constitution had deliberately separated the powers of the government into three branches—executive, legislative, and judicial. Allowing the president to override that carefully balanced arrangement in order to rule over the judicial system would "make that Department omnipotent," Johnson had written, and "danger to liberty is more to be dreaded from the executive than from any other Department of the Government."

For proof that the tribunal had overstepped its bounds, Johnson looked no further than America's cherished Bill of Rights. The Fifth Amendment to the Constitution states that the only exception to civil trials is "in cases arising in the land or naval forces, or in the Militia, when in actual service in time of War or public danger."

"According to this great authority every other class of person and every other species of offense" belonged to the civil courts, Johnson pointed out.

The Sixth Amendment is just as clear in stating that every citizen of the United States is entitled to be publicly tried by an impartial jury. The president's decision to try the accused conspirators in a military court had deprived them of those rights, violating the Fifth and Sixth Amendments. "If the Executive can legally decide whether a citizen is to enjoy the guarantees of liberty afforded by the Constitution," Reverdy Johnson asked, "what are we but slaves?"

Johnson gave no credence to the notion that the public's anger and grief over Lincoln's death would make it impossible to assemble an impartial jury. The very suggestion that the nation's collective emotions could prevent a jury from rendering a fair judgment in this case was "an unjust reflection upon the Judges, upon the people . . . and upon our civil institutions themselves," he said.

Further, Johnson reminded the court, laws do not exist solely to convict the guilty. Among the Constitution's most sacred duties is the protection of the innocent. Throughout history, innocent people have been unjustly accused of crimes. The framers of the Constitution, Johnson said, "deemed the right to a public trial vital to the security of the citizen and especially and absolutely necessary to his protection against

Executive power." If any member of the Constitutional Convention had suggested that the law be changed to allow the president to override this fundamental right, that person "would have been deemed . . . a traitor to liberty or insane."

Nor did Johnson see any sense in contending that the Constitution revoked these rights during times of war. "Not a syllable" of the document said such a thing. "All history tells us that war at times, maddens the people; frenzies government and makes both regardless of Constitutional limitations of power," Clampitt read. "Individual safety at such periods, is more in peril than at any other. Constitutional limitations and guarantees are then also absolutely necessary to the protection of the government itself."

Johnson had to grant that in particular circumstances the president does have some power over individual rights, such as to suspend habeas corpus (as Lincoln himself had done during the war) or to declare martial law. But that power "in no way impairs, or suspends the other rights secured to the accused."

The government had also backed itself into a tight corner when it came to the charges it had levied against the defendants. Over and over again, those charges specified that the crime was treasonous. That accusation came with a very specific definition and set of rules. According to the definition set down in article 3 of the Constitution, treason consisted solely of levying war against the states, or giving aid and comfort to enemies of the states. John Wilkes Booth was not an enemy of the United States, Senator Johnson contended. He was a murderer who'd chosen a political target. The accused were also not enemies or belligerents. "They were citizens of the District, or of Maryland and under the protection of the Constitution," Johnson insisted. Article 3 states that "no Person shall be convicted of Treason unless on the testimony of two Witnesses to the same overt Act, or on Confession in open Court." Neither of those conditions had been met in this case. Further, the

Crimes Act of 1790 states that anyone accused of treason is entitled to "a copy of the indictment, and a list of the jury and witnesses, . . . at least three entire days before he shall be tried." During jury selection, defendants accused of treason have the right to challenge thirty-five potential jurors. None of the accused conspirators had been granted those rights.

Public trial by jury was the "great right the American colonists brought with them as their birthright and inheritance," Clampitt read. At times during the Civil War, that right had admittedly been "disregarded and denied," Johnson's argument acknowledged. "The momentous nature of the crisis . . . involving as it did the very life of the nation, has caused the people to tolerate such disregard and denial. But the crisis, thank God, has passed."

Even Jefferson Davis, the recently apprehended president of the Confederacy, was to be tried in the civil courts. If he, "the alleged head and front of the conspiracy is to be, and can be so tried," Johnson demanded, "upon what ground of right of fairness or of policy, can the parties who are charged to have been his mere instruments be deprived of the same mode of trial?" The only legal exception to a citizen's right to a civil trial was laid out in the Fifth Amendment to the Constitution: only service members accused of committing crimes during active duty in time of war were subject to court-martial.

"A great crime has lately been committed," Clampitt read as Senator Johnson's argument wound to a close, "that has shocked the civilized world. Every right minded man desires the punishment of the criminals, but he desires that punishment to be administered according to law."

Administering justice "with integrity" was not enough. Johnson considered it "nearly" as vital that "the public should have undoubted faith in the purity of criminal justice."

In conclusion, Clampitt read, Reverdy Johnson would consider himself "dishonored" if he were to use jurisdiction simply as a loophole to "rescue" his client. The defense of the Constitution and the law was as important to him as the defense of Mary Surratt. "In my view in this respect, her cause is the cause of every citizen.

"As you have discovered I have not remarked on the evidence in the case of Mrs. Surratt, nor is it my purpose." Johnson would make but one remark specifically regarding Mary. "That a woman well-educated and as far as we can judge from all her past life as we have it in evidence, a devout Christian, ever kind, affectionate, and charitable, with no motive disclosed to us that could have caused a total change in her very nature, could have participated in the crimes in question, it is almost impossible to believe. Such a belief can only be forced upon a reasonable, unsuspecting unprejudiced mind by direct and uncontradicted evidence coming from pure and perfectly unsuspected sources. Have we these? Is the evidence uncontradicted? Are the witnesses Weichmann and Lloyd pure and unsuspected?" Johnson declined to say. He would leave the evidence to Aiken and Clampitt. If Weichmann's and Lloyd's testimony was true, Johnson contended, it established *their* involvement in the conspiracy "much more satisfactorily" than Mary Surratt's. "As far, gentlemen, as I am concerned, her case is now in your hands."

It was a fine argument—elegant, incisive, and firmly entrenched in the bedrock of the Constitution. And yet there was a great, gaping hole in it. Not in the logic, which was impeccable, but in what Senator Johnson had left unsaid.

The murder of Abraham Lincoln had not been mentioned until the close of the argument. Nor had Mary Surratt figured into it. Reverdy

Johnson's argument was so overarching, it might have been applied interchangeably to any one of the prisoners in the dock. "This was the easiest way for a lawyer to earn his fee in such a case," the *Daily National Republican* remarked, "but it seems that Mr. Johnson has troubled himself but little about the evidence. He has only theorized, drawing his arguments from the dusty volumes of his library."

Though he had tackled the critical issue of jurisdiction with the strength and tenacity of a charging bull, an odd sense of incompleteness lingered at the argument's close. It was almost as though he were dodging Mary herself entirely. If he had not touched on the evidence, had hardly mentioned his client's name, and had declined to appear in court on her behalf, did Reverdy Johnson truly believe Mary Surratt innocent?

While Clampitt read Reverdy Johnson's argument, another drama unfolded in the corner of the courtroom. At twelve-thirty that afternoon, Mary Surratt fell sick. Details are almost nonexistent. General Hartranft reported in the prison logbook, "Mrs. Surratt became so ill that it was necessary to remove her from the room." Whether it happened gradually or suddenly, with a great deal of fuss or hardly a whimper, he made no indication. Such a terse record was commonplace for the general. The newspapers, however, strayed far from their usual coverage where Mary was concerned.

After weeks of avidly tracking every swish of her fan and movement of her eyes, the papers were strangely mute, reporting the incident in a single sentence: "Mrs. Surratt is seriously ill this morning." No clues about the nature of her malady were to be found. That in itself may be as good a clue as any.

Clampitt later said he believed her illness was "contracted within her damp cell." However, other reports would eventually make vague reference to "the womb disease," specifying only that she "flooded for three weeks"—likely a reference to profuse menstrual bleeding. Whatever symptoms Mary experienced in the courtroom that day could well have been considered unfit to print.

Hartranft escorted Mary to a side room, "where she was still in the presence of the Court, and where the air was much more cool and pure." With the door open she was shielded from view, yet able to hear what was happening. At the close of the proceedings, Mary was not marched back to the cell block with the other prisoners—another potential hint to the nature of her illness. Many years later, Lewis Powell's lawyer would attribute her symptoms to menopause. "Her cell by reason of her sickness, was scarcely habitable," he wrote. In a stone cubicle furnished only with a wooden chair, straw mattress, and bucket, sanitation options were bleak.

Dr. Gray visited Mary that evening. Afterward, General Hartranft wrote to his superior, "Since Mrs. Surratt has been removed in this side room and as her illness seems to be growing more severe I would suggest that her daughter be allowed to remain with and wait on her as her illness is evidently such as to require a female attendant." Hartranft's suggestion was immediately adopted, and Mary remained confined in this more comfortable room for the duration of the trial.

☞

When court reconvened the next day, Mary Surratt did not return to her chair at the end of the prisoners dock, but remained sequestered in the semi-privacy of the side room. The Washington *Evening Star* explained that this anomaly was "for the benefit of fresh air." Free from prying eyes, she listened to Frederick Aiken pick apart the evidence against her as he argued her innocence before the tribunal.

"For the lawyer as well as the soldier, there is an equally pleasant duty," Aiken began, "an equally imperative command. That duty is to shelter from injustice and wrong the innocent, to protect the weak from oppression." That command came directly from God, he said. "Therefore, all things whatsoever ye would that men should do to you, do ye even so unto them; for this is the law and the prophets," he quoted from the book of Matthew. "Profoundly impressed with the innocence of our client, we enter upon this last duty in her case with the heartfelt prayer that her honorable judges may enjoy the satisfaction of not having a single doubt left on their minds in granting her an acquittal."

With that, Aiken launched into a discussion of "the principles of evidence." Those rules, "which time and experience . . . have unalterably fixed as unerring guides in the administration of the criminal law," were no different before a court-martial than they were before a civil jury. If the evidence would prove Mary innocent in a civil courtroom, Aiken said, then the commission would be obligated to acquit her. "This is a point which, in our judgment, we can not too strongly impress upon the minds of her judges," he emphasized.

Further, punishment for a crime as monumental as the murder of a president demanded a verdict "so well founded in reason as to satisfy and secure public confidence and approval." The evidence against Mary must be beyond reproach, Aiken warned, for although the public might be willing to overlook the controversy of jurisdiction where "acknowledged criminals" were convicted, "if citizens may be arraigned and convicted for so grievous an offense as this upon insufficient evidence, every one will feel his own personal safety involved, and the tendency would be to intensify public feeling against the whole process of the trial.

"Now, in all the evidence, there is not a shadow of direct and positive proof which connects Mrs. Surratt with a participation in this conspiracy alleged, or with any knowledge of it," he said. Knowledge was the key element in Mary Surratt's case. Both intent and malice must be explicitly shown, Aiken contended, because the three incriminating facts against her were not criminal acts by any stretch of the law.

Yes, John Wilkes Booth had frequented her home, Aiken acknowledged. Yes, she had delivered a message to John Lloyd on the day of the assassination. And, yes, she had claimed to not recognize Lewis Powell on the night of her arrest.

"These three circumstances constitute the part played by the accused, Mary E. Surratt, in this great conspiracy. They are the acts she has done. They are all that two months of patient and unwearying investigation, and the most thorough search for evidence that was probably ever made, has been able to develop against her," Aiken scoffed. "The acts she has done, in and of themselves, are perfectly innocent. Of themselves they constitute no crime. They are what you or I, or any of us might have done."

So much of the incriminating information against Mary came from Louis Weichmann and John Lloyd, Aiken said, that their testimony must be rigorously dissected in order that "error and duplicity may be exposed, and innocence protected."

First, Weichmann. It was patently ridiculous, Aiken declared, to presume that a group of men planning a conspiracy against the government would repeatedly meet and discuss their plot in the presence of an innocent man. More "singular and astonishing" than anything Weichmann had observed was the very fact of his "omnipresence" among the conspirators. He had seen Surratt and Powell playing with their stockpile of weapons, stolen Powell's fake mustache, and witnessed the conspirators' return from what was now known to be a thwarted kidnapping attempt. There was only one excuse for not warning his landlady of these strange things happening beneath her very roof—guilt.

"In order to have gained all this knowledge Weichmann must have been within the inner circle of the conspiracy," Aiken declared. "He knows too much for an innocent man." A "perfectly irresistible" conclusion naturally followed—if Mary Surratt had not only known what was going on but had also participated in the scheme, Weichmann would have known that, too. What Mary had done hardly compared "with the long and startling array of facts proved against Weichmann out of his own mouth."

Then there was the telegram Booth had sent to Weichmann. "What additional proof of confidential relations between Weichmann and Booth could the Court desire?" Aiken demanded.

In contrast to the all-knowing Weichmann, John Lloyd's erratic uncertainty made him worthy of skepticism in Aiken's eyes. Aiken implored the court to consider that even though John Lloyd had shown no sign of intoxication when he'd met Mary at Uniontown on the Tuesday before the crime, on the witness stand he had not been able to distinctly recall the most vital parts of the conversation. Yet when questioned regarding April 14, a day on which at least half a dozen people had witnessed "his absolute inebriation," Lloyd had claimed "that he positively remembers that Mrs. Surratt said to him: 'Mr. Lloyd, I want you to have those shooting-irons ready.'" How was that possible?

Why on earth was the court willing to take the word of a drunk who had tangled himself in the plot by hiding John Surratt's rifles, then denied any and all knowledge for two days before implicating Mary Surratt while in a condition of "maudlin terror"?

All these facts, Aiken said, "if they do not destroy" Weichmann's and Lloyd's testimony, "do certainly greatly shake their credibility." Even if events had unfolded just as Weichmann and Lloyd had reported them, Aiken pointed out, those facts still did not prove that Mary Surratt had been aware of the conspiracy, much less been a part of it. Without that awareness, there was no criminal intent, and without criminal intent, there was no crime.

"No evidence of individual or personal intimacy with Booth" had been brought out against Mary. No one could swear that the two had ever been engaged in "long and apparently confidential interviews." No one had noticed even a hint of them sharing "a private comprehension." And no proof existed to show that Booth had done anything more than come calling for John from time to time, and devote a few moments to chat with his friend's mother when John was not at home.

As his argument drew to a close, Aiken called upon the emotions of the tribunal. "When the mists of uncertainty which cloud the present shall have dissolved," who would believe that a respectable, law-abiding Christian mother "could so suddenly and so fully have learned the intricate arts of sin?" he asked. True, she was "a daughter of the South," but she had never said or done anything disloyal, excluded Northerners from her circle of friends, or refused food or shelter to Union soldiers.

"*This woman knew it not,*" Aiken emphasized. "This woman, who, on the morning preceding that blackest day in our country's annals, knelt in the performance of her most sincere and sacred duty at the confessional, and received the mystic rite of the Eucharist, knew it not." She would have "rejected it with horror," Aiken asserted, and found some way to save her son "from the evil influences and miserable results of such companionship."

The lawyer argued that "beautiful fairies and terrible gnomes do not stand by each infant's cradle" sprinkling fertile minds with the seeds of good or evil inclinations; a life of violence and crime was shaped from a slow accumulation of wrongdoing, or by some cataclysmic disaster. "In no such manner was the life of our client marked," he declared. "Remember *your* wives, mothers, sisters and gentle friends,"

Aiken implored. Those women were "not widely different from . . . the woman who sits in the prisoner's dock to-day.

"Let not this first State tribunal in our country's history, which involves a woman's name, be blazoned before the world with the harsh tints of intolerance, which permits injustice," Aiken demanded. "Let the ship of State launch with dignity of unstained sails into the unruffled sea of UNION and PROSPERITY."

CHAPTER TWENTY-FOUR

On Thursday, June 29, after devoting an entire day to hearing Congressman Bingham's closing arguments on behalf of the prosecution, the nine-member tribunal sat down to weigh the evidence. After six weeks of testimony, they quickly—and likely unanimously—convicted first George Atzerodt, then David Herold and Lewis Powell, and consigned them to the gallows.

Samuel Arnold, Samuel Mudd, and Michael O'Laughlen were also summarily convicted and sentenced to life imprisonment for their secondary roles in the conspiracy. For standing by as Booth fled from the stage and into the alley behind Ford's Theatre, Edman Spangler received the lightest sentence of all the men: six years in prison.

The question of Mary Surratt created a thornier issue. Her case was not so simple as Powell's or Herold's. At least one member of the tribunal, General August Kautz, believed her innocent. "Mrs. Surratt was shown to have been active in the conspiracy to kidnap prior to the capture of Richmond," he later wrote. "That she was a willing participant in [Lincoln's] death was not clearly made out. My own impression was that she was involved in the final result against her will by her previous connection with the conspiracy." Kautz also believed that Booth had not given "the order to kill" until after eight o'clock on the evening of April 14, which made it impossible for Mary to have understood the significance of the message she had allegedly relayed to Lloyd that afternoon. But General Kautz's inclination to give Mary the benefit of the doubt did not fit in with his fellow commissioners' thinking. "These nine soldiers constituting the judges in this case had but little sympathy or patience with the sentimental saying that 'It is better that ninety-nine guilty escape than one innocent should suffer,'" Captain Christian Rath said of the tribunal. The war had hardened them, Rath believed. "There was no place for sympathy here, and every attempt to create favor by appeals of that nature met with frowns and disapproval."

The exact vote is not known, but a majority of the nine commissioners voted her guilty of conspiring with Atzerodt, Herold, Mudd, and Powell. (No direct connection has been found to link Mary Surratt with Arnold, O'Laughlen, or Spangler.) Although a simple majority was sufficient to convict, the law required a two-thirds majority to impose the death sentence, and the thought of seeing a woman—even a woman they believed to be guilty—sent to the gallows did not sit well with the commission. "[General] David Hunter was the president of the court-martial and told me with his own mouth that the first vote of the commission in the case of Mrs. Surratt was not for capital punishment," John Clampitt would tell the *Chicago Times-Herald* years afterward. According to Clampitt, General Holt and Congressman Bingham recommended that the stymied commission reread the testimony. "That was done in violation of all principles of law or equity in the trial of such cases," Clampitt raged in 1895.

Six of the nine commissioners had to vote in favor of the death penalty in order to condemn Mary Surratt to the gallows, and on this question the men still could not agree. Both her age and her sex gave five of them pause. No woman had ever been executed by the United States federal government.

Deliberations stretched from Thursday into Friday, when Judge Advocate General Holt suggested a compromise: sentence Mary Surratt to death, but also submit a clemency plea to President Johnson. This document would formally petition the president to commute Mary's punishment to life imprisonment, thus shifting the burden of responsibility for her fate from their shoulders to Johnson's.

Congressman Bingham drew up the document. General James A. Ekin copied out its single paragraph appealing to Andrew Johnson to grant Mary Surratt mercy "if he could find it consistent with his sense of duty to the country." Then Ekin and the four other dissenting commissioners signed the paper.

General Holt gathered up the sheaf of papers. He would carry them to the president for approval. Only when Johnson affixed his signature to the documents could the sentences be carried out.

☞

Days passed. Friday, Saturday, Sunday, Monday, and Tuesday, Mary Surratt contemplated her fate, and the whole country with her. No one but the members of the tribunal knew that the verdicts and sentences had already been rendered. In the public mind a guilty verdict seemed both a foregone conclusion and an impossibility. "The question was whispered over the telegraphic wires, and in every newspaper, and in ten thousand homes, 'Will President Andrew Johnson sign Mrs. Surratt's death warrant?'"

Morning and evening, General Hartranft took the prisoners out into the yard for a chance to rid their bodies of the nervous energy that sluiced from their brains. Whether Mary was well enough to take advantage of this opportunity, Hartranft did not record. Those first days in July, Mary's name does not appear in the prison record book at all. How she coped with the dual assault of her agitated mind and her ailing body can only be imagined. But she had her daughter, and her prayer book. For Mary Surratt, that may have been enough.

⇥

The holdup was Andrew Johnson himself. Not indecision but illness. According to the *New-Orleans Times,* the president had been laid up due to "exhaustion by incessant attention to business." The only cure was complete rest. No visitors, no cabinet meetings. Certainly no contemplation of death warrants.

The Fourth of July—the first Independence Day since the end of the war—came and went without news. President Johnson remained indisposed until July 6, when the *New York Herald* reported that Johnson "hopes to be able to give attention to urgent public business daily hereafter."

And so the nation waited.

⇥

Within the Old Arsenal Penitentiary, ominous messages were passing between General Hartranft and his superiors. "I think we will need about six ambulances to-morrow," Hartranft wrote on July 6. "Will you be kind enough to order about that number to report to me at an early hour to-morrow morning?" Twenty cavalrymen arrived at the arsenal that same day, but Hartranft believed more would be required. "Will you be kind enough to order them to report to me at 8 o'clock to-morrow morning?" he asked the assistant attorney general. "I will need them only during the day."

Orders also went out to the commanding officer at the arsenal gate to distribute his entire regiment along Four-and-a-Half Street from the gate to Pennsylvania Avenue, beginning at six o'clock the following morning. "Every Officer & man must be at his post throughout the day and see that perfect order is preserved along the street & its vicinity."

☞

Mary Surratt was alone when General Hartranft brought her the long-awaited news, sometime between ten and eleven o'clock on the morning of July 6. Anna had "chanced to be absent in the city" that day.

First, the findings. Guilty, though not entirely so. General Hartranft informed Mary that the tribunal had conceded that she had not received, entertained, harbored, or concealed Arnold or O'Laughlen. Nor had she combined, confederated, or conspired with Edman Spangler. For an instant, Mary might have allowed herself to hope for mercy. Then came the sentence. "And the Commission does therefore sentence her," General Hartranft read, "the said Mary E. Surratt, to be hung by the neck until she be dead."

Hartranft left no record of how Mary received her death sentence. Nevertheless, the newspapers had plenty to say about what occurred in that room. "At the moment of reading the warrant no outward signs of emotion were visible on the part of the prisoners, save Mrs. Surratt and Atzaroth [sic], each of whom trembled and grew deathly pale," the New York Times disclosed. "Mrs. Surratt faintly uttered a few words, saying: 'I had no hand in the murder of the President.'" According to the Associated Press dispatch, Mary "sank under the dread announcement." But the Washington Evening Star claimed that she "burst into a violent paroxysm of grief." None of these reports revealed where or how they had come by this coveted, contradictory information.

Regardless of how she reacted outwardly, it is certain that Mary Surratt was shocked. "Her sentence surprised and stunned her," John Ford, co-owner of Ford's Theatre, would write, also without revealing his source. "She had faith . . . that it was impossible for a Court to find her guilty of what she was guiltless of. To hear herself condemned to be hung from a gallows must have been to her like listening to some horrible strange portent conveyed in an unknown tongue. The sound of it clanged against her brain; the vague terror of it bruised her heart."

The sentence itself was difficult enough to take in, but it was not the most staggering aspect of the news to absorb. For nearly two months she had lived under the shadow of this most dreaded of all possibilities, and now it was worse than she could have expected. She was to be "duly executed, in accordance with the President's order," General Hartranft informed her, between ten o'clock and two o'clock on July 7—the very next day. At most, twenty-seven hours remained to her on earth. Even the public at large would be jarred by this unprecedented haste. "At first the truth of the statement was doubted," the *New York Herald* wrote the next day, simply because of the abruptness of the execution.

Hartranft asked Mary if there were any friends he should send for, or "any special minister of the Gospel" he could summon to attend to her. She requested two priests, Father Jacob A. Walter and Father Wiget, as well as a Mr. John Brophy, the twenty-two-year-old principal of St. Aloysius School. And Anna, of course.

It was five o'clock in the afternoon of July 6 when John Clampitt and Frederick Aiken heard the first shouts of the newsboys in the street.

"The execution of Mrs. Surratt!"

Somehow the fearful news had reached the papers before either of them had heard a whisper of it. Dumbfounded, they struggled to make their minds function quickly enough to take action. "Amazed beyond expression" to learn that there was less than twenty-four hours until the sentence would be enacted, the two lawyers' first impulse was to bargain for a delay. Only President Andrew Johnson had the authority to override the commission. They hastened to the White House.

At the door they met former senator Preston King, who gestured to the foot of the stairs, where armed guards stood with fixed bayonets. It was "useless to attempt an issue of that character," King told them.

Flummoxed, the two lawyers concocted a scheme to bring Anna Surratt before the very man who had prosecuted her mother, Judge Advocate General Holt, to appeal for more time. It was the longest of long shots. "We thought that, touched by the unutterable woe of the poor girl, that pitying chords of sympathy might find a responsive echo in his heart," Clampitt explained of the ploy. Drenched in tears, Anna went down on her knees and begged the judge advocate general to grant her mother three more days to live. As Clampitt would recall it, Holt was unmoved. "His heart was chilled, his soul as impassive as marble," the lawyer said. And yet the pathetic scene must have had some effect, for Holt conceded to speak to President Johnson on their behalf. Perhaps it was the only way he could think of to stop Anna Surratt's tears from soaking his shoes. At any rate, he instructed the two lawyers to meet him at the White House later in the day.

✥

While Aiken and Clampitt scrambled to save Mary Surratt's life, preparations for her death were marching resolutely forward. A gallows had to be constructed, nooses tied and hung, coffins made, and graves dug. All of it fell to Captain Christian Rath to oversee.

The assignment proved more burdensome than he might have expected, and not only because of the looming deadline. Despite all the grief and fury that had followed Lincoln's murder, all the calls for revenge, Rath could find no workman at the arsenal who was willing to dig the graves for those who had been condemned to die for the crime. Superstition made them all wary, forcing Rath to turn to soldiers instead. The arsenal's carpenter, too, was reluctant to do his duty when informed that a scaffold wide enough to hang four people simultaneously would be required. "I thought he was going to faint," Rath remembered, "and he said, 'Captain, I have made everything out of wood except a gallows, and now you ask me to do that.'" But the carpenter had no more choice in the matter than Rath did.

While the carpenter worked, Rath stood before the assembled Invalid Corps to select the men who would assist him on the scaffold the next day. "I want four able-bodied men to volunteer for special duty," he announced.

"None of us waited to hear what the duty was," remembered William Coxshall, who'd lost his left forefinger at Petersburg. The light duties they'd been assigned while recovering from sickness or injury had bored them silly, and they were eager for "anything to break the monotony."

"I told these men that they must volunteer their services," Rath recalled, "as I could not command them to take part in the gruesome work." None of the potential volunteers backed down. In addition to lifelong bragging rights, the chosen soldiers could look forward to a day free from additional duties, and a drink "when the thing was over."

The true executioners would not be the men who handled the nooses but those stationed under the gallows to knock aside the posts that supported the hinged floor upon which the condemned would stand. Rath picked out "two husky fellows"—William Coxshall and D. F. Shoupe—to shoulder that duty. Four more soldiers were chosen to place the nooses around the necks of the condemned, and another three to lead Atzerodt, Herold, and Powell from their cells to the gallows.

For Mary Surratt's escort, Rath recruited a lieutenant colonel, explaining that "I didn't want an ordinary soldier to lay his hands on her." He also decided that Mary should be positioned beside Lewis Powell on the scaffold. Herold and Atzerodt, being cowards in the eyes of the masses, struck Rath as unworthy of sitting alongside Mrs. Surratt. Powell's courage and cheerfulness had earned him a sort of respect. It was the nearest Rath could come to giving her a place of honor.

Inside the arsenal, the condemned prisoners could hear the sawing and hammering, then the snap and clatter of the hinged platform as Rath and his volunteers tested the drops. For two hours Rath rehearsed his men with 140-pound shells standing in for the accused. William Coxshall called it "one of the grimmest things I have ever known." The sinister racket rattled even the infamously resigned Lewis Powell. "When I saw Payne last in his cell, even his fortitude seemed to be shaken by the hurried way in which he was to be executed," his lawyer recalled. "He had heard the noise of the hammers on the scaffolding. He was crouched like a tiger at bay, in the farthest corner of his cell, his eyes red and glaring."

Rath himself attended to the nooses, fashioning them from thirty-one-strand, three-quarter-inch Boston hemp. Carefully he coiled the four lengths of rope into the hangman's knot—seven turns each for Atzerodt, Herold, and Powell. When he came to the fourth noose, the one meant for Mary Surratt, he gave the knot only five turns, "for I fully expected that Mrs. Surratt would never hang."

To be absolutely certain the ropes would bear the weight of a plummeting body without snapping, Rath cut a length and tied it around a heavy bag of ammunition. Then he climbed a tree and tiptoed out onto a limb. "I threw the bag from the limb," Rath recalled, "first securing it to the rope. It brought up with a jerk, the limb broke off short, and I was precipitated to the ground with great force. But the rope held."

Bruised but satisfied, Rath concluded his preparations.

⇥

As evening shadows fell across the city, crowds moved up and down H Street, pausing across from number 541 to glance "over with anxious and inquiring eyes upon the house in which the conspirators met." A single light burned within. Mary's neighbors sat in their windows and doorways, watching as hundreds of people wandered past. For weeks the neighborhood had been inundated with curiosity seekers and their eager questions. Now the mood was different, more somber. The people tended to stay on the opposite side of the street, keeping a more respectful distance, and the murmur of their subdued comments floated though the hot summer air.

At around eight o'clock, a carriage drew up before the Surratt boardinghouse. Anna Surratt stepped out. "She appeared to be perfectly crushed with grief," the Washington *Evening Star* reported. Sorrow radiated so strongly from Mary Surratt's daughter that women on the street found themselves blinking back tears at the sight of her.

⇥

Aiken and Clampitt arrived at the White House just as General Holt emerged from his attempt to sway Andrew Johnson. "I can do nothing," the general said. "The president is immovable." The date of the execution was fixed, and Johnson saw no need to change it. "You might as well attempt to overthrow this building as to alter his decision," he told them.

Once again, the two lawyers were at a loss. Midnight was nearing. The only thing left to do was telegraph Reverdy Johnson at his home in Baltimore for advice. "It is very late," he replied. "There are no trains to carry me to Washington City. Apply for a writ of habeas corpus and take her body from the custody of the military authorities. We are now in a state of peace—not war."

A writ of habeas corpus would order Major General Winfield Scott Hancock, the commandant of the military district that included the arsenal, to bring Mary Surratt before a civil court and prove that he had a lawful reason to imprison her. Originally designed to prevent citizens from being arrested without cause and jailed indefinitely without being charged with a crime, "the Privilege of the Writ of Habeas Corpus" is a fundamental right, guarded by article 9 of the Constitution. In Mary's case, there had been no search warrant, and no probable cause shown for her arrest. Colonel Wells's verbal order to search 541 H Street and "bring away all that seems of importance, especially pictures, letters, and other witnesses," had been an explicit violation of Mary Surratt's Fourth Amendment rights. Abraham Lincoln had suspended habeas corpus in the midst of the war, but now that the conflict had ended, Reverdy Johnson believed no grounds remained for disregarding this civil right.

Aiken and Clampitt had only a few hours to find a judge to sign the writ—one willing to challenge the authority of both the War Department and the president of the United States.

☞

Clocks were tolling the hour of two in the morning when Frederick Aiken and John Clampitt jangled the bell at Judge Andrew Wylie's front door.

Above, a window lifted and a voice called out, "What do you want?"

"Important business of a judicial character," one of the lawyers replied, "upon which hangs life or death."

Aiken and Clampitt had aimed high. Judge Wylie was an associate justice of the supreme court of the District of Columbia. Rumpled from sleep, he came to the door and ushered them into his study so he could hear what had brought them to his doorstep in such a state of desperation.

The judge listened so solemnly—"immovable," Clampitt remembered, "sitting like a statue in the glimmer of the gas-light overhead"—that his dressing gown might have been a black judicial robe. Wylie did not interrupt as the lawyers read the petition they had drawn up and then presented their argument on behalf of Mary Surratt.

"Please excuse me, gentlemen," Judge Wylie said quietly when they had finished. He gathered up the papers Aiken and Clampitt had brought, and returned to his bedchamber.

"Our hearts fell within us as he closed the door behind him," Clampitt said. They could only assume that Wylie had gone up to dress himself before formally rejecting their petition. To their astonishment, he reappeared in just a few moments, still in his nightclothes.

"Gentlemen, my mind is made up," Wylie announced. "I have always endeavored to perform my duty fearlessly, as I understand it. I am constrained to decide the points in your petition well taken. I am about to perform an act which before to-morrow's sun goes down may consign me to the old Capitol Prison. I believe it to be my duty, as a judge, to order this writ to issue; and," he said, taking up his pen to sign the paper, "I shall so order it."

CHAPTER TWENTY-FIVE

July 7 dawned hot and mercilessly bright.

Mary had passed a miserable night. "She slept very little, if any," the Washington *Evening Star* reported, "and required considerable attention, suffering with cramps and pains the entire night, caused by her nervousness." Major Porter had given Mary wine of valerian, an herbal sedative, in hopes of calming her, according to the *New York Times*. She could not eat; only Lewis Powell was reported to have any appetite that morning.

"All that affection and love can do for her is being done," wrote the *Daily National Republican*. Anna was there, along with Father Wiget, Father Walter, and Mr. Brophy. But by eight-thirty, Anna was again at the White House, gambling her last few hours with her mother against one final attempt at persuading President Johnson to have mercy.

She made it no farther than the foot of the steps to the president's office. President Johnson had made it clear that his door would not be opened under any circumstances that day. "I can see no one on this business," Johnson had told his military secretary, Colonel R. D. Mussey.

"It was a disagreeable duty," Mussey remembered of Johnson's attitude toward the execution, "and there would be endeavors to get him not to perform it, and he wished to avoid them as much as possible." Anyone with "fresh evidence or any new reason" for Mary to be spared should be directed to Judge Advocate General Holt, the president decreed.

"These orders I regarded as peremptorily forbidding me to make any appeal to him in any one's behalf," Mussey later explained. Andrew Johnson's own private opinion was that Mary Surratt had "kept the nest that hatched the egg." Furthermore, Mussey recalled, "he told me that there had not been 'women enough hanged in this war.'"

Anna had neither fresh evidence nor a new reason. Her only weapon was her tears. At the sight of Colonel Mussey, she fell to her knees. Snatching at his coat, she begged and sobbed for help.

The colonel informed Anna, "in as tender a manner as possible," that the matter was out of his hands. Anna could not give up. She would not even move. Prostrate upon the stairs, she continued to wail and beg the help of any and all who passed by. Her mother was "too good and kind to be guilty of the enormous crime," she insisted. If Mary was put to death, Anna declared, she "wished to die also."

Through all the commotion, the president's office door stayed firmly shut, though "a number of hardy soldiers" could not keep the tears from their cheeks.

❧

At the arsenal, select members of the press were ushered into a room next to General Hartranft's office. The windows afforded a full view of the prison yard and gallows, where relic hunters were already scooping up chips of wood and fragments of rope. At the end of the hall stood a door "studded with massive rivets and bolts." That door opened into a passage leading out to the yard, and also into the hall of the prison-ers' cells. From time to time an officer of Hartranft's staff offered the reporters a tidbit regarding what had gone on in those cells over the previous twelve hours.

"Mrs. Surratt early in the evening became completely unnerved and somewhat flighty in thought and expression. She seemed not only overwhelmed with mental anguish, but utterly prostrated physically with the near approach of the terrible ordeal which was meted to her," the New York Herald reported. The possibility that they had misjudged Mary did not enter into the reporters' thinking. It had long ago become "customary to represent her as a monster," and the New York Herald, like so many others, saw what they wanted to see—a villain unmasked. "The intellectual resources and will that has sustained this dark and sin-ister woman throughout this session of the court of inquisition com-pletely forsook her when hope vanished and the gibbet from which she was to swing was already reared scarce fifty paces from the portals of her cells."

At four o'clock in the morning, Aiken and Clampitt had placed the writ of habeas corpus bearing Judge Wylie's signature into the hands of the United States marshal. The document demanded that Major General Winfield Scott Hancock bring Mary Surratt before Judge Wylie's court and prove that she had been lawfully detained.

General Hancock duly appeared. "So prompt was the performance of his duty, in the estimation of the Court, that Judge Wylie compli-mented him on his ready obedience to the civil authority," Clampitt recalled. "General Hancock's appearance before the Judge showed his respect for the civil process of the Court."

But to Aiken's and Clampitt's consternation, Mary Surratt was nowhere to be seen. Beside Hancock instead stood Attorney General James Speed, who handed a document to Judge Wylie.

"I, Andrew Johnson, President of the United States, do hereby declare that the writ of habeas corpus has been heretofore suspended in such cases as this, and I do hereby especially suspend this writ, and direct that you proceed to execute," it read.

Both Judge Wylie and General Hancock were powerless before the president's express order.

"All hope faded," Clampitt lamented, "and we proceeded to the Arsenal to take a last farewell of the doomed and innocent woman." All down Four-and-a-Half Street, Aiken and Clampitt saw cavalrymen lining the long blocks between the arsenal and the White House. General Hancock had stationed them there. If the president miraculously issued a reprieve or pardon at the last instant, the news would be relayed at a gallop. Every one of the soldiers sat idle in their saddles.

☞

At the same time, another chance for Mary Surratt was brewing in the most unlikely of places—cell 195 of the Old Arsenal Penitentiary.

Lewis Powell had not rested easy. More than his own imminent death troubled him. His conscience writhed at the thought of Mary Surratt's death sentence.

The *New York Times* correspondent who had gained entry to the arsenal the night before reported that Powell "says John Surratt is acting cowardly, most villainously, in failing to appear and die with his mother." With no family or friends of his own to bid him farewell, Powell's final thoughts seemed to be fixing themselves firmly on Mary. "He expresses the deepest regret that Mrs. Surratt is to be a sufferer by reason of any act of his, and evinces a solicitude for her not unlike that of a tender child for its parent."

As his last hours ticked down, Powell confessed his remorse to Dr. Abram Gillette, the minister of Washington's First Baptist Church. "Concerning the fate of Mrs. Surratt, Payne spoke with great feeling," Gillette's son later revealed. "Of a prior knowledge of their later deeds he declared her innocent, but did not, of course, deny her interest in their original actions and plans. He never ceased to upbraid himself for seeking the shelter of her home, as in that lay the misfortune of her doom. He hoped, fervently, that she might be spared."

"She at least does not deserve to die with us," Powell told Dr. Gillette. "If I had no other reason, Doctor, she is a woman, and men do not make war on women."

Powell also unburdened himself to Captain Rath that morning, telling him, "Captain, if I had two lives to give, I'd give one gladly to save Mrs. Surratt. I know that she is innocent, and would never die in this way if I hadn't been found in her house. She knew nothing about the conspiracy at all, and is an innocent woman."

Powell's revelations caused an immediate stir. Captain Rath sent word to the War Department and received orders to take Powell's statement. Soon Father Walter and Father Wiget were involved, along with Mr. Brophy and General Hartranft. Father Walter wrote a message to the president, relaying what Powell had said and adding that since Powell "was now beyond hope," there was no reason for him to hold back the truth.

"Believing that Judge Holt desired the best possible evidence," Hartranft added that he had spoken to Powell as well and felt that Powell was telling the truth. (Later, the general would clarify that he "did not by any means intend to express my own opinion of the guilt or innocence of Mrs. Surratt." Hartranft simply believed that Powell was in earnest and "had told the truth according to the best of his knowledge and belief.")

"I will furnish you an army conveyance and swift horses," General Hartranft told Brophy. "Take it and drive like mad to the White House and give the president this note. I will delay the execution until the last moment, or until I hear from you definitely and positively what the President's answer is."

Brophy set off sometime between ten and eleven o'clock. According to Andrew Johnson's order, the execution was to take place no later than two that afternoon.

⇒⊮

Lewis Powell was not the only person decrying John Surratt Jr.'s conspicuous absence. "If John Surratt could prove his mother innocent through confessing himself guilty, it has been open to him at any time to save his mother's innocent life at the expense of his own guilty one," the New York World wrote that same day, "and if she be innocent, as Mary Surratt says, her son is a murderer."

The entire country knew that Mary Surratt was mere steps away from the hangman's noose. Where *was* her son? And was he truly willing to let his mother hang?

The most prevalent speculation had put him in Canada all along—likely Montreal—though phantom John Surratts had been appearing and disappearing all across North America. "Surratt in a Nunnery," one Pennsylvania paper insisted in June. There had even been a rumor of his capture at Port Lincoln in Alaska.

As John Surratt himself would later tell it, the truth about his mother's situation had been deliberately kept from him. "Let me solemnly say that I never knew my mother was in serious danger," he said in 1885. "I do not believe that the temper of the people would have allowed any one to be saved, but that would not have mattered in the least. I would have come had I known. I would, as God is my judge."

Throughout the spring of 1865, letters from friends in Montreal promised him "there was no cause of anxiety," leading John to believe that "revulsion of public feeling" would eventually guarantee Mary's release. But soon the newspapers he received in his hiding place began to be censored, with choice sentences "mutilated with ink and pen." When he protested the redactions, his supply of newspapers abruptly ceased.

Without information, John's confidence in his mother's safety flagged. Rushing to her aid was no simple matter, either, for he could not reveal himself without also putting at risk the lives of those who had kept him hidden all these weeks. John claimed in an 1870 interview that his mounting agitation and anxiety led him to dispatch a messenger of his own to Mary's legal counsel. "God alone knows the suspense and anxiety of my mind during his absence." The reply, when it finally came at the end of June, was most reassuring: "Be under no apprehension as to any serious consequences. Remain perfectly quiet, as any action on your part would only tend to make matters worse. If you can be of any service to us, we will let you know, but keep quiet."

John Surratt did exactly that.

☞

At eleven-thirty on the morning of the execution, Captain Rath decided one last rehearsal was in order. He was not so much concerned with the soldiers' readiness as with the mechanism of the gallows itself. For the execution to proceed properly, it was imperative that the drops fall in tandem at his signal. The men assembled into their assigned positions. Rath gave the signal. One drop swung away just as it should. The other—the one where Mary Surratt and Lewis Powell would be standing in a matter of hours—stuck. Rath had to summon the carpenter to come with his saw and make the necessary last-minute adjustments. "We tried it a second time," said William Coxshall, "and though it worked perfectly, we had no great confidence that it would come off all right."

⇀≫

Around the same time, an officer who had just walked past the cells paused to feed a few details to the assembled members of the press. "Mrs. Surratt was lying full length upon her mattress, clothed in some white undress garment, looking very pale and debilitated," the *New York Herald* wrote. "Two ladies were also in the cell endeavoring to calm the almost continual shuddering of her shrunken figure and summon fortitude for her to bear the wretched fate that was at hand." If the report was true, these two ladies have never been identified.

⇀≫

At noon came a clicking sound from above the prison yard. All eyes turned upward, to the rising window of the arsenal's old workshop building, "and forthwith was seen protruding the familiar snout of the camera, showing that the inevitable photographer was on hand." Not just any photographer, but Alexander Gardner, the same man who had photographed Lincoln's funeral and taken portraits of Arnold, Atzerodt, Herold, O'Laughlen, Powell, and Spangler during their detention aboard the ironclads. Gardner's "good-humored face" and wild bushy beard appeared above the camera as he focused his lens, like all the waiting eyes in the prison yard, upon the gallows.

⇀≫

For an hour John Brophy tried again and again to make his way past the White House guards. Every direction he approached, he found himself barred by "a gleaming bayonet and beyond the bayonet the stern bronzed face of a soldier." The sentries would not even consent to deliver the note from Father Walter to the president.

Brophy stood on the steps in a lather of frustration. His mission was so urgent and yet so impossible, he could hardly think straight. Anna Surratt clung to him like a panicked child, "sobbing and choking with grief." The more frantic Anna became, the more slowly Brophy's mind seemed to churn. Yet he could not bear to pry her loose any more than she could bear to let go of anyone who might be able to help.

While the two of them stood paralyzed with helplessness, a fine carriage drew up at the entrance. Out stepped "a richly dressed and strikingly handsome woman." She was none other than Adele Douglas, widow of Senator Stephen A. Douglas, the "Little Giant" who had been Lincoln's fiercest rival during the election of 1860. She, too, had come to appeal to the president on behalf of Mary Surratt.

Brophy darted to her, imploring her to help him gain an audience with President Johnson. Mrs. Douglas's resolute bearing proved to be a weapon more powerful than the soldiers' firearms. "She dashed straight at the bayonets and they lowered almost in homage before her," the New York Sun reported. The unarmed guards within were no match for her, either. "She swept them aside with an imperious gesture."

No one dared stand in the way of Mrs. Stephen A. Douglas. She would reach the president. Anna and Brophy waited, daring to hope.

But it was not long before Mrs. Douglas emerged so bitterly disappointed, it showed "in her every feature and every movement." She couldn't bring herself to say the words to Anna. She only shook her head.

"Oh, don't give up so!" Anna pleaded. "Don't! Don't! Oh, do go to him again. He won't refuse you. He can't. Do go to him again!"

Brophy held out the letter from Father Walter. Mrs. Douglas could not refuse. In she charged again, just as though she, and not Andrew Johnson, occupied the White House.

But the president would not be budged.

Everyone but Anna could see that the situation was hopeless. Every minute she spent pleading now only subtracted from the few precious minutes she had left to spend at Mary's side. "Come with me if you would see your mother again while she lives," Brophy coaxed.

A "mad gallop" through the streets of Washington ensued, but blocks away from the arsenal the carriage halted. In every direction, a tide of people pushing doggedly toward the arsenal clogged the streets. "Everybody who had a cousin or a grandfather thought of course *they* could get in," wrote the *Daily National Republican,* "but they found they couldn't unless they had that little bit of paper called a pass, duly inscribed." Those who had been turned away and those intent on getting in pushed and shoved themselves into one great muddle. Cake and lemonade vendors milled through the crowd.

Just as had happened at the White House, a carriage came clattering to Anna and Brophy's aid—this one boasting a cavalcade of mounted soldiers as an escort. Recognizing an army conveyance and noticing the distressed young woman inside, the soldier in command halted his procession and stepped out of his carriage.

Major General Winfield Scott Hancock stood before them, hat in hand. What was the trouble, he wanted to know, and what could he do to help? This was the very same Major General Hancock who had just appeared before Judge Wylie in an attempt to comply with Aiken and Clampitt's writ of habeas corpus. He, too, was on his way to the arsenal, to carry out his duty of overseeing the execution.

Brophy introduced Anna, explaining that Miss Surratt was "trying to speak to her mother once more on earth." Brophy saw the hero of

Gettysburg's face flush with emotion and watched as "something very like tears" glossed Hancock's eyes.

"Poor child," the general said. He gave an order to an officer, and the mounted soldiers surrounded both carriages, clearing a swath through the crowd.

CHAPTER TWENTY-SIX

At twelve-fifteen, Father Walter administered the sacraments to Mary Surratt. All the religious rites and comforts she was entitled to were performed in her cell, Father Walter said afterward, "so as to save her from being too much exposed to the public gaze." Though Mary had not yet given up hope of clemency, her greatest concern, should the worst befall her, was for Anna rather than for herself. "What will become of her—what will be Anna's fate?" she asked "repeatedly and frantically" as she wrung her hands at the thought of leaving her fragile, fiercely devoted daughter orphaned.

Soldiers and spectators alike sweated in the treeless prison yard. Some men smoked cigars. Others debated the various methods of execution: firing squad, garrote, guillotine. Still others lolled in the narrow margins of shade cast by the wall. No one knew yet whether Mary Surratt would truly be put to death. The mere sight of four nooses shocked one spectator into exclaiming, "My God, they are not going to hang all four, are they?" The entire nation buzzed with that question. Would Mary Surratt truly hang? *Should* she hang?

"A mawkish sort of sympathy seems to be expressed in some quarters for Mrs. Surratt, on account of her sex," the *Philadelphia Inquirer* marveled, "but the same sort of people, I dare say, would sympathize with Satan himself, if there was any possibility of bringing him to justice."

"Against Mrs. Surratt the evidence was by no means conclusive," the *New York World* argued. "Her guilt might possibly have been established before a civil court. Whatever opinions of her guilt may be held by the public, the opinion is wide-spread that her guilt was not proven."

While the city of Washington waited and debated, a rumor took flight that Mary had made a confession. It was not so. She had only made the customary religious confession to Father Walter before he administered Holy Communion.

As the hour designated for her death crept nearer, Mary grew calmer rather than more frantic. Five minutes after Mary received the sacraments, Anna was once more at her mother's side. The reporters who had watched Anna enter the arsenal noted that "her bearing was quite firm, and her manner and step almost confident in expression." Anna seemed so uncharacteristically resolute that the journalists speculated she had succeeded in having her mother's sentence commuted.

Even Mary appears to have sensed the momentary change in Anna. "Is there any hope?" she asked her daughter as Anna entered the cell.

"Hope is gone," Anna replied. She slumped against the doorway and said again, "Hope is fled."

In that moment, it seems Mary Surratt realized there was but one task left for her to do on earth—to spare her daughter as much pain as she could manage.

"Mother, are you resigned?" Anna asked.

"Yes, my child," Mary assured her.

As Father Walter would tell it, Mary realized that Anna was no match for the ordeal to come. Waiting only made it worse. Mary summoned up all her fortitude and "appeared to rally in strength for a moment." The time for farewells had come.

"Annie, my child, this is no place for you," Father Walter remembered Mary saying to her daughter.

Anna removed a steel pin shaped like an arrow from her bonnet and fastened it to a black silk bow on her mother's collar, just below Mary's chin. What they said to each other is known to them alone. John Clampitt witnessed Mary and Anna's last moments together, but could not bring himself to commit them to paper. "My pen is too dumb to describe the heart-rending scene at the parting of mother and daughter," he said. Their farewell also "melted the hearts of the stern soldiers, used to scenes of anguish," said the Washington *Evening Star.*

At twelve-thirty, Anna left her mother's cell for the last time. The reporters needed no one to relay the information. "Loud sobs from Mrs. Surratt's cell told of the parting scene . . . and presently Miss Surratt was supported from her mother's cell in hysterics of grief. Her sobs and cries were heard for some moments until she had passed through the iron gates of the prison."

Ten minutes later, the remaining relatives and friends of the condemned were ordered to say their goodbyes. "The sounds of grief which emanated therefrom were so loud as to be distinctly heard outside." David Herold's seven sisters left "all in one chorus of weeping."

"A great quiet prevailed" in the prison yard after that. The soldiers whispered to one another. At five minutes to one, the reporters and spectators watched as four armchairs were placed upon the scaffold and the nooses arranged.

The heat was blistering. If not for the breeze, one reporter estimated, the temperature might have reached 100 degrees. The rays of the sun, he wrote, "shot down like the blasts from a fiery furnace." Now and then, one witness noticed, an eddy of the breeze sweeping down the Potomac would dart over the wall, and the dangling nooses could be seen to "writhe as I have seen wounded snakes."

Guards formed a square around the gallows a few minutes before one o'clock. An officer summoned the reporters and led them out to the yard, where they would be permitted to stand just outside the cordon of soldiers. These front-row privileges would put them within thirty feet of the gallows. On their way, "through the courtesy and kindness of General Hancock and General Hartranft, the representatives of the press were allowed to pass by the cells of the prisoners."

As Mary sat awaiting the order to proceed, she said to Father Walter, "Father, I wish to say something."

"What is it, my child?"

"That I am innocent."

The priest, known for his outspokenness, had been sternly instructed not to stir up the prison staff with his own proclamations of Mary's innocence. In an overabundance of caution, he dissuaded Mary from making a final statement. "The world and all that is in it has now receded forever," Father Walter advised. To speak out now would only "disturb the serenity of your last moments," he said.

Within minutes, the procession of the condemned assembled and the door to the prison yard swung open. Flanked by two soldiers, Lieutenant Colonel McCall and Sergeant Kenney, Mary Surratt stepped into the bright sunlight. Hundreds of eyes turned toward her—those of soldiers, spectators, reporters, and the photographer who had come to fix the scene of her death upon plates of glass. Fifty men looked down from the roof of a neighboring building. A line of sentries stood shoulder to shoulder along the thirty-foot wall that ringed the yard.

The heat and the attention alone almost could have smothered her to death then and there. Despite the protection of her veil and an umbrella to shield her from the sun, Mary Surratt's dread was plain to see in every step and breath she took. Father Walter and Father Wiget followed one step behind. Each carried a crucifix and breviary. Their lips were moving together, reciting a prayer as the procession passed the four shallow graves that lay in wait.

Though her steps were "comparatively steady" at first, Mary "faltered a little" at the base of the stairs leading to the top of the scaffold. "Her limbs seemed to fail her," the *New York Herald* noticed, which obliged her two escorts to almost carry her up the steps. (More than dread slowed her; several reporters noticed a chain joining Mary's ankles.) As the blazing sun shone across her veil, Mary's face became clearly visible to the public for the first time. Her cheeks were sunken now, her teeth "incomplete." The curl of her upper lip gave her an expression more of ghastly horror than plain fear that reminded one reporter of "the newly dead."

Lewis Powell, by contrast, was as amiable as ever. "He walked like a king about to be crowned," Captain Rath marveled, "his fearless blue eyes roving carelessly over the scaffold and his yellow hair shining like a golden halo in the sun." Indeed, Powell playfully crowned himself, sweeping a straw hat from the head of Lieutenant Colonel McCall and dropping it onto his own head. At the top of the scaffold, he sat on the chair placed behind his assigned noose—the one beside Mary Surratt—"as though he was sitting down to dinner."

George Atzerodt was petrified, so consumed with terror that it disgusted people to look at him as he quivered. "For mere relief they turned from him to rest upon the regal face of Payne."

"Last, and in every way least, came nineteen-year-old David Herold," the *New York Herald* observed, hobbling along in stocking feet "with bloodless, sallow cheeks."

At the top of the scaffold, Mary Surratt gave one look at the scene spread before her, then closed her eyes, shutting it all out. She seemed to turn inward then, taking refuge in silent prayer. Father Wiget held the crucifix to her lips while Father Walter "pour[ed] into her ear" every holy word of comfort and assurance at his disposal.

Without Anna, Mary had no one to protect, and fear began to take full possession of her. Her head lolled from side to side. Only the sight of the crucifix, which she kissed "fervently, several times," had the power to quiet the intermittent wails that welled up within her. Uplifted by her faith, "her face lost its deadly fear" and she could manage to look out at the crowd for a moment. But the sight of the dangling noose never failed to cow her. She seemed almost to flicker as her expression changed from one extreme to the other.

Father Walter and Father Wiget fanned her. They held the umbrella over her to shield her from the blast-furnace heat of the sun. Their lips moved endlessly in murmured prayer as they ministered to her.

When all the condemned were seated, General Hartranft removed his hat and began to read the sentences "in a low quiet tone." Just as quietly, Mary murmured prayers in Latin.

Reverend Gillette stepped forward. "Gentlemen," he called out over the crowd, "the prisoner Lewis Thornton Powell, known as Payne, requests me, on this occasion, to say for him that he thus publicly and sincerely thanks General Hartranft and all the other officers and soldiers who have had charge of him, and all who have ministered to his wants, for their unvarying kindness and attention to him. Not an unkind word was ever spoken, not an unbecoming gesture has ever been made toward him." Then he prayed aloud for the soul of Lewis Powell. Reverend Mark Olds and Reverend J. G. Butler likewise offered public thanks and prayers on behalf of Herold and Atzerodt. Father Walter and Father Wiget said nothing.

The time had come for the condemned to stand so that the nooses could be fitted.

"She half fainted," George Alfred Townsend of the *New York World* wrote, "and sank backward upon the attendants, her limbs yielding to the extremity of her terror, but uttering no cry, only a kind of sick groaning, like one in the weakness of fever."

Lieutenant Colonel McCall bound Mary's elbows behind her, while Sergeant Kenney tied long strips of cotton around her dress, just below the knee. "It was with a shudder, almost a blush," that Townsend watched the sergeant wrap the cords three times around her skirts to keep them from billowing upward when she dropped. Spectators saw Mary turn her head and speak to McCall. Through the wooden slats over his head, William Coxshall heard her say, "It hurts." As Coxshall would tell the story years later, one of the men above replied, "Well, it won't hurt long," but several others in the crowd saw McCall slackening the ties slightly to make her more comfortable.

Beside her, Lewis Powell "gave a slight shrug of the shoulders when the coil fell around his bare neck." At the other end of the scaffold, Atzerodt and Herold both appeared "half dead with terror and the consciousness of their awful situation" as their nooses were fitted. "About the same time Mrs. Surratt seemed, by a desperate mental effort, to nerve herself up specially for this occasion, looking forward and around her, for the only time, with an air of mingled determination and resignation."

The tension extended beyond the condemned. Beneath the platform, William Coxshall's stomach was roiling, "what with the heat and the waiting." It seemed the clergymen would go on speaking forever. Coxshall wrapped his arms around the wooden beam like a drunken man in need of support, leaned over, and vomited. "I felt a little better after that, but not too good."

Mary's noose was fitted last of all. Lieutenant Colonel McCall gently removed her bonnet. To Powell's lawyer, that moment was "the most harrowing part of her execution. . . . It was the meeting of the extremes of what is esteemed sacred and what is deemed infamous." Finally came a white hood—"the cap of doom"—that reached her shoulders.

To properly position herself under the beam that held her noose, Mary had to step forward. She knew that the floor beneath her was hinged, and beyond that, the edge of the platform loomed. Mary was so overcome, she could hardly hold herself upright, much less move. Even on the ground, from thirty feet away, it was clear to the spectators that she might "give way." At that moment, it was not the imminent drop of the platform that terrified Mary most but the thought of collapsing or stumbling blindly over its edge.

"Please don't let me fall," she begged; "hold on!"

To prolong the wait now would only be torture, but Captain Rath had not yet given up hope. "All is ready, Captain," General Hancock prompted him. "Proceed."

"Her, too?" Rath asked.

"Yes," Hancock replied. "She cannot be saved."

Captain Rath silently signaled the attendants to step back from the drop. Little more than ten seconds passed before William Coxshall heard the much-anticipated signal—the clap of Rath's hands. Once. Twice. "On the third clap, Shoupe and I swung with all our might." The wooden beams broke free, and Mary Surratt felt the platform drop from beneath her feet.

Powell, Atzerodt, and Herold plunged straight down and bounced upward as the nooses caught. "They were literally *jerked* into Eternity," wrote a lieutenant of the Fourteenth Indiana Regiment.

Mary had been standing with her body pitched slightly forward when the platform fell. "This gave a swinging motion to her body, which lasted several minutes," a reporter noted. The shortcut Captain Rath had taken with Mary's noose had done her no harm. There was no sign of struggle—only the reflex to throw out her hands to catch her balance. One witness saw her left hand clench, and that was all.

George Atzerodt went just as quickly. His body continued to quiver after his neck had snapped, as if the fear lingered longer within his flesh than his life did.

Lewis Powell was not so fortunate. His powerful neck did not snap, which left him to die of strangulation. "Payne was a strong brute," said William Coxshall, who likely stood mere feet away from Powell's body as it jerked and shuddered, "and died hard." Herold, too, struggled to die.

For almost fifteen minutes more, the bodies dangled from their nooses while the civilians in the crowd were dispersed. "She hangs and swings as if within the dark folds of her puffed dress no life has ever been," the New York Herald observed of Mary Surratt. "A bag of old clothes it might be but for that flesh we see between the rope and the cap." Then Major Porter examined the bodies and pronounced them dead.

Ten minutes after that, Rath gave the order to cut down the corpses. "An over zealous corporal" scaled the scaffold and slashed through George Atzerodt's rope with a single cut. The dead man's body plummeted to the ground with a thud. Though the corporal was soundly reprimanded for his disrespect, discipline remained shaky.

"The soldiers performing this task whacked off as much rope from each dangling quil as they could reach, and, cutting it into small pieces, threw it among their comrades below," a lieutenant who'd watched from beneath the scaffold wrote later to a compatriot. The scuttle and scramble for these "rope-relics" was so great that some men tumbled into one of the open graves. Before they could clamber out, they found themselves showered with dirt as their "laughing comrades" above slung a half dozen shovelfuls of earth over them.

"When Mrs. Surratt was being taken down, as the rope was cut, her head of course fell over upon her breast, and an individual standing by made the heartless remark, 'She makes a good bow.'" As if it had all been nothing but a performance.

This was precisely the kind of derision Captain Rath had hoped to avoid. "I took charge of Mrs. Surratt myself," he said, "not being willing that any hand should desecrate her. I lifted her tenderly in my arms, her limp body bending as I held it." Rath removed the noose and noticed as he loosened the rope that "pieces of the delicate skin came with it. The rope had cut in deeply. That rather sickened me, and I remember it to this day," he recalled thirty years afterward.

With his own hands and no one else's, Rath "placed her in the box." "Box" was the word for it, for the coffins were not made in the traditional shape, instead resembling the sort of packing crate used to ship firearms. The white hood remained over Mary's head. Assistant Adjutant-General R. A. Watts wrote the name of each of the condemned on a slip of paper and put the slips into bottles, which were then placed in the coffins for future identification. By four o'clock, all four coffins lay beneath three and a half feet of dry prison yard clay.

That ought to have been the end of it. But the Surratt affair was not over—not by half. "This trial settled nothing," Powell's lawyer observed. "It lead to four executions but a lynching would have done that."

CHAPTER TWENTY-SEVEN

Rumors of Mary Surratt's restless spirit walking the hallways of the house on H Street began without delay. The first tenant, it was said, lasted only six weeks before fleeing with his nerves in tatters. Those that followed never failed to make "a shuddering exit."

Plenty of people would find themselves haunted by Mary Surratt in the years to come, though these hauntings had nothing to do with ghostly footfalls or transparent figures draped in black.

For Louis Weichmann, the haunting began almost the instant he was released from prison. Within a week of Mary Surratt's execution, the *Daily Constitutional Union* was aflame with a story that effectively cast him as his landlady's murderer.

In this story, John Brophy claimed to have spoken with Weichmann the day after his release from prison. During the course of their conversation, a troubled Weichmann confessed a litany of undisclosed information so important that Brophy wrote it all down and submitted it in an affidavit to the War Department.

The original document was given to President Johnson, the *Daily Constitutional Union* said, and so the newspaper could not guarantee that the version it printed was identical—"but the *facts* and *entire sub-stance* are precisely the same."

In essence, John Brophy swore before a notary public that Louis Weichmann was a disloyal, lying coward who had testified against Mary Surratt to save his own neck. Specifically, Brophy alleged that Weich-mann admitted that he'd been threatened by Secretary Stanton and Colonel Burnett, that he had lied on the witness stand, and that he was "an avowed secessionist" who'd wanted to go to Richmond and had refused to fight for the Northern cause. "He told me he would rather be hooted at as a spy and informer and do anything rather than be tried as a conspirator, and have his future hopes blasted," Brophy's af-fidavit read.

More unsettling yet were Brophy's allegations regarding what Louis Weichmann had said about Mary Surratt. Brophy swore Weichmann had told him that Mary "wept bitterly and constantly" over her son's clandestine missions to the Confederate capital, "and that she begged and implored [John] not to go to Richmond, but to stop at home, and not bring trouble upon himself and upon the family."

Another incident concerned Mary's suspicions about what had been going on under her roof. One day Mary had taken her son aside and said, "John, there is something going on I am afraid, and I cannot see what it must be. Why do these men come here? Now, John, I cannot allow this; and you must tell me what you are about." According to Weichmann, John had refused to tell his mother what the men were up to.

The most disquieting admission of all alleged that "since this trial closed, he told me he thought Mrs. Surratt to be innocent, saying her son John was the guilty one." Weichmann had even offered to give Brophy a letter to President Johnson "in her favor," if Brophy would "keep it a profound secret" and personally deliver the letter into the president's hand. When Brophy asked why Weichmann didn't write directly to Judge Advocate General Holt, Weichmann said he "had no confidence in Holt."

At first, Louis Weichmann didn't appear to take any notice of Brophy's bombshell. But two days later, the *Philadelphia Inquirer* printed "evidence" that had never been given in the courtroom—some of the very same details Weichmann had provided to Colonel Burnett from prison on May 5, after being "confused and terrified" by the assistant judge advocate. No one outside the War Department ought to have had access to those details. And yet a newspaper in Philadelphia, the very city where Louis Weichmann had recently taken a job, was privy to this information. Surely that was no mere coincidence.

On July 16, Louis Weichmann officially retaliated with a column and a half of admonishments in the Philadelphia *Sunday Dispatch*. "Mrs. Surratt is dead," he wrote, "and what I now have to say can do her no harm." Brophy's claims were "a tissue of lies from beginning to end," he said.

"The War Department had all the information which I possessed, on the morning of the 16th of April," Weichmann lied, omitting any mention of the document in the evidence files labeled "Items not brought out in the examination of Weichmann, or that he has since recalled," as well as his own letter to Burnett on May 5.

"Mrs. Surratt is to be much blamed. She should have exercised a woman's influence and a mother's love, and then she could have prevented all." In other words, a real woman—a properly feminine lady—could have thwarted the entire conspiracy.

In terms of his testimony, there was "nothing to regret," Weichmann declared. "Conscious of my integrity, and of my desire to do right to all, I stand to-day in the pure light of heaven without one sin on my soul to answer for as regards the trial of the conspirators." And then in contradiction to that declaration, he began to justify himself.

Once again, a fresh stream of information came gushing out of Louis Weichmann—information regarding Mary Surratt that appears nowhere in the War Department records of his interrogations, nor in his testimony.

"Before the 4th of March," he wrote, "Mrs. Surratt was continually remarking to everybody that *something* was going to happen to 'Old Abe.'" When Richmond fell and Lee surrendered, Weichmann alleged, Mary wept and closed her house, keeping it "gloomy and forlorn" while the rest of the nation celebrated with displays of light and song. But on the afternoon of April 14, as they drove toward Surrattsville, she turned "lively and cheerful." That was also when she allegedly asked the sentries outside the city whether they remained out all night, and was "glad to know" that they left their posts at eight o'clock. They chatted about Booth, Weichmann said, and Mary told him that Booth was done acting and would "very soon" leave for New York, "never to return."

"When about a mile from the city, on our return, and having from the top of a hill caught a view of Washington swimming in a flood of light and glory, raising her hands, she said, 'I am afraid all this rejoicing will be turned into mourning, all this glory into sadness.'" When Louis asked what she meant, Mary replied "that after sunshine there was always a storm, and that the people were too proud and licentious, and that God would punish them."

Most incriminating of all, Weichmann told the nation that when the detectives had come knocking at her door on the night of the assassination, Mary Surratt had commanded, "For God's sake let them come in! I expected the house to be searched!" After the authorities had gone, Weichmann claimed, Anna had exclaimed, "Oh! ma, just think of that man having been here an hour before the assassination! I am afraid it will bring suspicion upon us!"

"Anna, come what may, I am resigned" was the reply Weichmann alleged Mary had made to her daughter. "I think J. Wilkes Booth was an instrument in the hands of the Almighty to punish proud and licentious people."

Weichmann had put himself in an odd bind. To defend himself against Brophy's allegations, little served him better than feeding the public details that made Mary Surratt appear more conclusively guilty. But if Weichmann had known these details all along, if he could have proven her guilty during the trial, why hadn't he?

John Brophy was not in the least intimidated by Weichmann's tirade. Brophy had sworn to his allegations in an affidavit, while Weichmann's claims were no more than "loose newspaper paragraphs, nearly every one of which is a contradiction of the other."

Brophy jeered at Weichmann's "perfect diarrhoea of information" and the convoluted thinking he dubbed "Weichmann logic." No better example existed than Louis's claim that he had surrendered every bit of information he possessed to the War Department two days after Lincoln's murder. "Now, will Mr. Weichmann condescend to tell us where, in the wide world, he found, since the 16th of April, enough of EXTRA charges against Mrs. Surratt to fill a whole column of very fine print!" Brophy demanded.

In reply, Louis Weichmann offered no proof to support his fresh accusations against Mary Surratt—only derision of Brophy and defense of his own character. "I had hoped that after the excitement and turmoil and agony of mind which I have undergone, after a month's *honorable* imprisonment in my country's service, that I would be permitted to regain that enviable obscurity from which I have been so mercilessly dragged into public notice," Weichmann said in the *Philadelphia Inquirer.* He also outed Brophy as Amator Justitiae, the author of the anonymous pamphlet in Mary's favor that had appeared all over the city the month before. "The fact is, Brophy deems Mrs. Surratt to have been innocent, and he wishes, at my expense, to cram it down everybody's throat. But the pill won't go."

To hear Louis Weichmann tell it, no one suffered more than he did in the years following the conspiracy trial. For the rest of his life, he felt persecuted for his role in Mary Surratt's execution.

His feelings were not wholly without cause. At his job at the Philadelphia customhouse—granted to him by the government because, in General Holt's own words, it was "the solemn duty of the government to protect this man"—he reported overhearing remarks like "See, that man there, well he has got his position by the blood of Mrs. Surratt."

Although Christianity remained a central tenet in his life, Weichmann never mastered the knack of turning the other cheek. He simply did not have the sort of temperament that allowed him to brush off such remarks. Insults lodged themselves permanently in his consciousness as if each one were an individual shard of glass. His reflex would always be to strike back—however long it took. Five years after a comment had provoked his ire, for instance, he still considered the man who'd made it "the most contemptible dog that ever lived," vowing "if I ever meet him face to face, I will give him a good pounding."

Louis Weichmann further believed the United States government owed him a debt that could never be fully repaid. When he was nearly ousted from the customhouse after the election of 1866, he appealed to none other than General Holt for help. "I can make just as easy and good a living elsewhere, but I feel that my reputation is everything, and hence, the position is a desirable strength, because of the strong protection shown around me by the government." The notion that his coworkers were "seeking to overthrow me" because they disagreed with his political views was only a pretext, he told Holt. The real cause of their disdain, Weichmann was sure, was "because I was a witness against the assassins of Abraham Lincoln, and especially against the woman Surratt whom copperheads and traitors revere as a martyr."

"I feel that my reputation is everything." No other single phrase encapsulates Louis Weichmann more aptly. To be known as the man who "wove the thread of testimony which closed on Mrs. Surratt, and in doing so escaped the gallows himself" when he believed himself the hero of the conspiracy trial was more than Weichmann was willing to bear.

While John Brophy and Louis Weichmann feuded in print, Anna Surratt grieved. None of the arguments or debates would bring her mother back.

In the eyes of the public, Anna was the sole Surratt unquestionably worthy of sympathy. "If there is anywhere among all the desolate souls of earth one who deserves the charity of a merciful thought, that one is this doubly orphaned girl,—whose father died a rebel,—whose mother died on the scaffold,—whose brother is an outcast in every quarter of the civilized globe," the *Boston Daily Advertiser* had observed the day after Mary's execution.

Any support Anna received from her family went unnoticed by the press. Always, the newspaper stories mentioned "friends." Her brothers were nowhere to be found. The day her mother died, Anna found solace in the arms of Sister Blanche of St. Vincent's School. Eliza Holohan helped her clean up the house on H Street and stayed there with her.

On July 9, Anna wrote to General Hartranft:

> *Genl. Hancock told Mr. Holohan that you had some things that belonged to my poor Ma, which, with my consent sent you would deliver to him. Don't forget to send the pillow low upon which her head rested and her prayer beads, if you can find them—these things are dear to me. Someone told me that you wrote to the President stating that the Prisoner Payne had confessed to you*

the morning of the Execution that Ma was entirely innocent
of the President's assassination and had no knowledge of it.
Moreover, that he did not think that she had any knowledge of the
assassination plot, and that you believed that Payne had confessed
the truth. I would like to know if you did it because I wish to
remember and thank those who did Ma the least act of kindness.
I was spurned and treated with the utmost contempt by everyone
at the White House. Remember me to the officers who had charge
of Ma and I shall always think kindly of you.
Yours Respectfully—
Anna Surratt

A little more than a week following the execution, Anna received a package from General Hartranft—the contents of her mother's pockets at the time of her arrest. It was not much—a five-dollar bill, a small assortment of receipts and notes, two pocketknives, three keys, a gold watch ring, a thimble, and a scrap of red velvet containing a few needles. No sign of the precious pillow or beads.

That was a long and melancholy summer for Anna Surratt. "Her health has greatly improved within a week or two," a New York journal reported in early September, "although she is far from being the happy, joyous girl that she once was." Hundreds of friends had come to console her, the paper reported, but Anna sadly declined to see all but a few of them. Her grief was still too deep, too central, to allow her to be gracious company. "She never smiles, and the expression of her face is that of agony struggling with resignation." Only the solace of religion brought relief.

The deepest wound she bore was the thought of her mother's body lying under just a few feet of dirt in the prison yard. While Mary had still dangled from the noose, Anna's friends had appealed to General

Hancock for permission to receive her body for a proper Christian burial. According to the Washington *Constitutional Union*, Hancock "said he had no authority to grant the request" and referred the matter to the secretary of war, who in turn deferred to General Holt. Holt's reply had been curt and formal: "Request will be considered and at a proper time may be complied with, but not at present."

CHAPTER TWENTY-EIGHT

In late November 1866, John Surratt's name suddenly appeared in newspaper headlines. The papers were cautious at first—"Curious News, if True" said the *New York Herald*—but the news, however improbable it sounded, was indeed true. John Surratt had spent most of the last two years engaged in a sequence of events worthy of an adventure novel.

Immediately following the assassination, he fled Montreal and sheltered for three months in the rectory of a Catholic priest in Saint-Liboire, Quebec, until a servant peeking under the stove spied him and mistook him for a woman hiding in the priest's bedroom. Then, with the help of an assumed name and a flimsy disguise worthy of "Reverend Paine," John crossed the Atlantic to England, and eventually turned up in Italy, where he reinvented himself as "John Watson" and enlisted in a regiment of Zouaves at the Vatican. As if that were not improbable enough, a college acquaintance who also happened to be serving in the Ninth Company of Pontifical Zouaves recognized John and reported him to the authorities. John Surratt was promptly arrested on November 6, 1866, and sent to the prison at Velletri to await extradition to the United States.

Two days later, as he was being escorted from the prison, John requested permission to relieve himself at the latrine beside the gate. To the surprise of the corporal and six guards in charge of him, John grabbed hold of the rail and vaulted over the ledge. A fall of twenty or thirty feet landed him in "the filth from the barracks" that had piled up on the rocks beneath the privy. He survived the fall, cushioned by excrement, and scrambled off into the valley below with minor injuries as his dumbfounded captors watched.

John managed to evade capture and make his way 125 miles south to Naples, where he boarded a freighter bound for Alexandria, Egypt, on November 17. American authorities intercepted John Surratt in Alexandria. "I have nothing to say," John told the American consul who took him into custody. "I only want what is right."

⟿

Thanks to an Indiana man named Lambdin P. Milligan, John Surratt did get "what is right."

In 1866, the United States Supreme Court had ruled in *Ex parte Milligan* that subjecting civilians to military tribunals while civil courts are in operation is unconstitutional. Justice David Davis declared in his majority opinion that "martial law can never exist when the courts are open."

Justice Davis included a silent nod to Mary Surratt and her co-defendants, acknowledging that "during the late wicked Rebellion, the temper of the times did not allow that calmness in deliberation and discussion so necessary to a correct conclusion of a purely judicial question." The "correct conclusion" Davis alluded to was the new certainty that the accused conspirators should never have been tried before a military tribunal. The civil courts had been open during the conspiracy trial, and therefore subjecting Mary Surratt to a military trial had been a violation of her rights.

"The Constitution of the United States is a law for rulers and people, equally in war and in peace, and covers with the shield of its protection all classes of men, at all times, and under all circumstances," Davis wrote. Nothing had "more pernicious consequences" than the idea that the Constitution's protection does not apply during a crisis or emergency. Trial by jury, Justice Davis declared, "is a vital principle, underlying the whole administration of criminal justice."

This landmark decision guaranteed that, unlike his mother, John Surratt would be tried in a civil court before a jury of his peers.

The trial of John Surratt commenced on June 10, 1867, in the Criminal Court for the District of Columbia, the Honorable George P. Fisher presiding. John's defense team consisted of three high-profile attorneys: the father-and-son duo of Joseph H. Bradley Sr. and Joseph H. Bradley Jr., and Richard T. Merrick (the same Richard T. Merrick who had been forced to refuse Mary Surratt's request to defend her two years prior). Unlike his mother's lawyers, John's defense team had had months to review the prosecution's evidence and prepare to refute it. Selecting twelve jurors that were acceptable to both sides became a monumental task that consumed the entire first week of the proceedings, but it was duly accomplished.

For the next two months, those twelve men listened to hundreds of witnesses testify as to John Surratt's involvement with the Confederacy and his whereabouts in mid-April 1865.

Two people seemed to be on trial: John and Mary Surratt. "I have not come here for the purpose of proving that Mrs. Surratt was guilty, or that she was innocent, and I do not understand why that subject was lugged into this case in the mode that it has been," the prosecuting attorney complained. Nevertheless, a feeling pervaded that if John were convicted, it would somehow justify the verdict against his mother. "It is *Mrs. Surratt's ghost* vs. Stanton, Holt, Bingham, Andy Johnson, and others," as one New York paper put it.

In fact, the most historically significant aspect of this trial would *not* be what the public learned about John Surratt's alleged role in Lincoln's assassination. Instead, new information regarding the government's evidence against his mother took center stage. The questions the witnesses brought to light about how the government had obtained its strongest evidence against Mary Surratt would be little short of revelatory.

Many of the same witnesses who had appeared before the tribunal in 1865 now returned to the stand. Chief among them were John Lloyd and Louis Weichmann. But their testimony was not identical to what they had sworn to two years earlier.

Likely mindful of the weight of his prior testimony against the accused conspirators, John Lloyd was hesitant to revisit the same topics now. He was particularly reluctant to give testimony relating to Mary Surratt, preferring to avoid her altogether. "I do not wish to go into the examination of Mrs. Surratt, as she is not here to answer," he said when asked if he had seen his landlady a few hours before the assassination. He refused to answer "unless the court compels me." Judge Fisher did so.

Lloyd remained careful, answering the questions with a stubborn precision that stymied the prosecution. He did not relish the power his words could wield, and so refrained as best he could from handing the prosecution anything that might be used as a weapon against his former landlady. Even reminders that he had previously answered questions regarding Mrs. Surratt in court could not budge him. "I do not wish to state one solitary Word but what I am positive of," he declared. And due to the drinking he'd done that day, there was little he could be positive about.

Now John Lloyd was much more forthright about his condition on the afternoon of Abraham Lincoln's murder—the afternoon when Mary Surratt had dropped a package off at the tavern. He'd been so drunk, he testified, that he had not even wanted to talk to her.

"How long did she stay after this conversation?" Surratt's lawyer asked.

"That I do not remember. I went into the house, into my back room, and threw myself down on the lounge, and immediately turned sick from the effects of the liquor."

The defense wanted to make the "effects of the liquor" perfectly clear to the court, and this time, Lloyd gave direct answers to such questions. The impact on his mind was "very singular," Lloyd said. "It makes me forget many things that I would say." He was, he admitted, his own best customer at the tavern. Sick though he'd been that night, Lloyd had "no doubt" that he had taken more to drink after Mary Surratt had left, though he could not specifically remember doing so. "I was drinking very free," he explained. The morning following Booth and Herold's midnight visit, he "commenced drinking as soon as I got up" without giving a thought to what had passed the night before. When the authorities arrived with their questions and informed him that the president had indeed been murdered, just as Booth had said, Lloyd panicked. "After the soldiers told me, I did not know what to do or how to act," he told the jury.

When it came to his discussions with the authorities following his arrest, however, Lloyd became far more candid. Asked whether he'd been offered any rewards, he told the court that Detective Cottingham had promised him "that the Government would protect me in my property, &c, and see that I would return home."

Cottingham had offered no further incentives. Nor had he issued any ultimatums. But there had been another incident later, during Lloyd's incarceration at the Old Capitol Prison, that had not been at all aboveboard. One day a military officer summoned him, Lloyd told the jury. "He told me he wanted me to make a statement," Lloyd testified. He explained to the officer that he had already made a statement to Colonel Wells, "while the things were fresh in my memory," and that he could not hope to make a fuller statement than that. The officer's response was as unethical as it was ominous. Lloyd relayed, "His reply was that [my statement] was not full enough." When the officer asked Lloyd to confirm that he had heard a particular foreboding remark, Lloyd answered that he had never heard anyone say such a thing. The officer was incredulous. "'Why,' said he, 'I have seen it in the newspapers.'"

For several minutes the prosecution argued mightily to halt this line of questioning, only to fail. "Now, did he say any thing to you in the way of an offer of a reward, or use any threat towards you, for the purpose of getting you to make it fuller?" Mr. Merrick asked.

When Lloyd had failed to produce the information the officer had expected to hear, the man "jumped up very quick off his seat, as if very mad, and asked me if I knew what I was guilty of," Lloyd testified. "I said, under the circumstances, I did not. He says, 'You are guilty as an accessory, the punishment of which is death.'"

It was a stunning revelation. Here in open court, John Lloyd was accusing the government of coercion. Not only of coercion but of attempting to manufacture evidence based on newspaper reports rather than reality.

Louis Weichmann's attitude on the witness stand was just the opposite. Where John Lloyd had sought to diminish his role in the verdict
against Mary Surratt, Weichmann seemed intent on vindicating his
prior testimony against her. Everything he had testified to in 1865, he
repeated—and more. Now he swore under oath to all that he had told
the papers when the Brophy affair had exploded. For Weichmann, John
Surratt's trial seemed to be an opportunity to ensure that his version of
the story became part of the official record.

In Weichmann's mind, he had been "providentially thrown in the
way of [the conspirators]." God had assigned his purpose as "an instrument prepared to convict them." As such, it was imperative that every
last detail he could provide be made public.

☞

Unfortunately for Louis Weichmann, he was not the only person who
wanted to present a fuller picture of the evidence than had been given
in 1865.

John Holohan informed the court that anytime he had seen Weichmann and Atzerodt together, "they were always the same as friends
could be." In fact, on one occasion he had seen Atzerodt wearing
Weichmann's blue military coat and hat. On at least four occasions,
he had even seen Booth and Atzerodt and Weichmann conferring together. Holohan also refuted Weichmann's testimony regarding the
morning after the assassination.

"That morning at breakfast did Mr. Weichmann say to you and Mrs.
Surratt that he had his suspicions about this business, and was going
to the Government to state his suspicions about it?" the defense asked.

"No, sir; he made no such declaration at all," Holohan replied. Holohan had heard nothing of the kind. On the contrary, he said, he was the
one who had delivered Weichmann to the police.

Mary's niece Olivia Jenkins perfectly corroborated Holohan's recollections about the breakfast conversation, and also challenged almost every inch of Weichmann's testimony regarding her aunt's behavior on the night of the assassination. There had been no late-night visit by John Wilkes Booth, Miss Jenkins said—only a man from the navy yard who'd rung the bell at suppertime and left some newspapers for Miss Jenkins. It was Anna who had answered the door anyway, not Mary. The business about an agitated Mary shooing the young people off to bed early was contrary to her recollections, too. Miss Jenkins remembered being up until almost ten o'clock that night, later even than Weichmann himself.

"Tell these gentlemen whether or not you noticed any thing peculiar in Mrs. Surratt's manner or not," the defense attorney requested.

"No, sir," Miss Jenkins answered. "I noticed nothing; she seemed the same as usual. I did not notice any excitement at all."

And though Miss Jenkins had been in the parlor all evening, she had not heard Mary ask Weichmann to pray for her intentions. "You heard no such conversation?" John Surratt's lawyer repeated.

"No, sir," Miss Jenkins confirmed.

Honora Fitzpatrick's testimony also meshed with John Holohan's and Olivia Jenkins's as though they were all threads weaving through the same length of cloth. To her fell the additional task of refuting Weichmann's most damaging claim—that when the detectives had come knocking at 541 H Street in the wee hours of April 15, Mary Surratt had exclaimed to him, "For God's sake let them come in; I expected the house to be searched." Miss Fitzpatrick, who had been asleep beside her landlady, remembered a much calmer Mary instructing, "Mr. Weichmann, ask them to wait a few minutes, and I will open the door for them."

Mary Surratt's friends and relatives were not the only ones who found Louis Weichmann less than trustworthy. John T. Ford, who had been in the Carroll Annex with Weichmann for thirty-nine days, told the court that Weichmann's testimony before the military commission had "rather startled me" because it "contradict[ed] to such an extent his statements to me." James J. Gifford, also an inmate at Carroll in the spring of 1865, testified that he had witnessed a government officer threaten Weichmann with hanging "unless he testified to more than he had already stated."

And in a series of leading questions worthy of the conspiracy trial, the defense brought out Louis J. Carland's claim that Weichmann had been "very much troubled in his conscience about the testimony he had given at the trial."

According to the young man's recollections, Weichmann had asked Carland to accompany him to St. Aloysius Church one day in the spring or summer of 1865. "He said he wished to make a confession, for his mind was so burdened with what he had done that he had no peace," Carland testified.

"Did he say to you that he was going to confession to relieve his conscience?" John Surratt's lawyer asked.

"Yes, sir; he did."

"Did you say to him, 'That is not the right way, Mr. Weichmann; you had better go to a magistrate and make a statement under oath'?"

"I did."

"Do you remember his replying to you, 'I would take that course, if I were not afraid of being indicted for perjury'?"

"He did make that remark to me," Carland said, finally speaking for himself, "and I then asked him the particulars. He said that if he had been let alone and had been allowed to give his statement as he wanted to give it, it would have been quite a different affair with Mrs. Surratt from what it was." Carland did not mention any names of those who had pressured Weichmann, making reference only to "the parties who had charge of the military commission." That strongly suggested Holt, Bingham, or Burnett.

"Did he say to you that he had been obliged to swear to a statement that had been prepared for him, and that he was threatened with being charged as one of the conspirators unless he did so?" the defense attorney asked, unabashedly leading his witness.

"Yes, sir, he did," Carland replied, "that it was written out for him and he was threatened with prosecution as one of the conspirators if he did not swear to it."

If Carland was to be believed, Weichmann had revealed that in 1865 the authorities in the Carroll Annex had informed him that he'd been overheard talking in his sleep—not just talking but confessing—and that he was impelled to sign a record of the things he had confessed while unconscious. It would seem an utterly outlandish story, if not for Weichmann's May 1865 admission of having been "confused and terrified" by Colonel Burnett's questioning. Something distressing had indeed happened to Louis Weichmann at the hands of government officers, but he would never say for the record just what had taken place.

"I asked him why he should swear to it if he knew it was not true," Carland told the court. "He said part of it was true, but it did not contain all the points he could have given if he had been let alone." If "let alone," Weichmann allegedly would have told the authorities that on April 11, *he* had been the one to suggest borrowing Booth's carriage, and that Mary had not known Booth was in town at all. Further, at the close of their trip to Surrattsville on the afternoon of April 14, he and Mary Surratt had just set out for Washington when someone at the tavern called them back. In turning the buggy around, the spring broke. If not for the delay caused by the breakdown, Mary would not have remained in Surrattsville long enough to have seen John Lloyd at all.

After Weichmann disclosed all of this, Carland waited on the steps of St. Aloysius while Weichmann went inside, presumably to confession. Then the two men went to a nearby saloon, where Weichmann's mood turned morose. As Carland watched, still shocked by what he'd learned, Weichmann downed several drinks and then recited Hamlet's soliloquy on death while gazing down the barrel of a pistol.

It is almost too astonishing to believe. Yet one fact is inescapable. Every time Louis Weichmann had been challenged in some way, his story had grown. Colonel Burnett had frightened additional details out of him in 1865. John Brophy's accusations had provoked more yet following the execution. Now, in 1867, John Surratt's trial allowed Weichmann to put the final flourishes on his version. With every fresh revelation, Mary Surratt appeared more culpable. Which raises the question of whether Weichmann had been holding back information in hopes of protecting his landlady or had invented it to protect himself.

☞

Louis Weichmann and Mary Surratt were not on trial, however—only John Surratt was. And he was not found guilty. But neither was he found innocent.

When it came time to decide whether John had been collecting information on Union prisons in upstate New York, as the defense maintained, or had been outside Ford's Theatre in Washington, DC, coordinating the timing of the attack on Lincoln and Seward, as the prosecution contended, the jury could not agree. For every defense witness that had claimed to have seen John Surratt in Elmira, New York, the prosecution had produced three more people to swear that witness was a notorious liar. Then the process had reversed, with the defense summoning two or three or more witnesses to discredit anyone who'd testified to having seen John Surratt on the streets of Washington. The result was a seemingly endless spiral of contradictory testimony.

The jury split along predictable lines, with eight Northerners in favor of conviction and four Southerners voting for acquittal. The charge of murder ended in a mistrial. Unless a purely Northern-leaning jury could be assembled, there was almost no chance of convicting John Surratt for the murder of Abraham Lincoln, as Edward Carrington, the United States attorney for the District of Columbia, well knew. "There was a revulsion of feeling because of the execution of Mrs. Surratt," Carrington believed, "and it was scarcely possible to convict." He filed the case as *nolle prosequi,* formally abandoning any intent to pursue the murder charge against John Surratt.

Carrington was not willing to turn John loose just yet, however. In the months that followed, he successfully obtained two new indictments against John Surratt Jr. on charges of treason. Judge Fisher dismissed the first treason charge. He had no choice. By the time the indictments finally reached his docket in the summer of 1868, over three years had passed since the president had been assassinated, and District of Columbia law carried a two-year statute of limitations on every crime except fraud and murder. When the second treason indictment was put before a grand jury on November 5, 1868, it was returned marked *ignoramus*—"we ignore."

After nineteen months on the run and two years in prison, John Surratt Jr. was a free man.

CHAPTER TWENTY-NINE

Mary Surratt was dead, and her son was free. And still, the Surratt matter would not die down.

Near the end of John's trial, the nation jolted when his lawyer mentioned the clemency plea for Mary Surratt in court. No one outside the White House and the War Department had known that five of the nine commissioners had petitioned the president to show mercy to Mary Surratt. A greater jolt yet came when word broke that President Johnson himself claimed to have been unaware of the plea's existence.

As his secretary recalled, Johnson sent to the War Department for the records of the conspiracy trial as soon as he heard the news: "The President very emphatically declared that he had never before seen the recommendation."

"A careful scrutiny convinced me that it was not with the record when submitted for my approval, and that I had neither before seen nor read it," Johnson himself would write in 1873.

"He distinctly remembered the great reluctance with which he approved the death warrant of a woman of Mrs. Surratt's age," the president's secretary would later reveal, "and that he asked Judge Advocate Genl. Holt, who originally brought to him the papers, many questions, but that nothing whatever was said to him respecting the recommendation of the Commission for clemency in her case."

Johnson did acknowledge that he and Holt had discussed the advisability of putting a woman to death, but the president remained adamant that no mention of a recommendation for mercy had been made during their two- or three-hour meeting. Further, Johnson's secretary would report that the president "felt satisfied that it had been designedly withheld from his knowledge." Shortly thereafter, "an unequivocal denial" from the president appeared in the papers, disavowing himself of any knowledge of the clemency petition.

Judge Advocate General Holt was horrified. The president of the United States had accused him of deliberately thwarting the commission's attempt to save Mary Surratt's life, as if Holt had taken the law—and with it, the power of life and death—into his own hands. Rumors even circulated in the papers that the stack of court documents, bound with a length of ribbon or tape threaded through eyelet holes at the top of each page, showed evidence of tampering. The eyelets punched into the clemency plea were larger, one report went, which suggested the page had been added to the record later.

"A more groundless calumny was never conceived or proclaimed against any public officer," Holt fumed.

Efforts to exonerate himself from this mortifying charge would consume General Holt for the rest of his life. For the next twenty-seven years, he lived in constant dread of reaching the moment of his death "darkened by a consciousness that this cloud, or even a shred of it, is still hanging over me."

A dozen officers of the government knew about the clemency plea—so many, Holt said, that any attempt to withhold the document from Johnson would have amounted to "a stupidity on my part verging upon idiotcy [sic]."

For proof, Holt offered up a barrage of evidence in a thirteen-page

Vindication pamphlet. First, a letter from Congressman Bingham. Bingham had drafted the clemency plea with his own hand, and hearing the rumors against General Holt, he spoke with Secretary Seward and Secretary Stanton. Both assured Bingham that the plea had been "duly considered" by Johnson and his cabinet before the president had signed Mary Surratt's death warrant. At Holt's request, James Speed, who had been the attorney general at the time, also verified in writing that he had seen the document at a cabinet meeting. And James Harlan, who had served as secretary of the interior, wrote to Holt confirming that he "distinctly" remembered the question of clemency being discussed by at least three cabinet members in Johnson's presence. Either Stanton or Seward had advised the president against commuting the sentence, Harlan said, telling Johnson that "it would amount to an invitation to assassins hereafter to employ women as their chief instruments."

Holt also presented the word of a clergyman, Reverend J. G. Butler of St. Paul's Lutheran Church, who recalled having a conversation with the president on the very evening following the execution. The pastor recalled President Johnson speaking "without reserve" of the "earnest appeal" for mercy on behalf of Mrs. Surratt. The president had made his belief in her guilt abundantly clear, "in terms as forceful as figurative," Reverend Butler wrote to Holt.

And finally, Holt procured a statement from the chief clerk of the Bureau of Military Justice. The clerk explained that because of the way the sheaf of court documents had been fastened together, "[Johnson's] eye necessarily fell" on the clemency petition as he signed the death warrants. All the other sheets in the stack were one-sided, except Mary's death sentence, which ran over to the back. As the president turned that page over to affix his signature at the bottom, he must have seen that there was one final page in the stack—the clemency plea.

Holt's evidence did not faze Andrew Johnson in the slightest. As far as the president was concerned, Holt's evidence was nothing but a snarl of contradictions. If he and Holt had met privately to discuss the commission's findings, for example, how could so many cabinet members have known about the plea? And if the document had been there all along, why hadn't it been included in the official government-sponsored publication of the complete records of the trial in 1865?

Ultimately, the controversy would never be resolved. Only one thing was clear: neither of the two men wanted Mary Surratt's blood on his hands.

While the rest of the nation was largely content to lay the Mary Surratt case to rest, one man quietly labored to ensure that those who did remember it would do so in a very particular light. That man, of course, was Louis Weichmann.

In 1887, Weichmann wrote to Secretary of War Stanton's biographer, anxious to learn how he himself might be portrayed in the section dealing with the conspiracy trial. The public's changing perception of the whole affair in the intervening years had given Weichmann much cause for concern. Left-leaning newspapers had "hounded" him, Weichmann claimed, simply for telling the truth. If he appeared in Stanton's biography, he wanted "fair credit for duty performed." To Weichmann's immense satisfaction, the resulting volume was favorable to both Edwin Stanton and General Holt, and omitted Weichmann entirely. "Every step in the direction of truth and justice, now-a-days, counts," Weichmann wrote to his old friend Holt of his success.

Five years later came the publication of *Assassination of Lincoln* by T. M. Harris—the very same General Harris who had objected to Reverdy Johnson's presence at the conspiracy trial. This work carried an additional weight of authority. Who could write a more reliable account of the trial than a man who had been present every day at the commissioners' table, who'd heard every word of testimony directly from the witnesses' mouths?

What the public did not know was that the chapter on Mary Surratt was essentially ghostwritten by none other than Louis Weichmann. After initiating a correspondence with the general and offering to share information to aid in research, Weichmann earned Harris's trust as well as the task of writing the portion of the manuscript he most coveted.

"So earnest and persistent have been the efforts of rebel priests, politicians and editors to pervert public opinion in regard to the case of Mrs. Surratt that it becomes necessary to devote some special consideration to it even at the expense of some repetition," the chapter began. "Immediately after her execution a wild howl was set up by these people for the purpose of making political capital out of the sympathy and tender feeling which we all have for her sex."

Under the cloak of Harris's name, Weichmann asserted that Mary's supporters had lied and suppressed evidence, and that all who had done so were "enemies of the government." He scoffed at John Lloyd's drunkenness and erased the contradictions and confusion of the officers who'd arrested Mary Surratt. The points of evidence most favorable to his position were elevated to the level of facts, so that in Weichmann's version, everything Mary had done was unambiguously suspicious. The combination of his testimony and Lloyd's was "completely conclusive of the guilt" of both Mary and her son, he declared, omitting any gray areas or uncertainty that might have perplexed Harris's readers. When evidence from John Surratt's trial bolstered his point of view, Weichmann included it. When it did not, he ignored it.

The effort to turn Mary Surratt into a false martyr "has never been abandoned," Weichmann warned, "and the case of Mrs. Surratt continues to be worked for all that it is worth by that portion of the Northern press that inherits the old copperhead animus."

Weichmann carried on using Harris's name as a cover for his own opinions even after the general's book was published. When a *Washington Post* article offended Weichmann in the summer of 1901 by claiming he'd said that Mary Surratt was innocent, Weichmann retaliated with an article in his own defense. But Louis Weichmann did not sign the article himself. Instead it was submitted in the name of General Harris. "I think it is a great deal better that this should have been over the signature of a high officer of the commission than over mine," he confessed to yet another assassination historian, Osborn Oldroyd, that same August. "It has more weight." Weichmann pulled the same sleight of hand in September, when a *Chicago Post* article accused him of perjury. For the second time General Harris appeared to rush to Weichmann's defense. In reality, the elderly general wrote only the first paragraph of the rebuttal. The rest of the article was Weichmann's handiwork.

Meanwhile, Weichmann had befriended Osborn Oldroyd for the same reason he'd sought out General Harris. In 1901, Oldroyd published *The Assassination of Abraham Lincoln*. Yet again, Weichmann had ingratiated himself with the author and succeeded in ghostwriting chapter 9 of Oldroyd's history. It was titled simply "Louis J. Weichman [*sic*]." Weichmann wanted no acknowledgment for his contribution. "It must appear as if coming from yourself," he wrote to Oldroyd.

Consequently, Weichmann had free rein to portray himself as the picture of innocence. Regarding the arrival of "Reverend Paine," for instance, Oldroyd's book declared that Louis Weichmann "had never seen him before, did not know him, and he might just as readily have dropped from the clouds of heaven or from anywhere else for all he knew." Weichmann saw to it that not one speck of fault fell upon him, or even near him.

He also took the opportunity to make sure that the public knew just how much he had sacrificed for the sake of duty. "Probably no one has suffered more persecution and misrepresentation because of his testimony and his duty to the Government at the trial of the conspirators than has Mr. Weichmann. It has been almost continuous, and has been done for the purpose of striking him down and disparaging him before the country, so that the people who were in sympathy with the conspirators could claim that the Commission was wrong in its verdict of 1865." As far as Louis Weichmann was concerned, *he* was the victim.

Weichmann would go on to write his own history of the assassination, incorporating his previous contributions to Harris's and Oldroyd's works into his manuscript. "I am egotist enough to think that I have written the best and most complete history of this subject, better than any which has yet been given out to the public." The book, however, would not be published in his own lifetime.

In the end, Weichmann did achieve a measure of the influence he'd sought. Those who would read about Mary Surratt in decades to come would not have access to original evidence files or court transcripts. His manipulation of the history of the assassination trial would not come to light for over a century.

And yet for all his efforts to exonerate himself, Louis Weichmann never found peace. As years passed, his friends would desert him. His marriage would fail. More than once he appealed to General Holt for financial assistance. Eventually he left Philadelphia and moved to Anderson, Indiana, where he opened a small business school and taught shorthand, typing, accounting, and a sampling of the eight languages he spoke. Talk in Anderson was that Weichmann refused to sit with his back to a door and hated to venture out at night. The specter of Mary Surratt always remained just over his shoulder.

CHAPTER THIRTY

Unlike Louis Weichmann and General Holt, Anna Surratt wanted to put the ordeal and all its horrors to rest. Nearly four years passed before Andrew Johnson saw fit to honor Anna's request to claim her mother's body. In early February 1869, she finally received permission to exhume Mary's remains from the arsenal yard.

By three o'clock the next afternoon, Mary Surratt's shallow grave had been opened. When unearthed, the pine box Mary had been buried in was found to be "in tolerable condition." As was the custom of the era, the undertaker lifted the lid so that Anna could see her mother's face once more. The sight that greeted her is difficult to describe, not so much because gazing upon a four-year-old corpse is unimaginable to people in the twenty-first century but because the accounts differ so widely. According to the Philadelphia *Press*, Mary's remains "were in an excellent state of preservation." Her face had reportedly turned black, yet still looked "perfect in feature." The rest of her body had also resisted decay, being "compact and firm." The *Evening Star*, on the other hand, described the contents of the coffin as "much decomposed, there being but little flesh remaining."

In either case, Anna's arrow pin still gleamed in the black silk bow beneath Mary's chin, just where Anna had fastened it as she'd bidden her mother goodbye. Mary's dress and shoes were in fine shape, and her hair was in a state of "perfect preservation." At the family's request, the undertaker snipped a lock of Mary's hair as a memento. Then he gently placed the coffin in his wagon so as not to shift its contents, and drove to Mount Olivet Cemetery, where Mary's body was transferred from its pine box to "a handsome walnut coffin."

The next day, Father Walter presided over a burial service "conducted with the strictest privacy," laying Mary to rest in a piece of consecrated ground donated by sympathetic cemetery officials. Honora Fitzpatrick, who had boarded at Mary's home and testified on her behalf, was one of the select few who attended. John Brophy had been invited as well.

Thereafter, "unseen hands" kept her grave "constantly covered with flowers." No stone was placed until 1875, when a local sexton arranged for a marble marker reading only "Mrs. Surratt."

EPILOGUE

Over 150 years after Mary Surratt's death, debate still rages. The question of Mary's involvement in the conspiracy to murder Abraham Lincoln has never been definitively answered. In the years immediately following her execution, the nation's collective horror at her death transformed her into a martyr. When President Johnson pardoned Samuel Arnold, Samuel Mudd, and Edman Spangler (Michael O'Laughlen had died of yellow fever in prison) just three and a half years after their conviction, Mary Surratt's execution stood out in even starker relief. The tide of public opinion would shift yet again by the end of the twentieth century, mirroring the sentiments at the time of her trial.

Since 1865, novels, plays, and a film have attempted to fill the tantalizing gaps in the historical record. But the true Mary Surratt remains a mystery.

The house on H Street still stands, in what has since become the Chinatown neighborhood of Washington, DC; it has been home to the Wok and Roll restaurant for many years.

In 1870, John Surratt embarked on a lecture tour to regale audiences with his thrilling adventures. But his first performance, glib and scattered with sly insults aimed at the police who had failed to catch him, incited a public outcry. The *New York World* condemned him for "making his living by hawking his mother's corpse," and attendance promptly withered. ("No wonder the New York editors do not like to hear of Mrs. Surratt," a Southern newspaper wryly remarked, "for each and almost every one of them aided and abetted in the 'hanging of a woman.' They do not like to be called 'lady killers.'") When news broke that John had booked Lincoln Hall as his Washington venue, outrage boiled so high that authorities feared John's presence in the capital might endanger public safety. So a US deputy marshal arrested him in Baltimore on a pretext (two years earlier John had done business as a tobacco dealer without paying the proper licensing fee) to ensure that the lecture tour would proceed no further. After paying a $1,500 bail, he discovered that even Richmond, the former capital of the Confederacy, had no taste for his "brazen-faced impudence," and a chastened John permanently retreated from public life.

He taught school, married, and fathered seven children. Until his death in 1916, he worked quietly as the treasurer of the Baltimore Steam Packet Company, a Chesapeake Bay steamship firm that ferried passengers from Baltimore to Norfolk.

John Surratt professed incredulity over his mother's hanging for the rest of his life. "Knowing that she was entirely innocent of any connection with the so-called conspiracy, though her sympathies were undeniably with the Confederacy, I could not imagine she was in any danger," he said in 1901. "I did not then dream of the intense bitterness and prejudice that was manifested in her trial."

Anna Surratt married a chemist named William Tonry on June 18, 1869. In an odd quirk of fate, Anna's husband's office was located in the former Ford's Theatre building where Lincoln had been shot. Four days after the wedding, Professor Tonry was promptly fired from his position in the surgeon general's office, presumably due to his connection with the disgraced name of Surratt. The couple moved to Baltimore, where they raised three sons and a daughter (another child died in infancy or early childhood).

In 1904, Anna died at age sixty-one. Her obituary in the *Washington Post* noted that "she had been an invalid for several years." No cause of death was given. She was always viewed as a fragile and emotional woman, so it is easy to suppose that the anguish Anna had endured in 1865 had remained with her always, cutting her life short. Devoted even in death, she was buried beside her mother.

AUTHOR'S NOTE

To my way of thinking, nothing plays a more vital role in piecing together the story of Mary Surratt than chronology. The fact that information emerged so gradually, and under an array of circumstances ranging from voluntary to possibly coerced (or, as one Surratt scholar put it, with witnesses "testifying with ropes around their necks"), makes it necessary to consider not only the evidence itself but, just as critically, who provided it, and when, and why. What motivated some witnesses to share information freely and others to withhold it for weeks, months, or years?

Those questions have made me even more judicious than usual about which sources I've chosen to trust, as well as about the manner in which I've chosen to quote from them. In particular, I've taken care to draw deliberate distinctions between what is known to have happened and what a witness *said* happened. Memory is fallible, and even the most honorably intentioned of witnesses can make mistakes.

The Lincoln Assassination: The Rewards Files proved surprisingly useful. The statements in this volume, submitted by those who aided in the capture of the conspirators and hoped to win a portion of the $100,000 reward, are told in the claimants' own words and allow their voices to emerge in a way that is often not possible in court. Though most of the statements date from the months immediately following the conspiracy trial rather than from the April 1865 investigation, they are nevertheless sprinkled with details that lend greater depth and reality to the telling. This became my main source for the dialogue during Mary's arrest, as well as during the apprehension of John Wilkes Booth.

It is wise to keep in mind that, with the exception of her interrogations and her letters to Father Finotti, Mary Surratt's words are all secondhand, filtered through the memories of both friends and foes. Who would more faithfully recall her words: Anna Surratt, Louis Weichmann, or arresting officer Major Smith, for instance?

Last of all, I have approached Louis Weichmann's posthumous memoir (*A True History of the Assassination of Abraham Lincoln and of the Conspiracy of 1865,* edited by Floyd E. Risvold) with special caution, primarily relying on it to enliven scenes with additional color and atmosphere—such as the specific title of the book Weichmann was reading on the afternoon of the assassination.

A WORD ABOUT COURTROOM DIALOGUE

None of the dialogue in this book is invented. Everything in quotation marks appears in printed transcripts, books, articles, or archival documents.

Nevertheless, it may come as a surprise to some Lincoln scholars that I have chosen to quote from Benjamin Perley Poore's transcription of the conspiracy trial rather than the "official" version published by chief phonographer Benn Pitman. Though Pitman's 1865 account of the trial, *The Assassination of President Lincoln and the Trial of the Conspirators,* earned the hearty endorsements of Stanton, Holt, and Burnett, his is not in fact a verbatim transcript—far from it. For the convenience of the reading public, Pitman rearranged the entire structure of the trial, gathering all the scattered evidence regarding each prisoner into eight separate sections. He also largely dispensed with the question-and-answer format, omitting the bulk of the lawyers' questions and stringing the witnesses' answers into long paragraphs that read like the narration in a novel. It is as if each witness stepped onto the stand and recited a chapter of the story without the slightest reluctance, hesitation, or prompting. Pitman's version, therefore, is not so much a transcript as a summary. His alterations stripped away the natural push and pull of examinations and cross-examinations, imbuing the testimony with an air of confidence and certainty that the witnesses often did not possess. In my opinion, the Pitman version thus represents a highly skewed version of reality.

Poore, by contrast, is a true word-for-word transcript, painstakingly compiled from the full phonographers' records that were printed each day of the trial in the *National Intelligencer*. Only Poore makes it possible to see how, when, and in what manner the evidence was revealed in real time, conveyed in the actual words spoken in the courtroom. Poore's version is not without its own flaws, however. His introduction is marred with superficial errors. Worse, the third volume abruptly ends partway through the events of June 13 (possibly due to a printer's error), leaving out the testimony of six witnesses on that day, as well as every witness who testified on June 14, 16, 23, and 27, and the closing arguments of both the prosecution and the defense. Thankfully, Mike Stewart took on the task of tracking down the four and a half missing days of testimony from the columns of the *National Intelligencer* and appending them to the existing Poore version in his own 2015 digital edition of the transcript. For the closing arguments, I had no choice but to fall back on the Pitman version, most recently edited by Edward Steers.

The first two volumes of Poore's transcripts are available free online at the Library of Congress: loc.gov/item/05023015.

Transcripts of John Surratt's trial are also available in the Library of Congress's free digital collection (note that they are somewhat confusingly labeled Volume III and Volume IV—these are the volume numbers of the law journal that printed them serially between June and September 1867): loc.gov/item/34015158.

ACKNOWLEDGMENTS

Thanks to:

Christopher Czajka, for his serendipitous January 2020 trip to the Surratt House Museum. The dozens of photos he took there came to my rescue when COVID-19 restrictions thwarted any chances for a research trip of my own.

Colleen Puterbaugh, collections manager of the Surratt House Museum, for patiently answering questions, emailing finding aids, and searching for documents in the James O. Hall Research Center.

Jerry and Marilyn Zaetta, for access to their personal collection of Lincoln assassination literature.

And finally, a nod to Grand Valley State University's Seidman House and its near-complete collection of Surratt Society Newsletters, donated by Harvey Lemmen. Accessing that information during the first weeks of 2020 was a stroke of purest luck.

SOURCES

TRANSCRIPTS

Poore, Ben[jamin] Perley, ed. *The Conspiracy Trial for the Murder of the President, and the Attempt to Overthrow the Government by the Assassination of Its Principal Officers.* 2 vols. Boston: J. E. Tilton, 1865. archive.org/details/conspiracytrialf00poor.

Stewart, Mike, ed. *The Lincoln Assassination Conspiracy Trial Transcripts.* Vol. III. Self-published, 2015. Kindle.

"Trial of John H. Surratt." In *The Reporter: A Periodical Devoted to Religion, Law, Legislation, and Public Events.* Published serially from vol. III, no. 47 (June 17, 1867) through vol. IV, no. 103 (September 24, 1867). Washington, DC: M'Gill & Witherow, Printers and Stereotypers, 1867. loc.gov/item/34015158.

BOOKS

Arnold, Samuel Bland. *Defence and Prison Experiences of a Lincoln Conspirator.* Hattiesburg, MS: Book Farm, 1943.

Baker, L. C. *History of the United States Secret Service.* Philadelphia: L. C. Baker, 1867.

Buckingham, J. E., Sr. *Reminiscences and Souvenirs of the Assassination of Abraham Lincoln.* Washington, DC: Press of Rufus H. Darby, 1894.

Burnett, Henry L. "The Controversy Between President Johnson and Judge Holt." In *Personal Recollections of the War of the Rebellion,* edited by James Grant Wilson and Titus Munson Coan, 211–234. New York: Commandery, 1891.

Burnett, Henry L. "Some Incidents in the Trial of President Lincoln's Assassins." In

Personal Recollections of the War of the Rebellion, edited by James Grant Wilson and Titus Munson Coan, 183–210. New York: Commandery, 1891.

Busch, Francis X. *Enemies of the State.* London: Arco Publications, 1954.

Chamlee, Roy Z., Jr. *Lincoln's Assassins: A Complete Account of Their Capture, Trial, and Punishment.* Jefferson, NC: McFarland, 1990.

Clarke, Asia Booth. *The Unlocked Book: A Memoir of John Wilkes Booth by His Sister Asia Booth Clarke.* New York: G. P. Putnam's Sons, 1938.

Colby, Colonel N. T. "The Old Capitol Prison." In *The Annals of the War Written by Leading Participants North and South,* edited by A. K. McClure. Philadelphia: Times Publishing, 1879.

Crook, William H. *Through Five Administrations: Reminiscences of Colonel William H. Crook, Body-Guard to President Lincoln.* Edited by Margarita Spalding Gerry. New York: Harper and Brothers, 1910.

DeWitt, David Miller. *The Judicial Murder of Mary E. Surratt.* Baltimore: John Murphy, 1894.

Doster, William E. *Lincoln and Episodes of the Civil War.* New York: G. P. Putnam's Sons, 1915.

Douglas, Henry Kyd. *I Rode with Stonewall.* Chapel Hill: University of North Carolina Press, 1940.

Edwards, William C., ed. *The Lincoln Assassination: The Rewards Files.* Self-published, Google Books, 2012.

Edwards, William C., and Edward Steers Jr., eds. *The Lincoln Assassination: The Evidence.* Urbana: University of Illinois Press, 2009.

Forney, John W. *Life and Military Career of Winfield Scott Hancock.* Boston: W. H. Thompson, 1880.

Harris, T. M. *Assassination of Lincoln: A History of the Great Conspiracy.* Boston: American Citizen, 1892.

Harrison, Burton, Mrs. *Recollections Grave and Gay.* New York: Charles Scribner's Sons, 1912.

Holt, Joseph. *Vindication of Hon. Joseph Holt, Judge Advocate General of the United States Army.* Washington, DC: Chronicle Publishing, 1873.

Hoyt, Harlowe Randall. *Town Hall Tonight.* Englewood Cliffs, NJ: Prentice-Hall, 1955.

Jones, Rebecca C. *The Mystery of Mary Surratt: The Plot to Kill President Lincoln.* Centreville, MD: Tidewater Publishers, 2004.

Kauffman, Michael W. *American Brutus: John Wilkes Booth and the Lincoln Conspiracies.* New York: Random House, 2004.

Larson, Kate Clifford. *The Assassin's Accomplice.* New York: Basic Books, 2008.

Leale, Charles A. *Lincoln's Last Hours: Address Delivered Before the Commandery of the State of New York Military Order of the Loyal Legion of the United States.* New York: Estate of C. A. Leale, 1909.

Lewis, Lloyd. *Myths After Lincoln.* New York: Harcourt, Brace, 1929.

Lomax, Virginia. *The Old Capitol and Its Inmates.* New York: E. J. Hale and Son, 1867.

Marshall, John A. *American Bastile.* Philadelphia: Thomas W. Hartley, 1884.

Moore, Guy W. *The Case of Mrs. Surratt: Her Controversial Trial and Execution for Conspiracy in the Lincoln Assassination.* Norman: University of Oklahoma Press, 1954.

Oldroyd, Osborn H. *The Assassination of Abraham Lincoln.* Washington, DC: O. H. Oldroyd, 1901.

Ownsbey, Betty J. *Alias "Paine": Lewis Thornton Powell, the Mystery Man of the Lincoln Conspiracy.* Jefferson, NC: McFarland, 2015.

Porter, Mary W. *The Surgeon in Charge.* Concord, NH: Rumford Press, 1949.

Roscoe, Theodore. *The Web of Conspiracy: The Complete Story of the Men Who Murdered Abraham Lincoln.* Upper Saddle River, NJ: Prentice-Hall, 1959.

Smoot, Richard Mitchell. *The Unwritten History of the Assassination of Abraham Lincoln.* Clinton, MA: Press of W. J. Coulter, 1908.

Steers, Edward, Jr. *Blood on the Moon: The Assassination of Abraham Lincoln.* Lexington: University Press of Kentucky, 2001.

Steers, Edward, Jr. *The Lincoln Assassination Encyclopedia.* New York: HarperCollins, 2010.

Steers, Edward, Jr., ed. *The Trial: The Assassination of President Lincoln and the Trial of the Conspirators.* Lexington: University Press of Kentucky, 2003.

Steers, Edward, Jr., and Harold Holzer, eds. *The Lincoln Assassination Conspirators: Their Confinement and Execution, as Recorded in the Letterbook of John Frederick Hartranft.* Baton Rouge: Louisiana State University Press, 2009.

Steiner, Bernard C. *The Life of Reverdy Johnson.* Baltimore: Norman, Remington, 1914.

Swanson, James L. *Manhunt: The 12-Day Chase for Lincoln's Killer.* New York: William Morrow, 2006.

Townsend, George Alfred. *The Life, Crime, and Capture of John Wilkes Booth.* New York: Dick and Fitzgerald, 1865.

The Trial of the Alleged Assassins and Conspirators at Washington City, D.C., May and June, 1865 : for the Murder of President Abraham Lincoln. Philadelphia: T. B. Peterson and Brothers, 1865.

Trindal, Elizabeth Steger. *Mary Surratt: An American Tragedy.* Gretna, LA: Pelican Publishing, 1996.

Wallace, Lew. *Lew Wallace: An Autobiography.* New York: Harper and Brothers, 1906.

Weichmann, Louis J. *A True History of the Assassination of Abraham Lincoln and of the Conspiracy of 1865.* Edited by Floyd E. Risvold. New York: Knopf, 1975.

Zanca, Kenneth J. *The Catholics and Mrs. Mary Surratt.* Lanham, MD: University Press of America, 2008.

NOTES

EPIGRAPH

Let the rest: Mary Surratt to Father Finotti, January 15, 1855, in Joseph George Jr., "'A True Childe of Sorrow.' Two Letters of Mary E. Surratt," *Maryland Historical Magazine* 80, no. 4 (Winter 1985): 404. (Note: spelling has been corrected from the original.)

The living can: John T. Ford, "Behind the Curtain of a Conspiracy," *North American Review* 148, no. 389 (April 1889): 493.

CHAPTER ONE

"very violently" through **"Let us in anyhow":** Louis J. Weichmann in "Trial of John H. Surratt," vol. III, no. 63, 4.

"Mrs. Surratt, there are": Louis J. Weichmann, quoted by Honora Fitzpatrick, in "Trial of John H. Surratt," vol. IV, no. 76, 8.

"Mr. Weichmann, ask them": Mary Surratt, quoted by Honora Fitzpatrick, in "Trial of John H. Surratt," vol. IV, no. 76, 8.

"For God's sake, let them": Mary Surratt, quoted by Louis J. Weichmann, in "Trial of John H. Surratt," vol. III, no. 63, 4.

"For God's sake, gentlemen": Louis J. Weichmann in "Trial of John H. Surratt," vol. III, no. 63, 4.

"Do you pretend to" and **"I will tell you":** John Clarvoe, quoted by Louis J. Weichmann, in "Trial of John H. Surratt," vol. III, no. 63, 4.

"What do you think": Louis J. Weichmann in "Trial of John H. Surratt," vol. III, no. 63, 4.

"Oh, my God, Mr. Weichmann": Mary Surratt, quoted by Louis J. Weichmann, in "Trial of John H. Surratt," vol. III, no. 63, 4.

CHAPTER TWO

"This reminds me": Kauffman, *American Brutus,* 224.

"vociferous cheering": Henry R. Rathbone in Poore, *Conspiracy Trial,* vol. I, 196.

"Mrs. Lincoln rested": Charles Sabin Taft, "Abraham Lincoln's Last Hours," *Century Magazine* 45 (February 1893): 634–36.

"I heard the discharge": Henry R. Rathbone in Poore, *Conspiracy Trial,* vol. I, 196.

"Sic semper tyrannis!": John Deveney in Poore, vol. I, 37; James P. Ferguson in Poore, vol. I, 191; Isaac G. Jacquette in Edwards and Steers, *Lincoln Assassination: The Evidence,* 741.

"Revenge for the South!": James P. Ferguson in Poore, vol. I, 192.

"Stop that man!": Henry R. Rathbone in Poore, vol. I, 196.

"I told him" through **"When he went up"**: William H. Bell in Poore, vol. I, 472–74.

"He's asleep" and **"Fred, Father is awake now"**: Kauffman, *American Brutus,* 22.

"He made the impression" and **"It is not worth while"**: Frederick W. Seward in "Trial of John H. Surratt," vol. III, no. 57, 3.

"Well, if I cannot": Lewis Powell, quoted by William H. Bell, in Poore, *Conspiracy Trial,* vol. I, 472–73.

"Don't walk so heavy": William H. Bell in Poore, vol. I, 473.

"There was no time" and **"I remember noticing"**: Frederick W. Seward in "Trial of John H. Surratt," vol. III, no. 57, 3.

"hallooing 'Murder!' ": William H. Bell in Poore, *Conspiracy Trial,* vol. I, 473.

"As soon as I could": George F. Robinson in Poore, vol. I, 480.

"But immediately on taking" through **"On reaching the hall"**: Augustus H. Seward in Poore, vol. II, 6.

"I am not dead": "The Attack upon Secretary Seward," Washington *Evening Star,* April 18, 1865; see also Kauffman, *American Brutus,* 26.

"beseeching me to attend to his wound" through **"Then a feeble action"**: Leale, *Lincoln's Last Hours,* 4–6.

CHAPTER THREE

"Send here immediately": Swanson, *Manhunt*, 114.

"undertaking" through "Sam": Poore, *Conspiracy Trial*, vol. I, 420–21.

"hit me on the face" and "For God's sake": Jacob Ritterspaugh in Poore, vol. II, 461.

"evil disposed persons": April 16, 1865, report of John Lee in Edwards and Steers, *Lincoln Assassination: The Evidence*, 798.

"villainous-looking fellow": April 16, 1865, report of John Lee in Edwards, *Rewards Files*, 256–57; see also Edwards and Steers, 799.

"could be identified" and "My firm conviction": April 16, 1865, report of John Lee in Edwards and Steers, 798.

"Coming back he spoke" and "Your acquaintance is staying": April 23, 1865, statement of John Fletcher in Edwards and Steers, 513.

"I would not like to ride": John Fletcher in Poore, *Conspiracy Trial*, vol. I, 328.

"Well, she is good": George A. Atzerodt, quoted by John Fletcher, in Poore, vol. I, 328.

"there was something wrong" and "He apparently saw me": April 23, 1865, statement of John Fletcher in Edwards and Steers, *Lincoln Assassination: The Evidence*, 513.

"You get off that horse": John Fletcher in Poore, *Conspiracy Trial*, vol. I, 328–29.

"taken up any horse": May 3, 1865, statement of John Fletcher in Edwards, *Rewards Files*, 220.

"John is not": Mary Surratt, quoted by John Clarvoe, in "Trial of John H. Surratt," vol. IV, no. 75, 10.

"Mrs. Surratt, I want": John Clarvoe in "Trial of John H. Surratt," vol. IV, no. 74, 14.

"That was a night": "Tragic Memories," Washington *Evening Star*, April 14, 1894.

"As fast as we could" through "Mark you, this was": "Tragic Memories," Washington *Evening Star*, April 14, 1894.

"Secretary Seward and both": Chamlee, *Lincoln's Assassins*, 11.

"A shock from heaven": Horatio King, "The Assassination of President Lincoln," *New England Magazine*, December 1893.

"Washington was a little delirious": Crook, *Through Five Administrations*, 64–65.

"This is terrible, awful horrible": Kauffman, *American Brutus*, 11.

"No person, not present": King, "Assassination of President Lincoln."

"just like a cat": James P. Ferguson in Poore, *Conspiracy Trial*, vol. I, 190.

CHAPTER FOUR

"He who had for years" and "Thank God! thank God!": Weichmann, *True History*, 179–80.

"state of great excitement" through "rode out with Booth often": Undated report of Lieutenant Colonel Foster regarding Louis J. Weichmann in Edwards and Steers, *Lincoln Assassination: The Evidence*, 1323.

"rather considered it" through "familiar with the tinsel": Weichmann, *True History*, 103.

"Mrs. Surratt some time": Undated letter of Louis J. Weichmann to Colonel Burnett in Edwards and Steers, *Lincoln Assassination: The Evidence*, 1320.

"scarcely audible": Louis J. Weichmann in Poore, *Conspiracy Trial*, vol. I, 97.

"but more in the direction" and "frequently": Louis J. Weichmann in Poore, vol. I, 71–72.

"John, can you": John Wilkes Booth, quoted by Louis J. Weichmann, in Poore, vol. I, 72.

"either a blockade-runner": Louis J. Weichmann in Poore, vol. I, 80.

"agitated the question" and "I thought it would": Louis J. Weichmann in Poore, vol. I, 381.

"notorious rebel": April 30, 1865, statement of Louis J. Weichmann to W. P. Wood in Edwards and Steers, *Lincoln Assassination: The Evidence*, 1318.

"to become a good": Louis J. Weichmann in Poore, *Conspiracy Trial*, vol. I, 77.

"One of the young": Louis J. Weichmann in Poore, vol. I, 109.

"he was a great looking": Louis J. Weichmann in Poore, vol. I, 77.

"I thought it rather queer" and "I put on a pair": Louis J. Weichmann in Poore, vol. I, 90.

"from the appearance of things" and "The moment the door": Weichmann, *True History*, 97–98.

"took up a sword": Louis J. Weichmann in Poore, *Conspiracy Trial*, vol. I, 107.

"playfully wrested": Weichmann, *True History*, 98.

"No, you are not": John H. Surratt, quoted by Louis J. Weichmann, in "Trial of John H. Surratt," vol. III, no. 62, 12; see also Weichmann, *True History*, 98.

"And, oh! Mr. Weichmann": Weichmann, 98–99; see also Edwards, *Rewards Files*, 352. (Note: spelling of "Payne" changed for consistency.)

"Never in my life": Weichmann, 119.

"talking very confidentially": Louis J. Weichmann in Poore, *Conspiracy Trial*, vol. I, 73, 102.

"private business": Louis J. Weichmann in Poore, vol. I, 81.

"like a saucer or two": Louis J. Weichmann in Poore, vol. I, 86.

"china dishes": Undated statement of Louis J. Weichmann in Edwards and Steers, *Lincoln Assassination: The Evidence,* 1321.

"I myself had": Louis J. Weichmann in Poore, *Conspiracy Trial,* vol. I, 378.

"special officer" through "I considered myself": Louis J. Weichmann in "Trial of John H. Surratt," vol. III, no. 64, 15.

"I delivered him up": John T. Holohan in "Trial of John H. Surratt," vol. IV, no. 74, 11.

"I ordered Mr. Weichmann": James A. McDevitt in "Trial of John H. Surratt," vol. IV, no. 76, 4.

"proved so useful": "Tragic Memories," Washington *Evening Star,* April 14, 1894.

"on the floor": Weichmann, *True History,* 219.

"I asked that we": James A. McDevitt in "Trial of John H. Surratt," vol. IV, no. 76, 6.

"a rebel hotbed": Kauffman, *American Brutus,* 233.

"I told them I had not": April 22, 1865, statement of John M. Lloyd to Colonel H. H. Wells in Edwards and Steers, *Lincoln Assassination: The Evidence,* 808.

"denied all knowledge": May 9, 1865, letter of A. C. Richards in Edwards and Steers, 1098.

CHAPTER FIVE

"became convinced, within the certainty": Edwards, *Rewards Files,* 144.

"low conversation" through "breathed hard to pretend": Statement of John Kimball in Edwards and Steers, *Lincoln Assassination: The Evidence,* 779.

"to some extent exaggerated": Edwards, *Rewards Files,* 163.

"bring away all": May 5, 1865, report of Colonel Henry H. Wells in Edwards, 328; see also Edwards, 196.

"Is that you, Mr. Kirby?" through "Madam, I will accompany you": Edwards, 196; see also Henry W. Smith in Poore, *Conspiracy Trial,* vol. II, 19.

"Please entertain these ladies": Edwards, 196; see also R. C. Morgan in Poore, vol. II, 11.

"broke out into loud" through "at least five minutes": Edwards, 197.

"remarkably powerful man": May 5, 1865, report of Colonel Henry H. Wells in Edwards, 327.

"I guess I have mistaken": R. C. Morgan in Poore, *Conspiracy Trial,* vol. II, 10.

"**Whose house are you**" through "**This is the house**": Edwards, *Rewards Files*, 197; see also R. C. Morgan in Poore, vol. II, 10.

"**Mrs. Surratt, please step**" through "**Before God, sir**": Edwards, *Rewards Files*, 198; see also Henry W. Smith in Poore, vol. II, 15.

"**She held up either**": William M. Wermerskirch in Poore, vol. II, 33.

"**Your story does not**": Edwards, *Rewards Files*, 198; see also Henry W. Smith in Poore, vol. II, 15.

CHAPTER SIX

"**That is the man**": April 19, 1865, statement of Officer Thomas Sampson in Edwards and Steers, *Lincoln Assassination: The Evidence*, 478.

"**The mother took it**": "The Assassination: The Last Marks of Respect to Our Late President," *New York Times*, April 19, 1865.

"**infuriated**": "By Telegraph from Washington," *Boston Morning Journal*, April 18, 1865.

"**Mrs. Surratt is**" and "**The house was found**": "Assassination," *New York Times*.

"**I do not remember**": B. F. Wiget in Poore, *Conspiracy Trial*, vol. II, 179.

"**Surratt's Villa**": Jones, *Mystery of Mary Surratt*, 12.

"**my husband wollars**": Mary Surratt to Father Finotti, January 15, 1855, in Joseph George Jr., "'A True Childe of Sorrow.' Two Letters of Mary E. Surratt," *Maryland Historical Magazine* 80, no. 4 (Winter 1985): 403.

"**My dearest Father**": Mary Surratt to Father Finotti, May 13, 1855, in Joseph George Jr., "'A True Childe of Sorrow.' Two Letters of Mary E. Surratt," *Maryland Historical Magazine* 80, no. 4 (Winter 1985): 404.

"**an inoffensive, good-tempered man**": "Trial of the Conspirators; The Parties Arraigned; Their Antecedents," Washington *Evening Star*, May 12, 1865.

"**Mr. Surratt has be come**" and "**I think some times**": George, "True Childe of Sorrow," letter of January 15, 1855.

"**that God may releave**" and "**Sometimes I try**": Mary Surratt to Father Finotti, April 12, 1853, Surratt House Museum, repository.

"**ten or twelve days**" through "**Good bye perhaps**": Mary Surratt to Father Finotti, undated letter (possibly February 1858), in Michael Kauffman, "New Surratt Letters Discovered," *Surratt Courier*, October 1988.

"**I have not had**": Mary Surratt, January 17, 1858, in Laurie Verge, "Mrs. Surratt's Other Son," *Surratt Courier*, August 1977.

"grace and strenth": Surratt to Finotti, April 12, 1853.

"Yours a true Childe of sorrow": George, "True Childe of Sorrow," letter of January 15, 1855.

"Beleave me my dearest": George, "True Childe of Sorrow," letter of May 13, 1855.

"prominent" and "while her husband": "Johnny Bouquet's Walks; 'Maryland, My Maryland,'" New-York Tribune, May 8, 1881.

"I pray you not" and "And if you would": George, "True Childe of Sorrow," letter of January 15, 1855.

"Please answer this cribble" and "I have found out": George, "True Childe of Sorrow," letter of May 13, 1855.

"I am trying evry day" and "Dear Farther": George, "True Childe of Sorrow," letter of January 15, 1855.

"on as cheap a scale" and "will all have to": Kauffman, "New Surratt Letters Discovered," undated letter.

"I find it nessary": Mary Surratt to Father Finotti, September 28, 1858, in Kauffman, "New Surratt Letters Discovered."

"unhealthy" and "But I care not": George, "True Childe of Sorrow," letter of January 15, 1855.

"it has almost caused" and "We hoped at first": Alfred Isacsson, ed., "Sidelights: Some Letters of Anna Surratt," Maryland Historical Magazine 54, no. 3 (September 1959): 310–13.

"I wanted to get": April 17, 1865, interrogation of Mary E. Surratt in Edwards and Steers, Lincoln Assassination: The Evidence, 1245.

CHAPTER SEVEN

Question: But why did you dislike his eyes? and I saw my brother three weeks ago: April 28, 1865, interrogation of Anna Surratt in Edwards and Steers, Lincoln Assassination: The Evidence, 1217.

"a plain unassuming girl": April 18, 1865, statement about Honora Fitzpatrick by W. P. Wood in Edwards and Steers, Lincoln Assassination: The Evidence, 511.

"That ugly man": Anna Surratt, quoted by Honora Fitzpatrick in Poore, Conspiracy Trial, vol. III, 468–69.

"in the matter of": "Letters Received and Statements of Evidence Collected by the Military Commission, Pages 70–104 and Letters Received by Col. H. L. Burnett with Endorsements, May 9–Jun 9, 1865," in Investigation and Trial Papers Relating *to the Assassination of President Lincoln* (College Park, MD: National Archives and Records Administration, 1865), 240, fold3.com/image/1/7414868.

"but not always" through "No, sir. I engage a black man": April 17, 1865, interrogation of Mary E. Surratt in Edwards and Steers, *Lincoln Assassination: The Evidence*, 1243–50.

CHAPTER EIGHT

"such unfortunate females": Lomax, *Old Capitol*, 13.

"with a hole": Kauffman, *American Brutus*, 330.

"There was a calm": Lomax, *Old Capitol*, 134.

"weeping bitterly" through "She rather avoided": Lomax, 133–35.

"When first arrested": Undated statement of George Cottingham in Edwards, *Rewards Files*, 176.

"uneasy": Edwards and Steers, *Lincoln Assassination: The Evidence*, 807, 815; see also John M. Lloyd in Poore, *Conspiracy Trial*, vol. I, 121.

"I told him": April 22, 1865, statement of John M. Lloyd in Edwards and Steers, *Lincoln Assassination: The Evidence*, 807.

"take them away soon": April 23, 1865, statement of John M. Lloyd in Edwards and Steers, 809.

"in a manner" through "Get them out ready": John M. Lloyd in Poore, *Conspiracy Trial*, vol. I, 117–21.

"Talk about the Devil": Mary Surratt, quoted by John M. Lloyd in Poore, vol. I, 122.

"got pretty tight": April 28, 1865, statement of John M. Lloyd in Edwards and Steers, *Lincoln Assassination: The Evidence*, 812.

"I was not aware" and "Well Mr. Lloyd": John M. Lloyd in Poore, *Conspiracy Trial*, vol. I, 122.

"I could not divine": April 22, 1865, statement of John M. Lloyd in Edwards and Steers, *Lincoln Assassination: The Evidence*, 807, 816.

"a little bundle rolled up": April 28, 1865, statement of John M. Lloyd in Edwards and Steers, 812.

"This matter seemed": April 22, 1865, statement of John M. Lloyd in Edwards and Steers, 807.

"I was pretty well": April 28, 1865, statement of John M. Lloyd in Edwards and Steers, 812.

"more in liquor": Stewart, *Conspiracy Trial Transcripts*, location ID 7102.

"Just at that time": April 28, 1865, statement of John M. Lloyd in Edwards and Steers, *Lincoln Assassination: The Evidence,* 812.

"Herold told me": April 22, 1865, statement of John M. Lloyd in Edwards and Steers, 807.

"I will tell you": April 28, 1865, statement of John M. Lloyd in Edwards and Steers, 813.

"of a serious nature": April 22, 1865, statement of John M. Lloyd in Edwards and Steers, 808.

"I am not particular" and "We have assassinated": April 28, 1865, statement of John M. Lloyd in Edwards and Steers, 813.

"partial" through "He knew the whole": April 29, 1865, report of Alexander Lovett in Edwards, *Rewards Files,* 265–66.

"Mr. Lloyd has made" through "My God they will": April 23, 1865, report of George Cottingham in Edwards, 178.

"virtually acknowledged complicity": April 24, 1865, statement of Samuel Beckwith in Edwards, 138.

"accessory to the murder": May 14, 1865, report of George Cottingham in Edwards, 181; see also May 1, 1865, letter of James O'Beirne to Edwin Stanton in Edwards, 281.

"Had it not been": April 23, 1865, report of George Cottingham in Edwards, 178; see also December 10, 1865, statement of Towsley B. Robey in Edwards, 179.

"strategy": May 14, 1865, report of George Cottingham in Edwards, 181; see also May 1, 1865, report of George Cottingham in Edwards, 182–83.

"be relived from": May 1, 1865, report of George Cottingham in Edwards, 183.

"I dragged it out of Lloyd": December 1, 1865, statement of J. W. Ridenour in Edwards, 180.

"Lloyd shed tears": Undated statement (written prior to August 2, 1865) of George Cottingham in Edwards, 176; see also May 1, 1865, report of George Cottingham in Edwards, 183.

"I hope Mrs. Surratt": April 23, 1865, report of George Cottingham in Edwards, 178.

"that the house": April 23, 1865, letter of Colonel Henry H. Wells in Edwards, 323.

CHAPTER NINE

"the weight of indignant": December 24, 1865, statement of E. J. Conger in Edwards, *Rewards Files,* 155.

"THE MURDERER of our" and "All persons harboring": US War Department, "$100,000 Reward! The Murderer of Our Late Beloved President, Abraham Lincoln, Is Still At Large" (broadside advertising reward for capture of Lincoln assassination conspirators, Washington, DC, April 20, 1865), loc.gov/resource/cph.3g05341.

"supposed that they were": Joseph George Jr., "Nature's First Law: Louis J. Weichmann and Mrs. Surratt," *Civil War History* 28, no. 2 (June 1982): 101–27; see also Kauffman, *American Brutus,* 309.

"sick and tired": April 27, 1865, statement of David Herold in Edwards and Steers, *Lincoln Assassination: The Evidence,* 676.

"and thus end": April 27, 1865, statement of Luther Baker in Edwards, *Rewards Files,* 133.

"Captain, That's rather rough": John Wilkes Booth, quoted in April 27, 1865, statement of Luther Baker, in Edwards, 133.

"We did not come": Edwards, 159.

"go away from me" and "damned coward": April 27, 1865, statement of Luther Baker in Edwards, 133–34.

"Captain! Here's a man": April 29, 1865, statement of Boston Corbett in Edwards, 163; see also Lewis Savage in Edwards, 168.

"Let him out": April 27, 1865, statement of David Herold in Edwards and Steers, *Lincoln Assassination: The Evidence,* 677.

"I own & have": April 27, 1865, statement of Luther Baker in Edwards, *Rewards Files,* 134.

"Put out your hands!": May 30, 1865, statement of Abram Snay in Edwards, 167; see also Lewis Savage in Edwards, 168; John Winter and John Myers in Edwards, 170.

"The poor little wretch": Betsy Fleet, "A Chapter of Unwritten History. Richard Baynham Garrett's Account of the Flight and Death of John Wilkes Booth," *Virginia Magazine of History and Biography,* October 1963.

"Well, you may prepare": John Wilkes Booth, quoted in April 27, 1865, statement of Luther Baker, in Edwards, *Rewards Files,* 134; see also John Winter in Edwards, 170.

"I made up my mind" through "but a moments": April 27, 1865, statement of E. J. Conger in Edwards, 125.

"sprung to the door": April 27, 1865, statement of Luther Baker in Edwards, 134.

"Is he dead?": April 27, 1865, statement of E. J. Conger in Edwards, 125.

"I put my ear down" through "We put the body": April 27, 1865, statement of Luther Baker in Edwards, 135–36.

CHAPTER TEN

"I have been sent by the Secty" through "Never in the world": April 28, 1865, statement of Mary E. Surratt in Edwards and Steers, *Lincoln Assassination: The Evidence,* 1236–50.

"the man of iron and blood": Weichmann, *True History,* 225.

"Items not brought out": Edwards and Steers, *Lincoln Assassination: The Evidence,* 1331.

"It seems extremely improbable": Undated report of Colonel Foster regarding Louis J. Weichmann in Edwards and Steers, 1323.

"the principle parties" and "On Tuesday it was": May 5, 1865, report of Colonel Henry H. Wells in Edwards, *Rewards Files,* 327.

"I am satisfied": Report of W. P. Wood (undated but after April 30) regarding Louis Weichmann, in Edwards, *Rewards Files,* 351.

"This corrupt scoundrel" and "Directly after the arrest": Curtis Carroll Davis, "In Pursuit of Booth Once More: A New Claimant Heard From," *Maryland Historical Magazine* 79, no. 3 (Fall 1984): 220–34.

"Mrs. Surratt, you are" through "That her position": Lomax, *Old Capitol,* 172–75.

CHAPTER ELEVEN

"necessary food and water" and "small quantities": Steers and Holzer, *Lincoln Assassination Conspirators,* 67.

"to prevent the use": Porter, *Surgeon in Charge,* 31.

"Mrs. Surratt was": George Loring Porter, "How Booth's Body Was Hidden," *Columbian,* April 1911.

"I am a catholic": Steers and Holzer, *Lincoln Assassination Conspirators,* 80.

"The prisoner in 157": Steers and Holzer, 78.

"your trial": April 28, 1865, statement of Mary E. Surratt in Edwards and Steers, *Lincoln Assassination: The Evidence,* 1236.

"enemy belligerents": Steers, *Blood on the Moon,* 211.

"The commission was organized": "Proofs Go in Fire," *Chicago Times-Herald,* March 23, 1895; see also Douglas, *I Rode with Stonewall,* 342.

"on the verge of a riot" and "unpleasant visits": "The Current Weekly News: The Feeling of the People," *New York Examiner and Chronicle,* April 27, 1865.

"wretches" through "entitled to the extremest": "Trial of the Assassins," Philadelphia *Press,* May 10, 1865. (Reprinted from *Washington Chronicle,* May 8, 1865.)

"No prisoner will be": Steers and Holzer, *Lincoln Assassination Conspirators,* 68.

"I had a quiet": Porter, "How Booth's Body."

"I have the honor" and "exactly remember whether": May 5, 1865, letter of Louis J. Weichmann to Colonel Burnett in Edwards and Steers, *Lincoln Assassination: The Evidence*, 1324–25.

"weeping bitterly": Louis J. Weichmann in Poore, *Conspiracy Trial*, vol. I, 370, 376.

"Oh, John is gone away": May 5, 1865, letter of Louis J. Weichmann to Colonel Burnett in Edwards and Steers, *Lincoln Assassination: The Evidence*, 1325; see also Louis J. Weichmann in Poore, vol. I, 370.

"rushed into the room" through "I will shoot any one": Louis J. Weichmann in Poore, vol. I, 370; see also Edwards and Steers, 1325.

"You are foolish": Weichmann, *True History*, 102; see also Poore, vol. I, 370, 376.

"They were very guarded indeed" through "thought Surratt would be recalled": Louis J. Weichmann in Poore, vol. I, 370–89.

"if the pickets remained" through "pray for her intentions": Edwards and Steers, *Lincoln Assassination: The Evidence*, 1331; see also Edwards and Steers, 1326.

"she chased the young ladies": May 5, 1865, letter of Louis J. Weichmann to Colonel Burnett, in Edwards and Steers, 1327; see also Edwards and Steers, 1331.

"Think of that man": Edwards and Steers, 1331.

"That all this testimony" through "He was not": "The Surratt Case," *New York World*, October 17, 1868.

"treated me kindly" and "I am responsible": Undated statement of Louis J. Weichmann to Colonel Burnett in Edwards and Steers, *Lincoln Assassination: The Evidence*, 1319–1320.

CHAPTER TWELVE

"maliciously, unlawfully, and traitorously, and in aid of" through "receive, entertain, harbor": Poore, *Conspiracy Trial*, vol. I, 13–19.

"dungeon-like": "The Scene of the Trial," *New York World*, May 19, 1865. (Reprinted from *Boston Daily Advertiser*.)

"headless men" through "How the Court viewed": Arnold, *Defence and Prison*, 10–12.

"The mystery and apparent severity" through "in this age": Charles F. Cooney, "At the Trial of the Lincoln Conspirators: The Reminiscences of General August V. Kautz," *Civil War Times*, August 1973.

"fresh from the shop": "Scene of the Trial," *New York World*.

"Judge Holt sat immovable": Arnold, *Defence and Prison*, 10.

"frequent" and "spirited": R. A. Watts, "The Trial and Execution of the Lincoln Conspirators [part 2]," *Adrian Daily Telegram*, April 20, 1914.

"watching the movements": Poore, *Conspiracy Trial*, vol. I, 6.

"the duty of preparing": Watts, "Trial and Execution."

"infusing into the proceedings": Poore, *Conspiracy Trial*, vol. I, 6.

"without injury to the": Poore, vol. I, 19.

"All the arrangements made": "The Conspiracy. Hon. Reverdy Johnson in Court," *Washington Evening Union*, May 13, 1865.

"furnished with tea": Steers and Holzer, *Lincoln Assassination Conspirators*, 88.

"already undergoing a living death": "The Conspirators. The Preparations for Their Trial," Philadelphia *Press*, May 10, 1865.

"No lawyer has yet": "Washington," *Philadelphia Inquirer*, May 5, 1865.

"Our families never visited": Trindal, *Mary Surratt*, 146.

"Treason never found" through "She is bold and cruel": George Alfred Townsend, "The Conspiracy. A Full Account of the Plot Against the Rulers of the Nation," *New York World*, May 3, 1865.

"displayed considerable force" through "she seldom fail[ed]": "Trial of the Conspirators; The Parties Arraigned; Their Antecedents," Washington *Evening Star*, May 12, 1865.

"because I deemed": DeWitt, *Judicial Murder*, 40.

"impudence" and "evinces her boldness": "Washington. The Great Conspiracy!," *Philadelphia Inquirer*, May 11, 1865.

"The prosecution had had": Doster, *Lincoln and Episodes*, 260.

"This was a contest": Doster, 257.

CHAPTER THIRTEEN

"very slovenly dressed" and "very much broken down": "Washington. The Treason Trials!," *Philadelphia Inquirer*, May 13, 1865.

"Mrs. Surratt, yesterday": "The Latest News, by Telegraph, from Washington. The Trial of the Assassins," Philadelphia *Age*, May 13, 1865.

"all attempts of interfering": "Washington. The Great Conspiracy!," *Philadelphia Inquirer*, May 11, 1865.

"appeared in clean clothes": "Washington. The Treason Trials!" *Philadelphia Inquirer*, May 13, 1865.

"it would be" and "I said that I": Edwards and Steers, *Lincoln Assassination: The Evidence*, 63.

"The secrecy which was": "Sentence of the Conspirators," *New York World*, July 7, 1865.

"some exceedingly hard-bottomed chairs": "The Assassination. Continuation of the Conspiracy Trials," Washington *Evening Star*, May 15, 1865.

"Under no circumstances": R. A. Watts, "The Trial and Execution of the Lincoln Conspirators [part 2]," *Adrian Daily Telegram*, April 20, 1914.

"A more clumsy set": "The Testimony," *New York World*, May 18, 1865.

"trifling boy": James Nokes in Poore, *Conspiracy Trial*, vol. II, 468.

"Passionately fond of" and "nearly every one": April 27, 1865, statement of David Herold in Edwards and Steers, *Lincoln Assassination: The Evidence*, 665–66.

"His whole bearing": "Trial of the Assassins. The Court Proceeding with Its Work," *Philadelphia Inquirer*, May 16, 1865.

"Whether she was guilty": Poore, *Conspiracy Trial*, vol. I, 13.

"In relation to Mr. Johnson" and "on the ground that": Poore, vol. I, 52.

"a very repellent": "Visitors from Congress: Reverdy Johnson (1796–1876)," Mr. Lincoln's White House (website), Lehrman Institute, accessed October 21, 2021, mrlincolnswhitehouse.org. (Quote attributed to Noah Brooks, *Mr. Lincoln's Washington*, March 13, 1863, 136.)

"dignified bearing": "Trial of the Assassins: The Court and the Place in Which It Is Held," *New York Times*, May 15, 1865.

"towering rage": Watts, "Trial and Execution."

"I have lived": Reverdy Johnson in Poore, *Conspiracy Trial*, vol. I, 53.

"his indignation was": Charles F. Cooney, "At the Trial of the Lincoln Conspirators: The Reminiscences of General August V. Kautz," *Civil War Times*, August 1973.

"I am here no volunteer": Reverdy Johnson in Poore, *Conspiracy Trial*, vol. I, 54.

"whose law creates armies": Reverdy Johnson in Poore, vol. I, 61.

"I have always": Doster, *Lincoln and Episodes*, 264.

"The senator and General Harris": Watts, "Trial and Execution."

"considerable sparring": "The Conspiracy. Hon. Reverdy Johnson in Court," *Washington Evening Union*, May 13, 1865.

"I cannot help believing": Doster, *Lincoln and Episodes*, 264.

"memory was so sure": "Visitors from Congress," Mr. Lincoln's White House (website).

"firing pistol shots": Doster, *Lincoln and Episodes*, 263.

CHAPTER FOURTEEN

"He was seemingly": R. A. Watts, "The Trial and Execution of the Lincoln Conspirators [part 2]," *Adrian Daily Telegram*, April 20, 1914.

"During the first days": "The Assassination: Our Special Dispatch," *New-York Tribune*, May 15, 1865.

"not more than": Louis J. Weichmann in Poore, *Conspiracy Trial*, vol. I, 105.

"Her character was exemplary": Louis J. Weichmann in Poore, vol. I, 93.

"Were you in the habit" through "No, sir. At one time": Reverdy Johnson and Louis J. Weichmann in Poore, vol. I, 84.

"Your only reason" through "Then, again, I thought": Reverdy Johnson and Louis J. Weichmann in Poore, vol. I, 90–91.

"the principle parties": May 5, 1865, report of Colonel Henry H. Wells in Edwards, *Rewards Files*, 327.

"From the tenor": "The Great Conspiracy. The Assassins in Court—an Open Trial," *Washington Evening Union*, May 15, 1865.

"picked up his hat": Watts, "Trial and Execution."

"seems more than": "The Scene of the Trial," *New York World*, May 19, 1865. (Reprinted from *Boston Daily Advertiser.*)

"Too much latitude": "Trial of the Assassins: The Charges and Specifications Against the Prisoners," *New York Times*, May 16, 1865.

"rake the whole Confederacy" and "were often forced": Watts, "Trial and Execution."

"tiresome": "Scene of the Trial," *New York World*.

"In the mass" and "great latitude": "Progress of the Trial of the Assassination Conspirators," *New York Herald*, May 20, 1865.

"The first day disgusted him": George Alfred Townsend, "The Trial. Complete and Graphic Picture of the Court-Martial at Work," *New York World*, June 2, 1865.

"the testimony of the witness": Frederick Aiken in Poore, *Conspiracy Trial*, vol. I, 114.

"a right smart bundle" and "he would call for": John M. Lloyd in Poore, vol. I, 116.

"Will you state whether or not" through "From the way he spoke": General Joseph Holt and John M. Lloyd in Poore, vol. I, 116–19.

"Lloyd, for God's sake": David Herold, quoted by John M. Lloyd, in Poore, vol. I, 119.

"Did she ever have" and "Never": Frederick Aiken in Poore, vol. I, 125.

CHAPTER FIFTEEN

"tottered visibly" and "and did not once raise it": "The Assassination. Continuation of the Conspiracy Trials," Washington *Evening Star,* May 15, 1865.

"Do you recollect seeing him" through "I wanted to explain": Poore, *Conspiracy Trial,* vol. I, 136–39.

"shooting-irons": John M. Lloyd in Poore, vol. I, 117, 121.

"Mrs. Surratt has lost": Untitled squib in *New York Evening Express,* of May 16, 1865.

"The witness himself was": "Trial of the Conspirators. The Appearance of the Assassins," *Springfield Republican,* May 20, 1865.

"To WEICHMANN, Esq." through "J. BOOTH": Poore, *Conspiracy Trial,* vol. I, 368.

"Who is the person" through "I asked him what": General Joseph Holt and Louis J. Weichmann in Poore, vol. I, 369.

"Probably all readers" and "This story furnishes": "The Assassination Trials," *Boston Evening Transcript,* May 18, 1865.

"Do I understand you as stating" through "My suspicions were not": Frederick Aiken and Louis J. Weichmann in Poore, *Conspiracy Trial,* vol. I, 384.

"laughed and hooted": Louis J. Weichmann in Poore, vol. I, 385.

"gave his testimony": "The Conspiracy. Interesting Sketches of the Scenes Attendant upon the Great Trial," *New York World,* May 19, 1865.

"I have never seen": Wallace, *Lew Wallace,* 848. (Note: Louis Weichmann was twenty-two when he testified.)

CHAPTER SIXTEEN

"As the prisoners are": "The Conspiracy Trial: Proceedings This Afternoon," Washington *Evening Star,* May 20, 1865.

"before God": Edwards, *Rewards Files,* 198; see also Henry W. Smith in Poore, *Conspiracy Trial,* vol. II, 15; William M. Wermerskirch in Poore, vol. II, 33.

"How was Payne dressed at that time?" through "Certainly": Frederick Aiken and Henry W. Smith in Poore, vol. II, 17.

"Have you not been in the habit" through "If it has, I never have seen it": Frederick Aiken and R. C. Morgan in Poore, vol. II, 13.

"Are you aware or not" through "I am, of *eminent* actors": Frederick Aiken and Henry W. Smith in Poore, vol. II, 15–16.

"as if weeping": "Washington. Interesting Incidents of the Great Trial," *Philadelphia Inquirer,* May 20, 1865.

"Did Mrs. Surratt express" and "No, sir: she did not": Poore, *Conspiracy Trial*, vol. II, 19.

"We had sent" through "She knelt down": Poore, vol. II, 36.

"for an instant" and "The incident was": "Washington. Interesting Incidents of the Great Trial," *Philadelphia Inquirer.*

"Had Mrs. Surratt left" through "No, sir": General Joseph Holt and R. C. Morgan in Poore, *Conspiracy Trial*, vol. II, 11.

"Yes, sir: very light": Henry W. Smith in Poore, vol. II, 19.

"the hall was not" through "as near . . . as can be": William M. Wermerskirch in Poore, vol. II, 37–40.

"Do you think" through "I think I would": Frederick Aiken and William M. Wermerskirch in Poore, vol. II, 37–38.

"That is the coat" through "It is hard to remember": Poore, vol. II, 19–21.

"very light": Henry W. Smith in Poore, vol. II, 19.

CHAPTER SEVENTEEN

"We read in unmistakable letters" and "Either from within": "Personal," *Boston Herald*, May 25, 1865. (Reprinted from *Washington Chronicle*, May 23, 1865.)

"It is said": "The Conspiracy. What Was Done in the Secret Session of Saturday," *New York World*, May 23, 1865.

"so near to Mrs. Surratt" through "The expression of her face": Jane G. Swisshelm, "Was Mrs. Surratt Manacled?" *New-York Tribune*, September 16, 1873.

"The first feeling": "The Assassination. Trial of the Conspirators," *New-York Tribune*, May 16, 1865.

"but an animal": "The Assassination. The Flight of Davis," *New-York Tribune*, May 11, 1865.

"not one capable": "The Assassination. Continuation of the Conspiracy Trials," Washington *Evening Star*, May 15, 1865.

"dingy and sallow" and "no sense of mental": "The Scene of the Trial," *New York World*, May 19, 1865. (Reprinted from *Boston Daily Advertiser.*)

"shallow-pated blab-mouth": "The Assassination Plot. Booth's Flight," Washington *Evening Star*, April 29, 1865.

"eminently Spanish": "Trial of the Assassins: The Court and the Place in Which It Is Held," *New York Times*, May 15, 1865.

"dark and vindictive": "The Testimony," *New York World*, May 18, 1865.

"tolerably intelligent" through "no evidence or capacity of guilt": "Trial of the Assassins," *New York Times*.

"The full forehead": "The Assassination. Continuation of the Conspiracy Trials," Washington *Evening Star*.

"would go far toward": "The Scene of the Trial," *New York World* (reprinted from *Boston Daily Advertiser*), May 19, 1865.

"The general impression": E. H. Arr, "An Hour in the Court Room," *Springfield Republican*, June 7, 1865.

"with a cold clear": "The Conspirators. The Preparations for Their Trial," Philadelphia *Press*, May 10, 1865.

"Treason never found": George Alfred Townsend, "The Conspiracy. A Full Account of the Plot Against the Rulers of the Nation," *New York World*, May 3, 1865.

"a large, Amazonian" through "too strong to be": "Trial of the Assassins: The Court and the Place in Which It Is Held," *New York Times*.

"Mrs. Surratt appears" and "long confidential talks": "The Trial of the Assassins: Review of the Testimony Thus Far Placed on Record," *New York Times*, May 22, 1865.

"In all the pages": John W. Clampitt, "The Trial of Mrs. Surratt," *North American Review*, September 1880, 223–40.

"complete or always trustworthy" through "But the perusal": "The Trial of the Conspirators. The Case as Presented by the Prosecution," *Boston Daily Advertiser*, May 31, 1865.

"Women are rarely hanged": "The Conspiracy Trial," Boston *Daily Evening Traveler*, May 22, 1865.

CHAPTER EIGHTEEN

"From these dismount": George Alfred Townsend, "The Trial. Complete and Graphic Picture of the Court-Martial at Work," *New York World*, June 2, 1865.

"The chain of circumstances" and "nowhere reveals the fact": John W. Clampitt, "The Trial of Mrs. Surratt," *North American Review*, September 1880, 223–40.

"They will have": "Telegraphic Communication with New Orleans," *Boston Daily Advertiser*, May 25, 1865.

"During all this acquaintance" through "Nothing but what I read": Poore, *Conspiracy Trial*, vol. II, 174–81.

"Were any objections made" through "I never heard of it": Poore, vol. II, 183–86.

"Did you learn whether" through "I remember once passing": Poore, vol. II, 186–88.

"Ceaseless and senseless chatter": "By Telegraph: Special "Despatches" to the *Boston Daily Advertiser,*" *Boston Daily Advertiser,* May 26, 1865.

"Remainder of the testimony" and "Lively comments upon": "The Conspiracy Trials. Proceedings This Afternoon," Washington *Evening Star,* May 25, 1865.

"What should be": "By Telegraph," *Boston Daily Advertiser.*

"As I was passing" through "No, sir. She gave": Frederick Aiken and B. F. Gwynn in Poore, *Conspiracy Trial,* vol. II, 190.

"She said, when she": Louis J. Weichmann in Poore, vol. I, 86. (Note: Weichmann's testimony mistakenly refers to Charles Calvert. Though the loan had been given by Charles, it was George Calvert who insisted upon its collection in 1865.)

"What was his condition" through "Well, I could hardly": Frederick Aiken and B. F. Gwynn in Poore, vol. II, 191.

"What information did Mr. Lloyd" through "He said, in the last interview": Frederick Aiken and George Cottingham in Poore, vol. II, 193–96.

"astonished beyond measure": "By Telegraph," *Boston Daily Advertiser.*

"Will you state again" through "I said not": Frederick Aiken and George Cottingham in Poore, *Conspiracy Trial,* vol. II, 215. (Note: Detective Cottingham's first name is mistakenly given as "Thomas" on pp. 215 and 216 of the official transcript.)

"gloried in the fact" and "unblushingly": "By Telegraph," *Boston Daily Advertiser.*

"I am now" through "I told you": Frederick Aiken and George Cottingham in Poore, *Conspiracy Trial,* vol. II, 216. (Note: Detective Cottingham's first name is mistakenly given as "Thomas" on pp. 215 and 216 of the official transcript.)

"the most striking": "By Telegraph," *Boston Daily Advertiser.*

"thoroughly cognizant of all": "Washington Correspondence," *Boston Recorder,* May 26, 1865.

CHAPTER NINETEEN

"did not recognize me": Augustus Howell in Poore, *Conspiracy Trial,* vol. I, 343.

"Mrs. Surratt sits veiled": "The Assassins," *Daily National Republican,* May 26, 1865.

"a good hater": "Washington Correspondence," *Boston Recorder,* May 26, 1865.

"weary, anxious look": "The Assassination. The Trial on Tuesday," *New-York Tribune,* May 31, 1865.

"death-like silence prevailed": "Washington: Trial of the Conspirators," *Philadelphia Inquirer,* May 31, 1865.

"a scene": John A. Gray, "The Fate of the Lincoln Conspirators," *McClure's,* October 1911.

"State whether or not" and "Yes, sir: her eyesight": Frederick Aiken and Anna Surratt in Poore, *Conspiracy Trial,* vol. II, 496–97.

"was quite haughty": "Trial on Tuesday," *New-York Tribune.*

"in a clear, distinct tone": "Trial of the Conspirators," *Philadelphia Inquirer.*

"Is she able" through "No, sir: she made": Frederick Aiken and Anna Surratt in Poore, *Conspiracy Trial,* vol. II, 497.

"marked consideration and delicacy": "Trial of the Conspirators," *Philadelphia Inquirer.*

"Are you acquainted" and "Yes, sir; I have": Frederick Aiken and Anna Surratt in Poore, *Conspiracy Trial,* vol. II, 497.

"her animus was unmistakable": "Trial of the Conspirators," *Philadelphia Inquirer.*

"Was he a boarder" through "No, sir; I did not": Frederick Aiken and Anna Surratt in Poore, *Conspiracy Trial,* vol. II, 497–501.

"Where is mama?" through "She snatched it": "Trial on Tuesday," *New-York Tribune.*

"wept like a child": "Report of the Testimony Taken on Tuesday," *New York Times,* May 31, 1865.

"burst into a violent": "Trial of the Conspirators," *Philadelphia Inquirer.*

"I didn't see" through "She gave me": Gray, "Lincoln Conspirators."

"When Annie saw" through "You think so?": Gray, "Lincoln Conspirators"; see also "Hangman of President Lincoln's Assassins Tells His Story," *New York Press,* September 4, 1898.

"Mrs. Surratt was" and "something she could administer": "Hangman," *New York Press.*

"The presence of her daughter": "Washington; Miss Anna Surratt Released from Custody," *Philadelphia Inquirer,* June 3, 1865.

"with a look": "The Latest News, by Telegraph. From Washington. Miss Surratt in Court," Philadelphia *Age,* June 3, 1865.

CHAPTER TWENTY

"The extreme heat of": "Washington; The Grand Court-Martial," *Philadelphia Inquirer,* June 5, 1865.

"a most uncomfortable appearance": "By Telegraph. News from Washington,"
  Boston Morning Journal, June 6, 1865.

"You are satisfied" through "Yes, sir: I believe he did": Poore, *Conspiracy Trial*,
  vol. III, 69.

"Has Mr. Lloyd been in the habit" through "He had at times": Frederick Aiken and
  Joseph Nott in Poore, vol. II, 482–83.

"a noxious and pestilential": George Alfred Townsend, "The Conspiracy. A Full
  Account of the Plot Against the Rulers of the Nation," *New York World*, May 3,
  1865.

"would turn around": "The Assassination. Trial of the Conspirators," *New-York
  Tribune*, May 16, 1865.

"State whether or not you were present" through "No, sir": Poore, *Conspiracy Trial*,
  vol. III, 466–68.

"because he could not": Doster, *Lincoln and Episodes*, 269.

CHAPTER TWENTY-ONE

"These are they": George Alfred Townsend, "The Trial. Complete and Graphic
  Picture of the Court-Martial at Work," *New York World*, June 2, 1865.

"are suffering very much" and "there may be some": Steers and Holzer, *Lincoln
  Assassination Conspirators*, 115.

"one of the most": George Loring Porter, "How Booth's Body Was Hidden,"
  Columbian, April 1911.

"to adopt such measures": Porter, *Surgeon in Charge*, 31.

"unhesitatingly" and "under heavy guard": Porter, "How Booth's Body."

"a small box": Steers and Holzer, *Lincoln Assassination Conspirators*, 126.

"was still a woman": John W. Clampitt, "The Trial of Mrs. Surratt," *North American
  Review*, September 1880, 225.

"apparently almost prostrated": "The Conspiracy Trials. Proceedings Today,"
  Washington *Evening Star*, June 12, 1865.

"Mrs. Surratt's Health Failing" through "The lady visitors": "Washington.
  Incidents in the Great Trial," *Philadelphia Inquirer*, June 8, 1865.

"considerably under the influence": Frederick Aiken in Poore, *Conspiracy Trial*,
  vol. III, 512.

"What was her treatment" through "If she took any pay": Poore, vol. III,
  550–52.

"You need not state" through "Yes sir, I know": Stewart, *Conspiracy Trial Transcripts*,
  location ID 7044–54.

"Did Mr. Lloyd" and "No, sir, he did not": Frederick Aiken and Emma Offutt in Stewart, location ID 7113–14.

"Mrs. Surratt, that vile" through "I do not think": Stewart, location ID 7442–84.

CHAPTER TWENTY-TWO

"Indeed, if there were" through "Her expression, for the several hours": Rev. B. H. Nadal, "The Conspirators. A Personal Description of the Assassins on Trial at Washington," *Bradford Reporter* (Towanda, PA), June 15, 1865. (Reprinted from *New York Methodist.*)

"very slovenly dressed": "Washington. The Treason Trials!," *Philadelphia Inquirer,* May 13, 1865.

"Profusely strewn": "An Injudicious Publication," Washington *Evening Star,* June 17, 1865.

"Her temper was never ruffled" through "Charity, forbearance, suspension of judgement": Joseph George Jr., "Trial of Mrs. Surratt: John P. Brophy's Rare Pamphlet," *Lincoln Herald,* Winter 1990.

"An Injudicious Publication" and "cannot fail of working": "Injudicious Publication," Washington *Evening Star.*

"certain parties are trying": Untitled squib in Bath *Daily Times and Sentinel,* June 22, 1865.

CHAPTER TWENTY-THREE

"That question in" through "danger to liberty": Steers, *Trial: The Assassination,* 251.

"According to this great authority" through "They were citizens of the District": Steers, 253–57.

"a copy of the indictment": "An Act for the Punishment of Certain Crimes Against the United States," First US Congress, Session II, Chapter 9, Section 29, April 30, 1790, loc.gov/item/llsl-v1.

"great right the American colonists" through "As far, gentlemen": Steers, *Trial: The Assassination,* 258–63.

"This was the easiest": "The Conspiracy Trials. Arguments for the Defense—Hon. Reverdy Johnson's Plea for Mrs. Surratt," *Daily National Republican,* June 19, 1865.

"Mrs. Surratt became so ill": Steers and Holzer, *Lincoln Assassination Conspirators,* 127.

"Mrs. Surratt is seriously": "From Washington—Consul to Zurich," *Albany Evening News,* June 20, 1865.

"contracted within her": John W. Clampitt, "The Trial of Mrs. Surratt," *North American Review,* September 1880, 225.

"the womb disease" and "flooded for three weeks": "Memories of 1865: The Hanging of Mrs. Surratt—the Evidence That Condemned Her," *Kalamazoo Gazette,* September 21, 1878.

"where she was still": Steers and Holzer, *Lincoln Assassination Conspirators,* 127.

"Her cell by reason": Doster, *Lincoln and Episodes,* 276.

"Since Mrs. Surratt": Steers and Holzer, *Lincoln Assassination Conspirators,* 127.

"for the benefit": "The Conspiracy Trials. Proceedings This Afternoon," Washington *Evening Star,* June 20, 1865.

"For the lawyer" through "Let the ship": Steers, *Trial: The Assassination,* 289–99.

CHAPTER TWENTY-FOUR

"Mrs. Surratt was shown" and "the order to kill": Charles F. Cooney, "At the Trial of the Lincoln Conspirators: The Reminiscences of General August V. Kautz," *Civil War Times,* August 1973.

"These nine soldiers" and "There was no place": R. A. Watts, "The Trial and Execution of the Lincoln Conspirators [part 2]," *Adrian Daily Telegram,* April 20, 1914.

"[General] David Hunter was" and "That was done": "Proofs Go in Fire," *Chicago Times-Herald,* March 23, 1895.

"if he could find": Moore, *Case of Mrs. Surratt,* 55.

"The question was whispered": A. Oakey Hall, "The Surratt Cause Célèbre," *Green Bag,* May 1896.

"exhaustion by incessant attention": "By Telegraph," *New-Orleans Times,* July 6, 1865.

"hopes to be able": "The Situation," *New York Herald,* July 6, 1865.

"I think we will" through "Every Officer & man": Steers and Holzer, *Lincoln Assassination Conspirators,* 139–40.

"chanced to be absent": Steers and Holzer, 143.

"And the Commission does": "The Conspiracy. Findings and Sentences," *Daily National Intelligencer,* July 7, 1865.

"At the moment" and "sank under the dread": "THE CONSPIRATORS: Finding of the Court," *New York Times,* July 7, 1865.

"burst into a violent": "EXTRA. The Execution," Washington *Evening Star,* July 7, 1865.

"Her sentence surprised": "The Surratt Case," *New York World,* October 17, 1868.

"duly executed, in accordance": "EXTRA. Four of the Conspirators Sentenced to Be Hung," *Daily National Republican,* July 6, 1865.

"At first the truth": "Our Special Washington Despatch," *New York Herald,* July 7, 1865.

"any special minister": Steers and Holzer, *Lincoln Assassination Conspirators,* 142.

"The execution of Mrs. Surratt!" and "amazed beyond expression": John W. Clampitt, "The Trial of Mrs. Surratt," *North American Review,* September 1880, 234–35.

"useless to attempt" through "His heart was chilled": Clampitt, "The Trial of Mrs. Surratt," 235.

"I thought he was": John A. Gray, "The Fate of the Lincoln Conspirators," *McClure's,* October 1911.

"I want four able-bodied" through "anything to break": Hoyt, *Town Hall Tonight,* 149.

"I told these men" through "I didn't want an ordinary": Gray, "Lincoln Conspirators."

"one of the grimmest": Hoyt, *Town Hall Tonight,* 150.

"When I saw Payne": Doster, *Lincoln and Episodes,* 271.

"for I fully expected" and "I threw the bag": Gray, "Lincoln Conspirators."

"over with anxious" and "She appeared to be": "Execution," Washington *Evening Star.*

"I can do nothing" and "It is very late": Clampitt, "The Trial of Mrs. Surratt."

"bring away all that": May 5, 1865, report of Colonel Henry H. Wells in Edwards, *Rewards Files,* 328; see also Edwards, 196.

"What do you want?" through "Gentlemen, my mind": Clampitt, "The Trial of Mrs. Surratt."

CHAPTER TWENTY-FIVE

"She slept very little": "EXTRA. The Execution," Washington *Evening Star,* July 7, 1865.

"All that affection": "EXTRA. The Execution. The Condition of the Prisoners," *Daily National Republican,* July 7, 1865.

"I can see no one" through "he told me that": R. D. Mussey to General Joseph
    Holt, August 19, 1873, in Holt, *Vindication of Hon. Joseph Holt,* 9–12.
"In as tender" through "a number of hardy soldiers": "Execution," Washington
    Evening Star.
"studded with massive" and "Mrs. Surratt early": "EXECUTION: Expiating the
    Great Crime," *New York Herald,* July 8, 1865.
"customary to represent": Jane G. Swisshelm, "A Woman's Sympathy for
    Mrs. Surratt," *Cincinnati Daily Enquirer,* July 12, 1865.
"The intellectual resources": "EXECUTION: Expiating the Great Crime," *New York
    Herald.*
"So prompt was" through "All hope faded": John W. Clampitt, "The Trial of
    Mrs. Surratt," *North American Review,* September 1880, 236.
"says John Surratt" and "He expresses the deepest": "Visit to the
    Prisoners—Preparations for the Execution," *New York Times,* July 7, 1865.
"Concerning the fate" and "She at least": Daniel Gillette, "The Last Days of
    Payne," *New York World,* April 3, 1892, in Ownsbey, *Alias "Paine,"* appendix 1.
"Captain, if I had": John A. Gray, "The Fate of the Lincoln Conspirators," *McClure's,*
    October 1911.
"was now beyond hope": Trindal, *Mary Surratt,* 212.
"Believing that Judge Holt" through "had told the truth": Steers and Holzer,
    Lincoln Assassination Conspirators, 152–53.
"I will furnish you": "Pleaded for Mrs. Surratt," *New York Sun,* July 7, 1901.
"If John Surratt could": "Sentence of the Conspirators," *New York World,* July 7, 1865.
"Surratt in a Nunnery": "Surratt in a Nunnery," *American Citizen* (Butler, PA),
    June 7, 1865.
"Let me solemnly say": Pilgrim, "John H. Surratt," *Philadelphia Times,* October 4,
    1885.
"there was no cause": "A Remarkable Lecture! John H. Surratt Tells His Story,"
    Washington *Evening Star,* December 7, 1870.
"revulsion of public feeling": Pilgrim, "John H. Surratt."
"mutilated with ink and pen" and "Be under no apprehension": "Remarkable
    Lecture!," Washington *Evening Star.*
"We tried it": Hoyt, *Town Hall Tonight,* 151.
"Mrs. Surratt was lying": "Expiating the Great Crime," *New York Herald.*
"and forthwith was seen" and "good-humored face": "The Great Execution. Full
    Details," Washington *Evening Star,* July 7, 1865.

"a gleaming bayonet" through "mad gallop": "Pleaded for Mrs. Surratt," *New York Sun*.

"Everybody who had": "Condition of the Prisoners," *Daily National Republican*.

"trying to speak" through "Poor child": "Pleaded for Mrs. Surratt," *New York Sun*.

CHAPTER TWENTY-SIX

"so as to save": Reverend J. A. Walter, "The Surratt Case," *United States Catholic Historical Magazine*, October 1891.

"What will become" and "repeatedly and frantically": "End of the Assassins," *New York Times*, July 8, 1865.

"My God, they are": "HUNG!," *Philadelphia Inquirer*, July 8, 1865.

"A mawkish sort": "From New York," *Philadelphia Inquirer*, July 7, 1865.

"Against Mrs. Surratt": "Sentence of the Conspirators," *New York World*, July 7, 1865.

"her bearing was": "EXECUTION: Expiating the Great Crime," *New York Herald*, July 8, 1865.

"Is there any hope?" and "Hope is gone": "The Assassins. A Minister's Visit to the Condemned—Sixteen Hours in the Cells," *New York Herald*, July 11, 1865. (Reprinted from *Washington Chronicle*, July 10, 1865.)

"Mother, are you resigned?" and "Yes, my child": Walter, "Surratt Case."

"appeared to rally": "End of the Assassins," *New York Times*.

"Annie, my child": Walter, "Surratt Case."

"My pen is too": John W. Clampitt, "The Trial of Mrs. Surratt," *North American Review*, September 1880, 236.

"melted the hearts" and "Loud sobs from": "The Great Execution. Full Details," Washington *Evening Star*, July 7, 1865.

"The sounds of grief": "EXTRA. The Execution. The Condition of the Prisoners," *Daily National Republican*, July 7, 1865.

"all in one chorus": "HUNG!," *Philadelphia Inquirer*.

"A great quiet prevailed": "The Execution at the Arsenal," *Washington Evening Union*, July 7, 1865.

"shot down like": Peterson and Brothers, *Trial of the Assassins*, 207.

"writhe as I": Mary E. Trindal, "History at Its Worst," *Surratt Courier*, June 1991.

"through the courtesy": "The Great Conspiracy. Execution of the Condemned," *Daily National Intelligencer*, July 8, 1865.

"Father, I wish to say something" through "That I am innocent": Walter, "Surratt Case."

"The world and all" and "disturb the serenity": "Mary E. Surratt's Good Name,"
    New York Times, March 24, 1895.
"comparatively steady" and "faltered a little": "Great Conspiracy," *Daily National
    Intelligencer.*
"Her limbs seemed" through "the newly dead": "Expiating the Great Crime," *New
    York Herald.*
"He walked like": John A. Gray, "The Fate of the Lincoln Conspirators," *McClure's,*
    October 1911.
"as though he was": "HUNG!," *Philadelphia Inquirer.*
"For mere relief" through "pour[ed] into her ear": "Expiating the Great Crime,"
    New York Herald.
"fervently, several times": "HUNG!," *Philadelphia Inquirer.*
"her face lost": George Alfred Townsend, "Last Scene of All," *New York World,*
    July 8, 1865; see also Peterson and Brothers, *Trial of the Assassins,* 207.
"in a low quiet tone": R. A. Watts, "The Trial and Execution of the Lincoln
    Conspirators [part 3]," *Adrian Daily Telegram,* April 21, 1914.
"Gentlemen, the prisoner": "Expiating the Great Crime," *New York Herald.*
"She half fainted" and "It was with": Townsend, "Last Scene of All."
"It hurts" and "Well, it won't": Hoyt, *Town Hall Tonight,* 152.
"gave a slight" and "half dead with terror": Trindal, "History at Its Worst."
"About the same time": "The Last Moments on the Scaffold," *Albany Evening Journal,*
    July 8, 1865.
"what with the heat" and "I felt a little": Hoyt, *Town Hall Tonight,* 151.
"the most harrowing part": Doster, *Lincoln and Episodes,* 276.
"the cap of doom": "Expiating the Great Crime," *New York Herald.*
"give way": "Great Conspiracy," *Daily National Intelligencer.*
"Please don't let me fall": "Full Details," Washington *Evening Star;* "Great
    Conspiracy," *Daily National Intelligencer.* (See also "Condition of the Prisoners,"
    Daily National Republican; "Execution at the Arsenal," *Washington Evening Union;*
    Walter, "Surratt Case.")
"hold on!": "Condition of the Prisoners," *Daily National Republican;* "End of the
    Assassins," *New York Times.*
"All is ready, Captain" through "Yes. She cannot be saved": Gray, "Lincoln
    Conspirators."
"On the third clap": Hoyt, *Town Hall Tonight,* 152.
"They were literally *jerked*": Trindal, "History at Its Worst."
"This gave a swinging": Peterson and Brothers, *Trial of the Assassins,* 207.

"Payne was a strong brute": Hoyt, *Town Hall Tonight,* 151.

"She hangs and swings": "Expiating the Great Crime," *New York Herald.*

"An over zealous corporal": "Great Conspiracy," *Daily National Intelligencer.*

"The soldiers performing" through "laughing comrades": Trindal, "History at Its Worst."

"When Mrs. Surratt": "Great Conspiracy," *Daily National Intelligencer.*

"I took charge": Gray, "Lincoln Conspirators."

"pieces of the delicate": "Hangman of President Lincoln's Assassins Tells His Story," *New York Press,* September 4, 1898.

"placed her in the box": Gray, "Lincoln Conspirators."

"This trial settled nothing": Doster, *Lincoln and Episodes,* 278.

CHAPTER TWENTY-SEVEN

"a shuddering exit": "Wraithes and Gobblins," *Boston Post,* December 3, 1866.

"but the *facts*": "The Case of Mrs. Surratt; Affidavit of Mr. John P. Brophy," *Daily Constitutional Union,* July 11, 1865.

"an avowed secessionist" through "said he would not": July 7, 1865, statement of John P. Brophy in Edwards and Steers, *Lincoln Assassination: The Evidence,* 206–7.

"evidence": "Mrs. Surratt. Her Guilt—Evidence Proving Her Connection with the Assassination," *Philadelphia Inquirer,* July 13, 1865.

"confused and terrified": Edwards and Steers, *Lincoln Assassination: The Evidence,* 1324–25.

"Mrs. Surratt is dead" through "The War Department had": "The Case of Mrs. Surratt," Philadelphia *Sunday Dispatch,* July 16, 1865.

"Items not brought out": Edwards and Steers, *Lincoln Assassination: The Evidence,* 1331.

"Mrs. Surratt is to be much blamed" through "Anna, come what may": "Mrs. Surratt," Philadelphia *Sunday Dispatch.*

"loose newspaper paragraphs" through "Now, will Mr. Weichmann": "Brophy's Rejoinder," *Washington Evening Union,* July 19, 1865.

"I had hoped that" through "The fact is, Brophy": "Weichmann vs. Brophy!!," *Philadelphia Inquirer,* July 26, 1865.

"the solemn duty": Joseph George Jr., " 'The Days Are Yet Dark.' L. J. Weichmann's Life After the Lincoln Conspiracy Trial," *Records of the American Catholic Historical Society of Philadelphia* 95, no. 1 (March–December 1984): 67–81.

"See, that man there": Louis J. Weichmann to General Joseph Holt, October 22, 1866, in Kenneth J. Zanca, "Two Overlooked Letters of Louis J. Weichmann to the Hon. Joseph Holt," *Surratt Courier,* February 2005.

"the most contemptible dog" and **"if I ever meet"**: George, "Days Are Yet Dark."

"I can make" through **"because I was"**: Louis J. Weichmann to General Joseph Holt, October 22, 1866, in Zanca, "Two Overlooked Letters."

"wove the thread": Victor Louis Mason, "Four Lincoln Conspiracies," *Century Magazine,* April 1896.

"If there is anywhere": Dixon, "By Telegraph. Special Despatch to the Boston Daily Advertiser. The Assassins Executed," *Boston Daily Advertiser,* July 8, 1865.

Genl. Hancock told Mr. Holohan: Trindal, *Mary Surratt,* 229.

"Her health has greatly" and **"She never smiles"**: "Miss Annie Surratt—Sympathy for Her," *New York Freeman's Journal,* September 9, 1865. (Quoted in Joseph George Jr., "Some Newspaper Clippings About the Surratts," *Surratt Society News,* March 1985.)

"said he had no" and **"Request will be considered"**: Joseph George Jr., "Some Newspaper Clippings About the Surratts," *Surratt Society News,* March 1985.

CHAPTER TWENTY-EIGHT

"Curious News, if True": "John H. Surratt—Curious News, if True," *New York Herald,* November 24, 1866.

"the filth from" and **"I have nothing"**: Alfred Isacsson, "John Surratt and the Lincoln Assassination Plot," *Maryland Historical Magazine* 52, no. 4 (December 1957): 316–42.

"martial law can never" through **"is a vital principle"**: Ex parte Milligan, 71 U.S. 2 (1866) [i.e., U.S. Reports volume 71, Wallace volume 4, December 1866], loc.gov/item/usrep071002a.

"I have not come": "The Latest by Telegraph. Washington Items," *Daily Illinois State Register,* August 5, 1867.

"It is *Mrs. Surratt's ghost*": "The Trial of Mrs. Surratt's Heirs, Against Holt, Stanton, Bingham, and Their Man Andrew Johnson!," *New-York Freeman's Journal and Catholic Register,* August 10, 1867.

"I do not wish to go into" through **"That I do not"**: John M. Lloyd and Richard T. Merrick in "Trial of John H. Surratt," vol. III, no. 58, 11–12.

"very singular" through **"After the soldiers"**: John M. Lloyd in "Trial of John H. Surratt," vol. III, no. 59, 6–7.

"that the Government" through " 'Why,' said he": John M. Lloyd in "Trial of John H. Surratt," vol. III, no. 59, 1–2.

"Now, did he say" and "jumped up very quick": "Trial of John H. Surratt," vol. III, no. 59, 3.

"providentially thrown in" and "an instrument prepared": George Alfred Townsend, "John H. Surratt; A Morning with His College Chum," *New-York Tribune,* May 20, 1867.

"they were always" through "No, sir; he made": John T. Holohan and Joseph H. Bradley in "Trial of John H. Surratt," vol. IV, no. 74, 8–10. (Note: the transcript does not specify whether this is Mr. Bradley Sr. or Jr.)

"Tell these gentlemen" through "No, sir": Richard T. Merrick and Olivia Jenkins in "Trial of John H. Surratt," vol. IV, no. 77, 10.

"For God's sake": Louis J. Weichmann in "Trial of John H. Surratt," vol. III, no. 63, 4.

"Mr. Weichmann, ask them": Honora Fitzpatrick in "Trial of John H. Surratt," vol. IV, no. 76, 8.

"rather startled me": John T. Ford in "Trial of John H. Surratt," vol. IV, no. 82, 1.

"unless he testified" through "Yes, sir, he did": "Trial of John H. Surratt," vol. IV, no. 80, 11–15.

"confused and terrified": Edwards and Steers, *Lincoln Assassination: The Evidence,* 1324–25.

"I asked him why": Louis J. Carland in "Trial of John H. Surratt," vol. IV, no. 80, 11.

"There was a revulsion": Pilgrim, "John H. Surratt," *Philadelphia Times,* October 4, 1885.

ignoramus: James E. T. Lange and Katherine DeWitt Jr., "The Three Indictments of John Harrison Surratt Jr.," *Surratt Courier,* January 1992.

CHAPTER TWENTY-NINE

"The President very emphatically": Colonel W. G. Moore, "Notes of Colonel W. G. Moore, Private Secretary to President Johnson, 1866–1868," compiled by St. George L. Sioussat, *American Historical Review* 19, no. 1 (October 1913): 98–132.

"A careful scrutiny": "Johnson vs. Holt," *Daily National Intelligencer,* November 12, 1873; see also DeWitt, *Judicial Murder,* 179.

"He distinctly remembered" and "felt satisfied that it": Moore, "Notes of Colonel W. G. Moore."

"an unequivocal denial": "The Recommendation of Mercy in the Case of
 Mrs. Surratt," *Daily National Intelligencer,* August 7, 1867.

"A more groundless calumny": Holt, *Vindication of Hon. Joseph Holt,* 3.

"darkened by a consciousness": Allen Thorndike Rice, "New Facts About
 Mrs. Surratt," *North American Review,* July 1888.

"a stupidity on my" through "distinctly": Holt, *Vindication of Hon. Joseph Holt,* 4.

"it would amount to": Moore, *Case of Mrs. Surratt,* 107–8.

"without reserve" through "[Johnson's] eye necessarily fell": Holt, *Vindication of
 Hon. Joseph Holt,* 5–6.

"hounded" through "Every step in the direction": Joseph George Jr., " 'The
 Days Are Yet Dark.' L. J. Weichmann's Life After the Lincoln Conspiracy
 Trial," *Records of the American Catholic Historical Society of Philadelphia* 95, no. 1
 (March–December 1984): 67–81.

"So earnest and persistent" and "enemies of the government": Harris, *Assassination
 of Lincoln,* 192.

"completely conclusive of the guilt": Harris, 200.

"has never been abandoned": Harris, 192–193.

"I think it is": George, "Days Are Yet Dark."

"Louis J. Weichman [*sic*]": Oldroyd, *Assassination of Abraham Lincoln,* 153.

"It must appear": George, "Days Are Yet Dark."

"had never seen him" and "Probably no one": Oldroyd, *Assassination of Abraham
 Lincoln,* 167.

"Probably no one": Oldroyd, 194.

"I am egotist enough": Louis Weichmann to George Loring Porter, August 16, 1900,
 in Porter, *Surgeon in Charge,* 18.

CHAPTER THIRTY

"in tolerable condition" through "conducted with the strictest privacy": Joseph
 George Jr., "Some Newspaper Clippings About the Surratts," *Surratt Society
 News,* March 1985.

"unseen hands" and "constantly covered with flowers": John F. Coyle, "Was
 Mrs. Surratt Guilty," *Washington Post,* July 28, 1901.

EPILOGUE

"making his living": "Surratt," *New York World,* December 9, 1870.

"No wonder the New York": Untitled squib in *Memphis Public Ledger,* December 16,
 1870.

"brazen-faced impudence": "The Height of Impudence," *Richmond Evening State Journal*, January 4, 1871.

"Knowing that she was": "John H. Surratt, Sole Survivor," *Brooklyn Daily Eagle*, October 13, 1901.

"she had been": "Daughter of Mrs. Surratt," *Washington Post*, October 26, 1904.

AUTHOR'S NOTE

"testifying with ropes": Joseph George Jr., "Nature's First Law: Louis J. Weichmann and Mrs. Surratt," *Civil War History* 28, no. 2 (June 1982) 101–27; see also Kauffman, *American Brutus,* 309.

INDEX